Bill Barnes
3/10/08

LOVE AND CONSEQUENCES

LOVE AND CONSEQUENCES

A MEMOIR OF HOPE AND SURVIVAL

MARGARET B. JONES

RIVERHEAD BOOKS A MEMBER OF PENGUIN GROUP (USA) INC. • NEW YORK 2008

RIVERHEAD BOOKS
Published by the Penguin Group
Penguin Group (USA) Inc., 375 Hudson Street, New York, New York 10014, USA ·
Penguin Group (Canada), 90 Eglinton Avenue East, Suite 700, Toronto, Ontario M4P 2Y3,
Canada (a division of Pearson Penguin Canada Inc.) · Penguin Books Ltd, 80 Strand,
London WC2R 0RL, England · Penguin Ireland, 25 St Stephen's Green, Dublin 2, Ireland
(a division of Penguin Books Ltd) · Penguin Group (Australia), 250 Camberwell Road,
Camberwell, Victoria 3124, Australia (a division of Pearson Australia Group Pty Ltd) ·
Penguin Books India Pvt Ltd, 11 Community Centre, Panchsheel Park, New Delhi–
110 017, India · Penguin Group (NZ), 67 Apollo Drive, Rosedale, North Shore 0632,
New Zealand (a division of Pearson New Zealand Ltd) · Penguin Books (South Africa)
(Pty) Ltd, 24 Sturdee Avenue, Rosebank, Johannesburg 2196, South Africa

Penguin Books Ltd, Registered Offices:
80 Strand, London WC2R 0RL, England

Library of Congress Cataloging-in-Publication Data

Jones, Margaret B.
Love and consequences : a memoir of hope and survival / Margaret B. Jones.
p.   cm.
ISBN 978-1-59448-977-8
1. Jones, Margaret B.   2. Foster children—California—Los Angeles—Biography.   I. Title.
HV885.L7A3   2008   2007044934
362.73'3092—dc22
[B]

Printed in the United States of America
1   3   5   7   9   10   8   6   4   2

Book design by Gretchen Achilles

While the author has made every effort to provide accurate telephone numbers and Internet
addresses at the time of publication, neither the publisher nor the author assumes any
responsibility for errors, or for changes that occur after publication. Further, the publisher does
not have any control over and does not assume any responsibility for author or third-party
websites or their content.

This book is dedicated to my daughter, my nieces, nephews, and Godchildren; to Romeo, who always pushed me to be the best kind of person; and most of all, to all the Bloods and Crips who lost their lives in the struggle—as well as those who are lost trying to find life within the struggle.

LOVE AND CONSEQUENCES

AUTHOR'S NOTE ON LANGUAGE, DIALECT, AND KONTENT

LOS ANGELES, CALIFORNIA, is home to 4 million people. Despite the popular perception of L.A. as a land of abundance, movie stars, and plastic surgery, for some 385,000 residents in its smaller neighborhoods—West Adams, Hyde Park, the jungle, Leimert Park, and the many others that make up the larger area commonly referred to as South Central—life is more comparable to that in an urban Third World country. Just three or four freeway exits from the upscale shops in Beverly Hills on Rodeo Drive, people buy guns out of car trunks in alleys off Rodeo Road and get shot over the color of their shoes.

My words and views were learned in the dirt and desolation of South Central Los Angeles. The streets where I grew up were run by the laws of the local gangs. Their laws shaped what we wore, how we talked, and how we navigated the city. When one resident of the urban core asks another where they live, the response often includes not only a street name but also which gang claims that area as its turf. I do now see that there is no difference between Bloods and Crips. We are all the same, the problems and conditions we all face are the same. We were just born into different neighborhoods. My particular street, however, was ruled by the mighty Blood Nation. You will see that reflected in the language and vision of the book.

Please do not confuse the use of slang and my replacing *c*'s with *k*'s as ignorance or stupidity. I choose to write as we chose to speak in the world of my childhood. A world where Bloods and Crips have such a deep-seated hatred for each other that Bloods smoke big-arettes and Crips celebrate C-days rather than B-days (birthdays). I do it in order to offer up the whole story.

I'm tired as I write this because I woke up last night at two A.M. to my phone ringing. I knew it was bad news because the homie who was calling me had not answered his phone for the last week, but I was instantly relieved because at least I knew he was alive. "Sup, ma?"

"Wassup with you?" I ask.

"Damn, ma, my cousin, lil Chris. I feel real fukked up rite now. I jus called to tell you he's chillin wit God now."

There is something beautiful and comforting about the slang to me. Despite the tragedy, it is not cold. It is in essence, alive, full of personality. I like the thought that "lil Chris is chillin wit God" a lot better than thinking of him as a victim of a gang-related homicide, another statistic in the saga of black-on-black crime. I like the idea that he is kickin' it somewhere with all the others, in the present tense, not just an open file at the Rampart Police Division with a fifty-fifty chance of ever getting solved. Something about the vernacular hints toward the will to strive to survive. It has a sense of authenticity, and with it the hope of pride.

America wraps itself in the idea that the problem with the ghetto is that its inhabitants are lazy hoodlums. It builds walls around the problem, both figurative and literal, and gets on with its life. "Luxury then," as Imamu Amiri Bakara points out in "Political Poem," "is a way of being ignorant, comfortably."

I have combined characters and changed names, dates, and places. I have done this for the sake of clarity and to protect the hearts, freedom, and egos of others. The experiences and sentiments, though blurred, are real. This is how we live.

To all the homies BIP/RIP along the way, everything I do, I do in your memory. You are never forgotten. I hope that in death you finally found the peace that you never had in life. Surely you all deserve that; maybe the next time around it will not have to come at such a great price. We learned too late that, as OGB Madd Ronald (from the W/S R.20s Neighborhood Bloods) said, we must be willing to live for each other rather than die for each other.

LOST

I WAS EIGHT AND A HALF when I moved to South Central Los Angeles, the city's large inner core divided among 775 different gangs—Blood, Crip, Sur, 18th St., or MS—which ran the different neighborhoods like training grounds, enforcing the laws of the street more strictly and consistently than the police enforced the official ones.

My foster family's particular neighborhood was controlled by one of the seventy-five-plus Blood gangs within L.A. County. While each gang's set varied in the size of its turf and number and activity level of its members, since our set was geographically located between two other Blood sets that we shared good relations with and referred to as "neighbors," we had power in our size and strength.

It was a completely unspectacular neighborhood, full of small bungalow-style homes and two-story apartment buildings, often carefully tended, but with burnt-out yards and Chevys that ranged from primered and dented with missing parts, to custom candy-colored lowriders with two-thousand-dollar gold Dayton hundred-spoke wire wheels. The area was shared by USC students, Black Muslim intellectuals, crackheads, prostitutes, and groups of gang members, some of whom were decked out in expensive clothing and gold jewelry. It was this latter group—the gang members—that caught my attention, and I watched in awe as their lowrider car club three-wheeled and bounced down the streets.

The leaders of the gang were the OGs—"original gangsters." To me they were like celebrities. One of the OGs went by the name of Kraziak. He was in his early thirties, light-skinned with long hair that he kept in meticulous braids. Every week, he had them freshly done in elaborate designs. He drove a candy-red 1969 Chevy Chevelle Malibu Super Sport with two black racing stripes up the middle and a red flag (bandana) neatly folded and tied around the rearview mirror. From the stories Kraziak told, it seemed as though he'd been around almost as long as the hood itself. He knew everything about L.A.'s history, not only the history of our gang's conception, but that of all the gangs. He told us about the Purple Hearts, and the Slausons, the gangs that preceded the Bloods and Crips, how they had formed in the forties and fifties to protect the community against the rampant racial violence.

Kraziak had moved out of the hood. He now stayed over in Hawthorne by the airport with his girlfriend, two sons, and baby daughter. He still came through on the daily, though, parking the Malibu on the street across from the park, its windows blatantly rolled down. Kraziak was so revered, no one would dare mess with his ride. Heading into the park, to the benches in the back grassy area where the homies usually hung out, he would stop and ask the women whose babydaddys, sons, or husbands were locked up in juvie or prison how things were going at home. When the ice cream truck came by, he'd treat all the kids to popsicles or candy bars, paying the driver with a crisp hundred-dollar bill.

Sometimes, he stopped and talked to me. We talked about L.A.

history, life at home, or maybe just how hot it was outside. He always ended the conversation by reaching into his pocket, pulling out a few extra bills and telling me, "Be true to the game, live by her rules, and she will always bless you." Then he'd hand me the money and wink. Him thinking that I was worth his attention made me more proud than any school award or honor ever could. It meant I was going somewhere.

I loved being in the neighborhood and took every chance I had to be out there among the hustle. It made me feel important, like I was—or could become—part of something. I emulated the gang members' style of dress and walk, studied the gang hand signs. At twelve, Kraziak finally hooked me up with a position. I was grateful for the work, eager to earn my own money toward the flame-red Nike Cortez with fat laces that everyone else wore, but even more excited to prove myself worthy of wearing the affiliated color and moving up in the ranks.

My job was to approach anyone wanting to buy drugs, see what they wanted, and check them out to make sure they weren't the police. Then, if I felt okay about it, I would take their money, tell them where to go, and gesture my approval to the homie who was holding the drugs. There were all kinds of people buying drugs in the area—white suburban teens, college kids in nice cars, and even the occasional businessman in a big luxury Mercedes or BMW. Usually, though, it was just the neighborhood crackheads, whom we called baseheads or smokers. It was sad seeing the strung-out and desperate begging in front of their kids, but some of the other baseheads were funny to watch. They would tell wild stories, trying to get you to front them some drugs or offer to do just about anything for the smallest amounts of cash. Once I saw a younger homie pay a basehead two dollars to eat dog shit. We all laughed over that for a week. But mostly it was a boring job with a lot of time sitting around, waiting and watching.

My foster mom liked for all of the girls in the house to wear braids. She said they looked neat and clean and she didn't want us running around looking like "ragamuffins." Because her long hours scrubbing floors and walls left her fingers stiff, and because I was the oldest girl, I would braid my foster sisters' hair for her; when I was done with them, Big Mom would do mine. It always came out in embarrassingly crooked, loose cornrows, made even worse by the fact that though thick and wavy, my hair didn't really have the texture to hold it. I killed a lot of time on the job unbraiding my hair and daydreaming about the shoes and things I was going to buy for myself and my two little foster sisters. I loved the thought that thanks to my after-school activities my girls wouldn't be teased for wearing hand-me-downs like I had in elementary school. Things were only gonna get better. "Sky's the limit," Kraziak would say as he handed me my cut of the money we made, usually giving me an extra twenty off the top as a reward for my good work.

This particular day I had just unraveled the last of my braids and was shooting the pile of small black elastic bands at a crack vial on the sidewalk, pushing it slowly toward the curb with each hit.

"Good aim, lil homegirl," said one of the homies in a red shirt, Dickies pants, and a thick gang tattoo in Olde English font just above his shirt line as he crossed the street. I didn't know him, but he looked over twenty so I knew he must be one of the big homies. I smiled, embarrassed at being caught playing a child's game. I brushed away the remaining rubber bands, sending them scattering over the thin strip of grass in front of the sidewalk and watched as he made his way through the park. In the distance, a silver Cadillac caught my eye. I stood up, running my hands over the deep waves my braids had left in my hair and pulled my red LA fitted cap onto my head. As the car pulled a U-turn in the intersection and slowed down to circle back onto the block for the second time, I stepped off the curb into the street. Something bad was about to happen. I started running toward the park, waving my hands and gesturing coded signs to Kraziak, Freddy, Slikk, and some of the other homies I knew standing under the palm trees that marked the park's entrance across the street. My stomach felt queasy.

The Caddy had dark tinted windows and Dayton wire wheels, while the businessmen and students who drove similar cars into the area almost always rolled on stock rims. Its unfamiliarity and slow speed were suspicious.

Kraziak turned, and I could hear the man on the passenger side start to talk. "Where you from, cuz?" The man spoke the words in a strong, confident voice. It was a trick question. "Cuz" is a word used only between Crips, and this street was clearly Blood turf.

"What's that neighborhood Crip like?" he then said even louder. Everyone started running away from the park or getting down under the tables. I looked down at my black Chuck Taylors with their wide red laces and tongues flipped and wondered if the driver's-side window was about to roll down, too. And then the street erupted. A blur of sound, everyone yelling at the same time, over which, Kraziak's voice carried: "This is Blood, homie."

The next sounds were explosions. Gunshots. I panicked, running back and ducking behind a car. I squeezed my eyes shut, but I could hear several different guns, the steady bursts of an AK-47 and the strong, hard single explosions of handguns. They sounded so close,

I thought for sure I was going to get hit. I thought the explosions and screaming might never stop.

Then tires peeled out. I opened my eyes. The Crip car, no longer slow and teasing, flew off around the corner, and I watched as homies from my neighborhood jumped into four parked cars and started off after them from all different directions around the small park. One ragtop Impala pulled out in front of me, slowing down just enough for one of the homies to jump in over the closed door. The sound of gunfire grew softer as the cars got farther away down the street. I struggled to get back on my feet, my legs wobbly and my breath stuck in my throat.

As the sound of gunfire faded, people started to come out of everywhere, running from the corners of the park, stepping out of houses and apartment buildings. I could hear women screaming, and a baby crying. I knew that with the number of bullets I had heard, someone had to have been hit. My head felt hot and light, as though I might faint as I crossed the street and pushed my way through the commotion.

As I got closer to the aftermath, I could see two men immobilized on the sidewalk, bleeding, and another in the street. I was scared to look and see who was hit, or how badly. My eyes stopped first on the man in the street. It was Freddy, a good friend of both of my two foster brothers. The homies were helping him stand up, and blood poured out of his shoulder and down his arm and chest, pooling on the sidewalk. The other man was a dark-skinned YG (young gangsta) in his late teens. He was from the hood, but my brothers had warned me to stay away from him, and I had listened. He was shot in the leg and the bullet must have hit the bone and shattered it because the leg was twisted, with the foot turned in against the ground and the knee a full quarter rotation to the right. I pushed a little deeper into the crowd and saw that the man farthest back toward the park was Kraziak.

I was in shock. I felt choked. I had seen people get shot before, seen bodies lying in the street while the homicide people looked for clues, but I had never seen anyone I cared about laid out like that. Everything else blurred. All I could see was Kraziak. He must have been hit more than ten times. Blood bubbled out of his mouth and neck and he gasped, trying to breathe. One of the homies clutched him in his arms and held him up to keep him from choking on his own blood.

"Kall nine-one-one!" people yelled.

"Fukk nine-one-one!" the homie holding Kraziak yelled, "Someone get a kar, we gotta get him to the hospital. Let's go!"

The blood was everywhere. I never realized how much blood was inside a person, or how much could come out. The smell enveloped the area. It smelled like life and death all at the same time, a sickly sweet and slightly rotten smell. It felt like it was smothering me.

"Let's go!" the homie yelled at everyone, over and over. "K'mon, let's go!" Three of them lifted Kraziak up and carried him right past where I stood. I wanted to look away but couldn't. I wanted to reach out and touch him, but I couldn't do that, either. His face and neck had started to swell and he was almost unrecognizable. He moaned as they lifted him into the car, the sound pushing blood out of his mouth and neck.

"Is he gone live?" I asked as the car pulled away. Tears ran hot and wet down my face.

"Hard ta say," one of the homies said and shook his head. "I known people who got shot once and died and people who got shot ten times and lived."

I didn't want Kraziak to die. I sat down on the curb where a few moments before I had felt proud, confident, and part of something greater than myself and tried to stop crying. My body shuddered with uneven breaths as I wiped at my eyes.

By the time the cops pulled up at the scene, the blood had dried and turned yellow on the concrete where the plasma had started to separate. They were the ones who told us Kraziak had been pronounced dead at the county hospital. His blood now belonged to the flies. The sky was starting to darken, and red streaks appeared against the hills. All of a sudden all I could think about was how Big Mom was going to whoop my ass if I came home after the streetlights clicked on.

The cops put up yellow crime-scene tape and established a perimeter, then started going around asking everyone if they had seen anything. No one said they had.

One cop looked over the crowd of people now quickly dispersing and pointed a gloved finger at me, probably hoping that the child in me would come out and tell him what he knew I had witnessed.

"Naw, man. I ain seen shyt," I bit down hard on my lower lip at the end of my words. The policeman looked at me and then held out a business card.

"In case you change your mind," he said. I hesitated but finally reached out and took it, both of us knowing I would never call. In a few hours the police would be performing the same task in the Crip neighborhood a few blocks to the north, a different set of onlookers shaking their heads, denying that they'd seen our homies catch up to the other car and execute a message of revenge.

In South Central, the myth of human kindness and compassion ends and self-preservation is the ruling principle. At the end of the day what you know and have seen is no one's business but your own. It's a cold game, but what you know can kill you just as fast as what you don't. Snitches and rats dig their own graves.

As the police pulled away, we started to pick up the remains of the crime-scene tape that lay on the ground, wrapped around lampposts and telephone poles or blowing into the park. I took a piece and tied it around my wrist.

One of the big homies I didn't know, obviously shaken, said he was going to the store. He drove the few blocks to Tony's Liquor and returned quickly with a bottle of Hennessey and a stack of plastic cups.

"Here," he said, offering me one. I shook my head no and pulled nervously at my new bracelet. I couldn't stop picturing Kraziak's face, swollen and covered with blood. "It makes the thoughts go down easier," he said, handing me a cup anyway.

I took the flimsy cup and watched as he poured a little of the amber liquid, first onto the ground and then into my cup. This was my first taste of straight Hennessey, although I had always seen the big homies drinking it that way. It tasted like burning, but almost instantly, as he had said, my head felt at least a little better.

The big homie smiled at me and then slipped the remaining cups over the neck of the Hennessey bottle, reaching into his back pocket with his spare hand.

"Chaser?" he asked, holding up a bottle of Pepsi. I nodded my head, still rubbing my tongue against the roof of my mouth, trying to kill the taste. "Here," he said and poured half the bottle on top of what was left of the Hennessey in my cup.

"Thanks," I said awkwardly. He smiled, tucking the Pepsi back into his pocket and walking off to pass out the rest of the cups.

I stood for a moment looking at the flies as they circled around the dried blood, landing and taking off over and over again in the day's last light. Then, eyes downcast, I started shuffling home. My foster sisters would be sitting on the sofa, watching cartoons and waiting for dinner—red beans or black-eyed peas, most likely. I knew Big Mom would make me set the table and then give me a whooping and send me to my room for coming home late. It didn't matter, though; I didn't want to sit at the table and listen to how everyone's day was, or have Big Mom ask me what I learned in school. I sipped the rest of the Pepsi and then threw the cup into the street.

As I watched it, a glint of light caught my eye and I bent down and pinched a bullet shell between my fingers, rolling it back and forth a few times before slipping it into my jeans. The whole walk home I kept the shell clenched tightly in my fist inside my pocket. I thought about Kraziak and the blood bubbling up out of his mouth and neck. It seemed impossible that he was gone, that I wouldn't see him at the park the next day or the day after that. I couldn't even imagine the place without him. I thought about how Kraziak always told me be true to the game and she would bless you. Would he still believe that now? For me, his death had disproved his maxim. If the Crips could kill Kraziak, it meant that no degree of love or respect from your homies could really protect you.

I quickened my pace as I walked the last few blocks from the park. The streets seemed different. I looked down the alleys and into the shadows thinking every movement was a threat and every stranger meant me harm. And that's when it happened. All the fear and sadness inside of me turned to rage. I hated that they had taken my big homie and even more that they had taken my sense of security. I hated that I felt as if no one could protect us: not our parents, not the police, not the game, not even ourselves. But the more I thought about it, the more I just hated the Crips. I thought about the homies speeding off after the Crip car. As I turned the corner and saw my house with Big Mom in the doorway, I vowed to be like those Bloods, to get even. We were on our own in the City of Angels, and we were smoking niggas, sending them to heaven every day just to keep the name.

THE HAND YOU ARE DEALT

BACK IN KINDERGARTEN, my teacher called my mom in for an after-school conference. She had asked each of the kids to draw a family portrait, and I had drawn myself standing alone, in front of a elegantly landscaped apartment building. The tall bird-of-paradise plants bloomed in orange and blue, but I had no hands or mouth. My mom, in tan pants and a neatly tucked white polo shirt, shifted in the undersized school chair and looked at me.

"I ran out of time," I said, looking at my hands as they rested on the big table. My mom smiled and nodded. Everyone seemed satisfied, and we went home.

The next day my teacher asked me to draw my family again, only this time with everyone sitting inside the apartment, watching TV. I drew my mom and my brother sitting on the sofa, and me standing off behind them in the doorway. In the new drawing, I still had no hands or mouth.

I showed no signs of physical abuse, no unusual bruises or scrapes, and never had a broken bone. There were things about my behavior, things that could mean something or nothing. I was from a decent-enough-looking, intact family, one concerned enough that a parent would actually show up for a conference if called. I had siblings who had gone through the same middle-class suburban school without a negative mark in their files, and a mom who stood waving at the entrance to the school every day as the ending bell rang. Those were good signs, very good signs, but my moods and behavior were erratic, and something felt wrong to this teacher.

She did what she could. She called the Department of Children and Family Services and reported that something didn't *seem* right, and my drawings were put in a file, where they sat until further notice. Years later, as an adult, I acquired copies of my files and looked at those pictures. Drawn in black crayon with the awkward, elementary lines of a young child, they were so clearly full of things a kid should never know. I can't imagine what it must have felt like to that teacher, to see them and be powerless to do anything but sit back and wait.

Three months after the drawing incident I walked up and tapped her on her shoulder during "rest time" to ask if I could go to the bathroom. When she turned to me to answer, I had blood running down my legs. Her whole face contorted. She told the other kids to stay where they were and to lie still.

"I'll be right back," she said in a stern, flat voice I had never heard her use before. It was a voice that meant business and showed panic, all at once. The other kids heard it, too, and they all looked up to see what was going on. I could feel all their eyes on me. I was a shy, polite child, never one to try to attract attention to myself. Under the other children's gaze, I could feel my skin burn and my cheeks redden. I turned back to my teacher, but the look in her eyes did nothing to ease my discomfort. Instead, it made me more scared. She almost looked like she was going to cry. Then she reached out to me.

I held out my hand, but instead of taking it like I expected, she lifted me up and carried me to the nurse. I reached my arms around her neck and laid my head on her shoulder to steady myself and keep from falling. With all the looks and my teacher carrying me, I figured I must really be sick, but how could they know that when no one had even felt my forehead? I let my body relax against hers as she quickened her step, rushing, almost running, to the nurse's office.

Once inside, my teacher set me on the table with the paper down the middle. I didn't understand what was going on, and I still had to go to the bathroom. When I looked at Ms. Appleby, there was blood on the front of her dress where she had held me.

"I'm sorry about your pretty dress," I said, embarrassed. I was sure it was one of her favorites and now I had ruined it. I started to cry. She hugged me to her, stroked my hair, and rested her head atop mine.

"Oh, Maggie, oh sweetheart," she whispered just above my ear. "I'm sorry. I'm so so sorry."

Why should she be sorry? I tilted my head up to look at her. Her eyes were closed, her hand still on my head, stroking my hair as she repeated it over and over again. "I'm so sorry."

The rest becomes a blur, a mix of words that I understood but could make no sense of. They talked about being safe, it not being my fault, and some friend of theirs who wanted to talk to me.

Next thing I knew I was in a car with an unfamiliar woman in a gray jacket, driving away from my school, away from my neighborhood, to a place I had never seen before. It went against every don't-talk-to-strangers, don't-get-in-strangers'-cars lesson I had ever learned. I felt anything but safe. I watched her face as we drove, focused on the road. She had green eyes like my teacher, but brown hair, like mine and my mom's, that fell to her shoulders. Her face looked young like my mom and teacher's did, but she had a deep crease in her forehead like the old principal Mr. Ramirez did. He smelled like mothballs and cough drops. She smelled like lemon pudding.

We pulled up next to a big building with dark windows and a mural of three angels on the top. I strained my neck to look up at it. Their faces were tilted down toward the ground and their eyes appeared closed. The angel in the middle had a halo made of stars that looked real and the two on the sides played trumpets that stretched down toward the sidewalk. I looked up at them as we walked through the front doors. Inside, the woman in the gray jacket fed me cookies, even though it was before lunch, and asked me questions. She smiled a lot. I guess she thought it would make me feel better, but it just made me feel worse since I couldn't figure out what she was so happy about. At first she just asked me simple things like what was my favorite toy and if I liked pizza. I tried to answer her quickly so that I could get back to school. I wanted to be there when my mom came to pick me up. Then she started to ask me all kinds of things about my family.

"Has anyone ever touched you where your underwear is?" Her face looked deadly serious. She placed a pink frosted cookie with rainbow sprinkles in front of me. I held it up in my hand and changed the subject.

"What animal do you think this is supposed to be?" I asked her. She looked irritated, but said that she thought it was supposed to be a camel.

"Has anyone ever touched you where your underwear is?" she repeated. I shook my head no.

"No?" she asked. I shook my head again. "Well, then," she said, "why do you think you are bleeding there?"

"I dunno," I said, shrugging my shoulders, my eyes focused on the cookie instead of on her. I thought of the time I saw blood on my mom's clothes and what she said. "My mom says that happens to women."

I knew what the woman in the gray jacket was asking me about. I knew, but I wasn't going to tell her.

"Don't tell," the voice had whispered in my ear. "They'll take you away if you tell."

The woman in the gray jacket put down the tablet she was writing on and leaned closer to me. I tried to keep my eyes down like the angels and look at the cookie so that I wouldn't feel anything, but her stare was upon me and it made it hard not to look up. It made my skin burn and my stomach ache. I wondered what "take you away" really meant. Was this woman trying to take me away?

"Yes," she said, nicely now, "that's true, but, Maggie, you aren't a woman yet. You're just a little girl."

I put the cookie down on the table, its icing melted and smudged from my touch, and I looked up at her. Her eyes looked sad and tired under her makeup. "I wanna go home now. And I'm not supposed to eat cookies before lunch, anyways."

If she saw what a good kid I was, surely she would have no choice but to take me home and this whole thing would be over.

The woman in the gray jacket reached out across the table and put her hand on mine. I looked at my fingers sticking out from under hers. They were waxy and tinted pink from the frosting, small dots of color speckling where the sprinkles had melted. I wanted to pull my hand back, but I didn't. The woman in the gray jacket then confirmed my worst fears. She told me that I wasn't going home. "Maybe someday," she said as she patted my hand, "but not today."

I wanted her to stop talking, to let go of my hand. I wanted to scream at her to stop, to shut up: I wasn't supposed to talk to strangers. I wanted to, but I couldn't because I was too scared.

I wanted to go home.

I started to cry. I tried to be big and to act strong. I tried so hard not to cry, but all my defenses melted away and then I couldn't stop it from happening. The tears just came. It made me feel bad that I was crying, and even more that I was letting her see me cry. I felt I had let her win. I raised my hands up over my eyes and covered my face, pushing my palms hard against my closed eyes, hoping it would stop the tears.

She kept saying that I was going to be safe now. I was surrounded by strangers in a place I didn't know and all they wanted to talk about was my safety. She told me that she would have someone go to my mom's house and get some of my favorite things. She asked if there was anything I wanted specifically and she would make sure that someone got it for me.

"I want Molly, I guess." With so much going on, it was hard to think of my room and what was in it, let alone what I wanted most out of it. I didn't know where I was going or for how long. I had never thought about leaving my house or what I would take with me if I did. Molly was an old doll, she had been my mom's when she was a little girl. Molly was dirt- and age-stained, but her color was still lighter than my own, an almost eggshell white. Her blond hair was dull and matted and her old flowered dress was torn in the front. When I tilted her up and down her blue eyes would close and open with a loud click.

Once I started to think of my room and my toys and everything I loved and would miss, I got intensely sad and scared. I couldn't stop naming the things I wanted; everything I thought of made me think of something else that I didn't want to say goodbye to.

"And my pink soft blanket and my pillow, the one with the butterflies on it. And my shiny black shoes and my new dress that I get to wear on Christmas. And my purple sweater. And my black teddy bear, not the brown one, the black one. My *Make Way for Ducklings* book. My rainbow pj's . . ."

"Well," she started and then paused. "I was thinking of maybe three or four things. Can you tell me which three of those things you want the most?"

I decided that I hated the woman in the gray jacket a lot. I hated her more than anyone I had ever met. My momma had always said never wish harm on anyone, not even your worst enemies, but in that moment I wished harm on the woman in the gray jacket with everything I had in my five-year-old soul.

"Just Molly, then. I just want Molly, then. Molly and my jewelry box." I started to worry that I wasn't going to get anything, that the woman in the gray jacket hated me just like I hated her and that that was why she was doing all of this.

She sent me to play in a room for what seemed like forever. Eventually, she walked in with Molly, the brown teddy bear that I said I didn't want, and a garbage bag half filled with my clothes. She told me to come with her. We walked through another room where another kid with a garbage bag full of things sat slumped down in a chair. Years later, helping another former foster kid move, we joked as we packed clothes into trash bags about how the trash bag was luggage for foster kids and wondered if in Beverly Hills and Century

City foster kids got genuine Hefty-brand trash bags that didn't tear at the top when you carried them. We laughed, but it wasn't funny, not really.

The woman in the gray jacket tried to hold my hand as we walked out of the building and to her car, but I refused. I shoved my hands deep into my coat pockets and looked at my feet as I walked. We drove for a while and I watched out the window as the city changed around us. We drove through side streets full of tall apartment buildings and signs in Spanish, onto the freeway, where we twisted through interchanges overlooking Korea Town and Little Ethiopia.

Finally, we pulled up in front of a white house with a red-tile roof. The woman in the gray jacket told me to wait in the car. I watched her walk up to the door where a white woman in a tight orange sweater and jeans stood holding a baby. I made a fist and dug my fingernails into my palm, concentrating on the pain instead of how scared I was of what was happening around me.

"Concentrate on something else," the nighttime voice would say. "Here"—and he'd make my hand into a fist, digging my nails into my palm, his weight pushing down on top of me. My nails had burned in my palm as they left deep imprints that filled with blood. "Concentrate on that."

After a few minutes, the woman in the gray jacket came back and told me to get out. I was going to stay at that house, she told me, but just until she found something else.

"That lady don't want me?" I asked, working up my nerve and looking up at the woman in the gray jacket. It was the first time I had looked at her since we'd left the big building, but she didn't notice.

"Doesn't," she corrected me. "The correct way to say it is 'doesn't want me,' and that's not it." She went on to say that Emma, the woman in the orange sweater, was a very nice woman, but that her house was already full of other kids. We walked inside. She carried the plastic garbage bag and I carried Molly in one hand and dug my fingernails into the palm of the other.

I sat on the sofa while the woman in the gray jacket and Emma talked some more. The house smelled good, like spaghetti sauce. I suddenly realized how hungry I was—I had missed lunch and left the cookies lying on the table in the big building. But I didn't say anything. The house was small and dark, with no pictures on the walls. I missed our apartment. My mom tried to make it look nice, with clean white walls and posters in big frames. Sadness crept over me. I held Molly up, tilted her backward and up and watched her blue eyes click open and shut.

Did my mom know that I'd been taken away yet? I thought of her going to my school to pick me up and them telling her I was gone. I knew she would cry. I thought back to the questions that the woman in the gray jacket had asked me in the office. The voice had said they would take me away if I told, but I hadn't told. I hadn't said anything. I replayed everything in my mind again to make sure. My mind kept getting stuck on one thing in particular: when I asked the woman in the gray jacket if I could go home, she said, "Maybe someday, but not today."

Someday could mean this weekend or it could mean never. Sometimes, when we were shopping and I wanted something, my mom would say "maybe someday" instead of "no," just so we wouldn't argue about it.

The woman in the gray jacket came over and said goodbye. I started to cry.

"I want to go home." I said it over and over. She tried to hug me, but I pushed her away, swinging small fists at her in anger and desperation. "I want my mommy."

Eventually she gave up trying to comfort me and said she'd be back in a few days when she found somewhere else for me to go. I stood there in the living room, crying and staring at the closed front door. I collapsed on the floor and cried and cried until I realized that no one cared and nothing was going to change. I dug my fingers into the brown carpet that smelled like cigarette smoke, and then I really started to cry.

That night, I met Emma's husband, a tall man named Gary, with freckles and hair the color of strawberries. The baby was their real kid, but they had two other foster kids: boys. Two was their limit, they said.

They seemed nice enough, but I wouldn't be staying there, so what did it matter? Mostly they left me alone.

Maybe the family didn't want to get attached to me because they knew I was going to leave, or maybe they didn't want me to get attached to them for the same reason. There is probably some foster-parent training class that tells you how you should act with a kid who is going to leave after a few days, but there certainly wasn't a class that taught foster kids how to act and adjust in the same situations. I walked around like a ghost for the next three days. I started to forget what my voice sounded like. The only time I heard it was at night when, alone on my cot in the extra room, I pulled my pillow over my head and cried. Once Emma heard me and came in, rubbed my back for a minute, and then turned on a night-light and left.

On the third day, the woman in the gray jacket reappeared. I sat on the front steps and held Molly while my trash bag of belongings was placed again in the backseat of her car. Then the lady approached Emma and the foster boys. The older boy said something I couldn't hear, and they all laughed. I wondered if it was about me. I tipped Molly backward and then up.

As soon as we were in the car I started pleading. No matter how much I hated her, she was all I had and she was in charge of my fate. It didn't make sense to leave me with people who didn't want me, I told her, when I was sure that my mom did. The lady stared dead ahead and listened to everything I said, nodding her head now and then. After about forty-five minutes, we pulled up in front of a yellow bungalow-style house in West L.A. As the engine shut off, she turned in her seat to face me and sighed. I knew then that all my talking had been in vain.

"Just be strong, sweetheart. Everyone likes a strong person. These are nice people. The stronger you are and the fewer problems you give them, the easier everyone's life will be."

I felt my body sink into the car seat with resignation. The woman in the gray jacket may have been all I had, but she had a lot of other kids with their own trash bags full of things. I wasn't special to her. I closed my eyes and thought about how my mom dropped me off at school every day with a reminder that she loved me. I wanted to hear that again. I longed for that love. I wondered if she was trying to get me back, if she was sad. I held Molly tight.

The woman in the gray jacket got out of the car, walked around to my side, and opened my door.

"You forgot the rainbow pj's I asked for," I said, getting out slowly, without looking at her.

"Come on," she said and smiled at me. "Let's do this."

. . .

The next three years were a series of temporary foster homes, and with each one came a change in neighborhoods and schools. My placements during those years numbered something like eight in total, although it was hard to keep track, since a few, like the one with Emma and Gary were only for a few nights. I had stayed in big houses and small apartments, had my own room, slept on a cot in a utility room, and slept on the top bunk of bunk beds in a shared room. Apparently a permanent placement was difficult to find for an "older" or "special needs" child, which basically meant anyone over toddler age.

Some homes were run by caring people, but most were far worse than the conditions I was removed from. It is rare to find a foster family that treats you as though you are a part of their family. In a city where people struggle to get by, a foster child is often just an extra paycheck. In poorer areas, they hung banners across streets like La Brea that said "Become a Foster Parent. Free Furniture. Generous Stipend."

One of the most important lessons I learned in foster care was that there is great variety within both good and bad. There are all different kinds of ways to love, just as there are all kinds of ways to abuse. The worst experiences are not always the most traumatic ones. People ask me if it was a good thing that I was removed from my parents' home, and I don't know the answer. I only know this: at a very young age, I learned what it meant to feel and be truly alone, and that is something one can never learn in her own home. In foster care I longed for the consistency and stability of a family and was taught that everyone in your life, no matter how much you love them, will leave you. I learned to walk into each new placement and look at each new face wondering how long it would be before I got moved again. I gave up trying to make friends. That perspective is my permanent scar, a deep and tender one, hidden where only those who really know me can see it. The child I was or could have been outside of the system was dead within the first year I entered it, and there was no reviving her. I had become a completely different person.

Ironically, considering the reason I was removed from my home, I found a full range of abuse in foster care. It came in all forms: physical, mental, and sexual. My foster parents and siblings stole from me: after about two years I had lost all the contents of my jewelry box, the teddy bear, and most of my photos. One family ate together each night, not allowing any of their foster kids to join them. After they had had their fill they would leave the table and allow us to eat the leftovers off their dirty plates. We would devour anything on the table and when there was not enough, the mother would tell us to break open the chicken bones and eat the marrow.

"That's the most nutritious part, anyway," she said as she walked out of the dining room. Young and hungry, we suffered the humiliation. We broke the bones open and scraped the marrow out with our forks. We ate. When there was nothing left to scavenge, we cleared the table and did the dishes. In that home, we always went to bed and woke up hungry.

Once someone has hit you, you learn what it feels like to be struck; maybe you even learn how to block the blows, or take them in the least painful areas of the body. I could look at the physical things and figure out how to survive them. The mental abuses were harder, because each time they played off a new fear, or a new broken space, within me. There was no way to expect or prepare for it.

Each abuse chipped away a new piece of my soul and brought me closer to giving up.

I still remember the morning when I stood in front of the bathroom mirror and decided not to hurt anymore. I was eight, and I was shocked that I hadn't thought of it before. I would watch my life from the outside rather than feel it from within. If I couldn't feel it, it couldn't hurt me.

That morning, even my shoes against the ground felt different, almost hollow. The little things that had made me happy, the candy at snack time, the softness of the violet I always picked from the yard and secretly rubbed in my pocket, those were hollow, too, but it was worth it. I felt free.

START FROM SCRATCH

AT THE END of the school year in 1982, when I was eight, the woman in the gray jacket showed up at Calvert Street Elementary School, one of the nicest schools I had attended, to move me one more time.

School let out each day at 2:40, and on this particular day I was doing as I always did, standing in the line of kids shuffling to get onto the bus. The schoolyard was a hub of commotion from the ring of dismissal to the departure of the last bus. Parents swarmed the yard and halls, searching for their kids and talking to other parents. Kids called to each other, waving and passing last-minute notes or making last-minute plans.

I was standing in the bus line, just watching, like I always did, when I noticed the woman in the gray jacket pull up. She parked her big brown, slightly outdated Caddy in the buses-only section and hung a laminated piece of paper with an official-looking emblem on it. I watched her exit the car and begin looking around. I knew she was looking for me. I hoisted my bag higher on my shoulder and started over to where she now stood with her back to me. Passing her car, I saw my things, back in their trash bag, sitting on the backseat. Molly lay on top. I turned and scanned the kids around me. When I saw a girl I recognized from my class, I went over to her and handed her my books.

"I'm transferring schools," I said without looking her in the eye, then turned around and quickly got in the car where the woman in the gray jacket, who had by now spotted me, was waiting.

"Where are we going?" I slammed the door shut. She hated it when I slammed the door, but her days of asking me to stop doing it were long over. She knew I was gonna do what I was gonna do.

By this point I had been labeled difficult and stubborn, diagnosed with attention deficit disorder, reactive attachment disorder, post-traumatic stress disorder, and now this new one: SED (severely emotionally disabled). At each new home she would run down my chart, mumble the doctors' terms, and then quickly add, "But she tests above average in IQ," as though it was some big consolation that after years of being deemed stupid, I was actually smart—just bad.

This time, the woman in the gray jacket said we were going to a placement in South Central Los Angeles. Her lips lingered on the words as if they were supposed to scare me. The name didn't sound any different than West Los Angeles or Van Nuys or Pacoma. I said it over in my mind a few times. South Central Los Angeles. South Central Los Angeles. Whatever it was, it was about to be home, at least for a few days.

The car twisted through side streets and onto the freeway. I didn't know anything about South Central. I didn't know about gangs and blue and red flags, turf, guns, drugs. I didn't know about poverty or bookless classrooms. But I knew by the way the woman in the gray jacket said it that I shouldn't expect anything good. I sat back in the seat and looked out the window so I could watch the neighborhoods shift.

This was the part I liked, watching the city evolve from one neighborhood to the next. The billboards and store signs would change languages and people would dress in different styles. The better areas had trees and flowers and the worse ones had stray dogs that bounded across the streets. I kept a tattered map that I had torn out of the yellow pages. L.A. was huge and the map was several pages, front and back. The foster-care system ran through all of L.A. County and covered all the small cities that filled it up. As we drove I would look for the names of places and try and remember them. Later, I would pull the map out, flip through its pages and draw over the places what they looked like, tall trees or dogs or foreign symbols on signs. I had seen and lived in a lot of cities: Pomona, Lakewood, Irvine, Pacoima, Van Nuys, West L.A., Burbank, Palmdale. I had been on freeways that passed through Whittier, Studio City, Beverly Hills, Santa Ana, Azusa, Fullerton, Brentwood, Santa Monica. I loved when we drove past the beach and I could smell the salt and seaweed in the air.

We rode the rest of the way in silence. The freeway began to climb uphill. Mulholland Drive, Sunset Boulevard, soon we were surrounded by green. In the distance, large houses looked out over the valley. Then the freeway rose up again and we arched onto a ramp and then another freeway: Robertson Boulevard, Crenshaw Boulevard. Large concrete walls blocked the view and I couldn't see anything, then we were on another freeway: Adams Boulevard, MLK Jr. Boulevard.

As we exited the freeway I sat up tall to get a better view. All the walls were covered with writing. It covered every surface, every fence, building, and wall. Large numbers and letters were shaded to per-fection in one spot and then crossed out in the next and covered partially by different ones. I didn't know it then, but this symbolized a borderland, a place where two gangs were clashing. When one set crosses out another's tag it is a statement that goes far beyond graffiti, it is an act of war and it will be fought over, sometimes to the death. The buildings, under their spray-painted surfaces, were small and close together. There were not the large familiar chains with big lighted signs like McDonald's and KFC; instead, they were small shops: Louisiana Fried Chicken, Johnny's Pastrami, and the simply stated Liquor Store. Unlike the people in my last neighborhoods, which had been mostly white or mixed-race, most of the people who hung out on corners and sat on top of parked cars here were Mexican or black. It was definitely more crowded and had a different feel than these other areas, but the biggest difference I saw was in the woman in the gray jacket. As we turned off the main street she reached across me and locked the door.

"What you locking the door for?"

"Well, it's just a good thing to do," she said without looking at me.

"How come you didn't do it when we got in the car, then?" I asked, curious now.

"Maybe I forgot." She sat straighter, closer to the steering wheel, looking from side to side every few minutes.

"What are you so worried about?" I asked. In my head I added: I'm the one getting a new place to live, with people I don't know. I'm the one changing schools again: new teachers, new books. I'd probably be behind again, too. I looked at the woman in the gray jacket as she looked nervously around and wondered if she knew how bad some of the homes she put me in really were. Then I wondered: If

she did know, didn't she care, or did she just not know what else
to do?

Finally, she stopped the car on a residential street. The freeway
was elevated here, and just a few houses down. You could see and
hear the cars speed by. The woman in the gray jacket's eyes darted
about, and then she sighed, "Well, then, this isn't so bad, is it?"

She still hadn't unlocked her door, so I just sat there and took it
in. Just in front of us a group of men and boys hung out, all of them
wearing red shirts, hats, or both. Some sat on a parked car, painted
a shiny red with gold rims and trim. It was the longest car I had ever
seen. I figured it was the size of a boat. One of the men rubbed the
car clean with a cloth, while some of the others sipped on big bottles of beer.

"All right then," the lady said, grabbing some files from the backseat. She took a deep breath and unlocked her door. "Come on now,
don't dawdle."

I climbed out and grabbed my trash bag of belongings. The
woman in the gray jacket walked around the front of the car, but as
she did, one of the older of the men turned and looked at her.
Noticing, she clutched her purse and looked sharply away.

"How you doin?" he said in a deep voice. The rest of the men and
boys looked back and forth among themselves and laughed as he
said it.

She said nothing, grabbed my hand, and pulled me toward a
small green house with a crumpled chain-link fence. There was a
short, plump, white-haired black woman sweeping the walkway and
a tall, thin, dark-skinned boy with closely cropped hair standing on
the porch rocking a light-skinned baby against his chest. I looked

back at the man by the car. He was still watching us. I felt bad that the woman in the gray jacket had ignored him. He hadn't done or said anything wrong. I smiled an apology at him. I understood—she made me feel like that, too. He noticed my acknowledgment and broke out in a wide smile. Then, with a slight yank, the woman in the gray jacket pulled me through the open gate.

"Maggie," said the woman in the gray jacket, "this is Evelyn." She held out some files. Evelyn smiled at me and motioned with her thick caramel-colored arm for the boy to come down off the porch. The woman in the gray jacket looked over her shoulder at her car.

"Well, dear, welcome home," she said, handing the broom to the boy. I smiled. I couldn't help it. She said "home," like I lived there, and she talked to me instead of to the social worker. "This here young man is my granson, Terrell, and that baby he holding is NeeCee, my grandaughter." The baby looked at me unblinking with hazel eyes. "You can go ahead an call me Big Mom. I ain sure I like it, sound too much like an old lady, but I guess that's me an everyone else calls me that anyway so you might as well call me that, too. Terrell, go put the broom in the shed, give that sweet baby to me." Evelyn slung the baby onto her hip and placed her other hand on my back. "Come now, lemme show you in." With that she led me away from the woman in the gray jacket and up the steps.

"Evelyn," called the social worker, "I'm going to leave these papers right here on the step. I just have to get going—busy, busy, busy."

Evelyn looked back at her with a look of acceptance. "Yes," she said, "I know you are. Go head then an jus leave em there." The woman in the gray jacket looked unsettled but set the folders down and turned to walk away.

"Oh, and Evelyn," she called out, "you have to get that board on the bottom step fixed. It's broken. That's a violation."

"Yes," said Evelyn, setting the baby down on the floor and winking at me. "Yes I know. I'll get that looked at." Her lips tightened a little as she spoke, as though she was holding back a laugh, and then broke out into a wide smile, the wrinkles around her eyes deepening.

The screen door banged closed and Big Mom called into the other room to turn off the TV. Outside, I could hear the woman in the gray jacket's car start up and pull away. She was on her way back to her own world, away from South Central, free of me, at least for now. She hadn't said anything about this being a temporary placement or that she would be back in a few days, so I guessed that this was it for a while. I looked away from the door and started to take in the house. It was smaller, dingier, and more crammed than most of the houses I had been in, but it looked livable. The front part of the house consisted of the living room and kitchen. The walls were tan and age-stained, but the air smelled of home-cooked food, and off to the left, two small children jumped up and down on the sofa laughing. The idea of food and happy kids would have made me okay with anything. I looked up at Big Mom, who was still looking down at me, and I smiled. I felt something like relief.

"Come on now, child, lemme show you where you gonna stay at." She put her hand on my back again and led me down the hall.

"Now, this first room here, that's the bathroom." She opened the door and leaned in, then pointed to the closet to the side of the door. "Towels, washcloths, soap is in there under the sink. I know it ain a lot, but it's home an we got each other, we got love and we got God.

An that, child"—she paused for a moment, for effect—"that is worth more than all the riches in the world." She smiled again, showing the whitest teeth I had ever seen and opened the next door. "Now, this is the girls' room. You gotta share with the other two, but you each got your own bed. Amen."

I looked in at the room: rose-colored walls and two twin beds on either side of a single window that was covered with bars. A weathered wooden crib stood against the back wall next to the closet. I still was not sure exactly who or how many people lived here. Each bed was neatly made with a white sheet and a pink pillow, and at the foot of each a hand-knit pink blanket lay atop a chest. Big Mom walked in, sat down on the bed to the right of the window, and pointed at the chest.

"This is your bed, and that chest right there, you can put all your things in that. Cept if you a have a few nice things that get hung up, then they go in the closet. You got a nice dress for church?"

I nodded my head that I did, wondering what exactly her definition of nice might be and hoping that she wouldn't be disappointed.

"You need some hangers, then?"

I nodded my head that I would.

"All right, then, ima get the rest ah the dinner together and then I'll bring a few in for you when I come back to let you know it's ready. Ima give you a few minutes to get settled in till then."

Big Mom reached over and used the post of the headboard to pull herself up. She moaned slightly under her breath as she got her footing. "Well," she said, "welcome home, an stay away from that window."

We stood in silence a moment, looking each other over, and then she did something that I will never forget. She leaned forward and kissed my forehead. I was completely unused to physical affection. I scrunched my eyes shut as her lips touched me and kept them that way until I heard the door shut behind her. I didn't know how else to react. In her absence, I reached up and touched my forehead where her lips had been.

I opened my clenched fist and the trash bag full of my things hit the floor. I lay down on the sagging bed which let out a squeak as my body pressed down on the springs.

I found that in these moments the worst thing to do was to start thinking too much, wondering about what it was going to be like, and for how long. It was going to be how it was going to be, good or bad, love it or hate it, and no amount of worrying would change that. I pulled the pillow tight over my head to block out the light. The pressure was a familiar comfort.

"God, please. I know I'm always asking you, but just let it be okay this time. I'm tired of always moving." I listened real close for a minute, just in case God felt like talking, but if he did, I couldn't hear him, so I closed my eyes.

I liked to think about my mom as I was falling asleep. The longer it had been since I'd seen her, the more beautiful and loving she became in my memories. I thought of her soft hands tucking me in and the way her laundry soap smelled on the blankets as they settled around my shoulders and neck. I thought about the way she kissed my cheek, the scent of her perfume and the sound of her voice as she told me to have sweet dreams. I was just starting to fall asleep when I was startled by loud and unfamiliar noises coming from outside Big Mom's house.

A combination of popping and tire screeching followed by

yelling that sounded so terrifyingly close, it seemed to be coming from the window above my head. Scared but curious, I rose to the window. Its thick bars partially blocked my view, but what I could make out was two men standing on the sidewalk where the big red car had been, and a third one sitting on the curb, hunched over. I leaned my head against the glass and found that if I squinted one eye and peered between the bars with the other, the scene came into focus. One man helped the one on the curb off with his shirt, and I could see then that blood was pouring down his back and his tattooed arm. His already red shirt on the ground caught blood as it fell, its fabric quickly changing from a bright orange-red to a deep, true blood red. The two unharmed men took turns studying the wound, leaning in close and talking intently. I was so absorbed in watching them, so scared and disgusted by the blood, that I didn't hear the door squeak open behind me.

When I suddenly sensed movement behind me I turned with a jolt to see two girls standing just inside the doorway: a little, wild-haired angel holding the hand of a girl about my age and size with long, neat braids and a dark, round face and almond-shaped eyes. The little one smiled and pulled her other hand from behind her back. Three hangers were clenched tightly in her small fist.

"Big Mom toldt me give you these and to tell you fifteen minutes ta dinner," the older one said and smiled. The younger one smiled again, too, a wide smile full of baby teeth and a deep dimple in each cheek.

"How old are you?" I asked the little one, taking the hangers.

"Two an a half." She ran over to the other bed and grabbed a half-disintegrated, one-eyed teddy bear. "Dis my bear."

"Oh yea?" I said as she handed it up to me for approval. "He looks kinda old."

She took him back and hugged him.

"It was her momma's," the older girl said. "I'm Tiffany. That's Nishia. She my cousin." She pointed to the little girl, who plopped the stuffed bear down on the bed and walked out the door. "I don't stay here. I'm jus here till my momma come back from the store. You know you ain supposed to look out that window like that, right? People be shootin outside." Tiffany talked like she thought she was a grown-up.

"Shootin?" I asked

"Shootin," she said, "like guns." We looked each other over for a minute, and then she sighed, reminded me that dinner was in fifteen minutes, and left.

I walked back to the window and looked out. I was suddenly well aware of what had happened. The one man had been shot, and the loud popping was the gun. The three men were gone now, as was the shirt that had lain on the sidewalk, but I could still see the blood staining the path. I watched as neighbors and passersby walked around it, either pointing and nodding or barely noticing at all. I walked back toward the little angel's bed and picked up her bear. I remembered Big Mom saying that the oldest boy was her grandson and the baby was her granddaughter. Where was their mother, I wondered—the original owner of this bear. I set the bear back down and went over to dump the contents of my trash bag onto my bed and see what was missing this time.

My belongings didn't even cover the top of the twin bed. I picked up my red button-up sweater and white dress and hung them on two of the three hangers. I opened the closet door and placed them on the far right, behind a few other lacy dresses, sweaters, and jackets of various sizes. Then I started folding my other clothes: three T-shirts, a pair of jeans, a nightgown, and two pairs of shorts. I opened the chest at the foot of the bed and placed the T's on one side and the jeans and shorts on the other. In the gap on the side I put my four pairs of socks and underwear. Then I closed the chest. I put the nightgown under my pillow and Molly on top. That left only two things on my bed: a toothbrush and my map. I took the map and ran my hands across it a few times to straighten it out. I looked for South Central L.A., but it didn't say that anywhere. I looked at the freeway numbers and found the ones we had traveled that day: 101, 405, 10, 110. I traced them until I found where we were. Still it didn't say South Central. It said other cities, though, West Adams, Watts, Inglewood, Hyde Park. I wondered what the name of this city was if it wasn't South Central. It was unsettling not to know the name of where I was.

I looked over to the small pile of toys in the corner and grabbed the box of crayons. I pulled out the broken half of a red one and colored the area I was now living in. I looked at the map and tried to think of what else I should draw. I thought again of the woman in the gray jacket, the way she had whispered the words "South Central Los Angeles," the way she had locked the door. I dug through the box and found a little stub of a black crayon and wrote the words "South Central." Then I put the crayons away and placed my map in my chest.

CONCEPTIONS OF SHADE

THE SUN SCORCHED all summer. Big Mom's old 1920s-style bungalow trapped the heat and magnified it. With no air conditioning, it was actually cooler to be outside. Big Mom would tell us to prop the front door open with old phone books to let in some air, but with no cross ventilation it didn't really help. "Well," she'd laugh and shake her head as it grew hotter and hotter and beads of sweat built up on our faces, "least it makes me feel like I'm tryin." When she laughed it was a deep sound that shook her whole body. I liked it because you knew she meant it.

I'd spent two months in my new placement and was starting to feel almost at home. I liked these people and they actually seemed to like me, too. The older kids had given me a new nickname, Bree, and it stuck. New name for a new life. They had even made me a cake on my ninth birthday, a first since I had turned five. The four other kids living in the house were Big Mom's grandkids by her daughter Rhonda, who had traded her once stable home life for crack addiction on the streets. Terrell, thirteen, was the oldest grandchild; two years younger was Taye, short for Jontaye, though no one called him that. Terrell and Taye had the same dad, but he had left them and their mom when the boys were six and four. They hadn't heard from him since. Then came the babies: Nishia was two and three-quarters, and NeeCee was almost eight months. Nishia's dad wasn't around and no one even knew who the baby's dad was. In addition to winning custody of her grandkids, Big Mom had become a state-certified foster parent, and one of the few willing to take in kids on an emergency basis.

Big Mom's biological kids had grown and moved on, with two exceptions, who had remained in L.A. Rhonda was occasionally spotted on the street, obviously addicted to crack, and another daughter, Denise, lived a few neighborhoods over with her daughter, Tiffany, in a big yellow apartment building. Big Mom and Denise would sometimes trade off watching the kids while the other shopped or ran errands. Tiffany was about my age and, having grown up in the area, understood everything I didn't. Over time she would teach me how to play video games; how to dress and talk; how to distinguish between Mexicans, blacks, Haitians, and Puerto Ricans; and how to tell a Blood from a Crip.

Out of everybody in the family, though, Terrell was my favorite, and in my nine-year-old way I tried to tag along after him in everything he did. He was handsome and charismatic, always had friends hanging around him, and always wore bright, starched, and perfectly ironed red shirts. Tiffany said it was because he wanted to be a Blood like the guys with the shiny cars and stereo systems. She said it was the Bloods in red and Crips in blue who were shooting outside my window and in the park. Terrell said he just wore red because red was his favorite color, but he and his friends adopted a sophisticated slang that advertised their homage to the Blood gang, replacing spoken *c*'s (letter of the enemy, Crips) with *b*'s, or crossing them out with *k*'s in writing. I was both fascinated by the complexity of it all and eager to top Tiffany's insider knowledge: I took note of every word.

We spent most of the summer in the yard or down in the park. Moms didn't care as long as the boys were keeping an eye on us and we came in when the streetlights switched on. I would help Nishia go up and down the slide, or push her on the baby swings while Terrell and Taye ran back and forth between watching us and talking to the older Bloods. Terrell always had some money, and on the walk home he would buy us all nickel candy to eat.

One hot August afternoon we sat outside in the yard, me listening to Terrell and his friends talking. The grass everywhere was dead, brown and dry, and rough against my bare legs. There was a drought, limiting lawn-watering to certain days of the week, but it didn't matter since water and electric rates had jumped and no one in our neighborhood could spare a drop for grass anyway. It killed Big Mom to see the flowers and grass she'd worked so hard to grow wither and die now. She would shake her head as she walked down the steps, eyeing the dead and dying plants, and say, "Poor things."

As always, I listened to the boys' slang and repeated the words over and over in my mind, committing their meaning and pronunciation to memory. I noticed Terrell's afro pick sitting on the ground next to him. Much to Big Mom's displeasure, he was trying to grow his hair out. In an attempt at what I thought was utter coolness, I grabbed it and ran it through my hair, turning to make sure Terrell was watching.

"You brazy, gurl?" he said. "What chu doin?"

I froze. Then I pulled myself up as tall as I could, scrunched my eyes up, and leaned into his face. "You brazy, turkey lips." Turkey lips. I had just turned nine. It seemed so brilliant.

"No, you brazy," he said, not to be challenged. "Uze white gurl. White gurls don't use that shyt." He and his friends, his "homies," as he called them, all burst into laughter.

I threw the black-pronged thing at him and ran in the house, jumping into the lap of Big Mom, who wrapped her giant, fat black arms around me.

It was the first time I had heard myself called white. I heard it as a powerful insult. Living here, white seemed to mean rich people who didn't understand or care.

"What's wrong, baby?"

"Terrell being mean," I offered as the arms pulled tighter around me. "He called me white," I bellowed. Big Mom said nothing, but rocked me gently back and forth, slightly chuckling, patting my shoulder.

"Well," Big Mom started, laughing outwardly a little now. "He's only part right on that, because you are white, but you white an Indian mixed. Jus like I'm black an Indian mixed. That's what us black folk call a redbone. But white folk, they jus call us black no matter what we mixed with. Black is black to them."

"What they call someone who's white and Indian mixed?"

"Well," Big Mom thought for a minute, "Indian people might got a word for it, but I'm not too sure. Ta white folk, if you look Indian, you Indian, an if you look white, you white."

I thought about that for a minute and then looked at Big Mom. Her eyes were the deepest brown I'd ever seen. "What if I don't wanna be white?"

"Well," she said, smiling a big smile, "that's white folk for ya. They thinking everyone wanna be white so they finna consider you white anyway. Like it or not." I wasn't sure that her answer made me feel better, but she laughed and kissed me on the cheek, like it was supposed to, so I smiled.

"Now you run along, child. Go an see what Nishia's doing. She came in to see what upset you and then jus disappeared." I climbed up off Big Mom's lap and watched as she pulled herself up out of the chair.

"What chu finna do, Momma?" I suddenly realized she'd been sitting down when I came in the house. Big Mom was never sitting down. She was a whirlwind of laundry, cooking, scrubbing, dusting, ironing, and baking. I loved watching her. She was a domestic super-woman.

"I'm jus fixin to talk ta Terrell for a minute," she said, patting at her hair where a few flat-ironed pieces flew out from under a yellow flowered head scarf. My heart sank. Big Mom was always mad at Terrell for some reason or another. It would start out with her talking to him about something small—his forgetting one of his chores, or coming in late—and would end up with her yelling at him about his friends and clothes. I didn't want her to end up yelling at him over my hurt feelings, too. I couldn't stand to have him mad at me, or worse, to stir up problems that would mean a new placement.

"Momma, I ain mad at him. He wasn't being mean. I take it back."

She smiled at me. "No, child, ima send those other boys on their way and tell him to get in here an take this trash out. Unless you wanna be doin his chores for him."

"Oh," I said. "Naw, ima just check on Nishia like you said." I walked out of the kitchen and through the living room, where Taye was playing Combat on Atari.

"Bam, nigga, take that. Yea, nigga, what now? Huh, punk? What's up now, nigga?"

He looked up and smiled when he saw me walk in the room. It was blistering hot and sweat was dripping down his forehead. He wiped it away with a bare arm.

"Bree, play me."

"Naw, Big Mom asked me to check on Nishia."

"I jus checked her, she straight. She playin wit her dolls. Now P-L-A-Y me."

"Naw, ima make sure. I don't want Big Mom be mad."

"You scurred to play me?" Taye wrinkled his forehead up.

"No."

"Fine, then, cause ima go easy on you." He nodded his head at me and smiled.

"Aiight, then come wit me to check on her, then I'll go ahead an whoop ure butt."

Taye cracked up at that, but I'd been secretly practicing at the game when he wasn't home so I could surprise him.

"Oh, like dat, then, huh, lil sis? Let's go check that baby cause I kan't wait ta whoop ya now, fa real."

We raced down the hall and to the left past the bathroom, where Taye took the opportunity to shove me in and hold the door shut briefly.

"Lemme out, turkey lips."

Taye opened the door, laughing. "Don't say turkey lips, that's wack. Say punk or faggot or mark ass nigga."

I tried to walk past him out the bathroom, but he dodged quickly to the side and blocked me. "Say it," he said, grinning.

I tried again to escape, moving quickly to the right and trying to slip by, but Taye was too big. I looked up at him and gave him my humblest okay-you-win expression, but he still wasn't satisfied.

"K'mon, say it, Bree. Say move, punk."

"Move, punk," I said meekly.

"Awww man, not like that. Ain no one finna move for that. Say Move, PUNK!"

"Move, PUNK!" I said louder.

"Well, that's better, but next time throw ure arms up like this when you do it." Taye put both his hands up by his face and demonstrated. "Now say punk ass nigga."

"Ima tell Momma you cussin."

"Momma ain finna protect you in skool. I mean daymn, it's like you wanna get ure ass beat."

I looked at him and narrowed my eyes. Again I tried to get past him and again he blocked me. I felt trapped, and that triggered panic.

"Punk ass nigga," I said and shoved him my hardest with both my hands on his stomach. He was roughly twice my size and the impact barely moved him, but he let me pass him. "Stoopid ass," I added as I walked toward the bedroom. Taye put his hands on my shoulders and walked behind me in love and pride at my growth. I was proud, too.

I turned the knob and opened the door, Taye behind me. There sat Nishia on the floor, ashy-kneed, with her hair all wild. She smiled when we walked in. Nishia had the best little-kid smile: her nose would squinch up and her eyes disappear into narrow slits as her jagged little baby teeth bit together. I put one finger over my mouth reminding her to be quiet so as not to wake eight-month-old NeeCee, and she smiled back as she nodded, pleased at her self-reliance and good behavior. That's when something else caught my eye, and my stomach dropped.

"Pretty, lookit," Nishia said quietly and held up Terrell's scrapbook. Red, blue, yellow crayons, and a broken half of an orange one lay scattered around the brown shag carpet.

"Tell me it's jus that page," I whispered as I sat down on the floor next to Nishia. I lifted the prized book out of her lap.

Terrell was the self-appointed historian of his family. He held on to everything and kept an up-to-date record of all things that happened to any of his siblings, something that Big Mom didn't have time or energy to do. His care and reverence for history were impressive. I had no pictures of my own birth parents or any of the people that I'd lived with since I left; the few I had got stolen or misplaced along the way. I never got my yearbooks, which cost money to purchase at the end of the year. In a way, I'd stopped existing anywhere but in the moment. Life was easier and less painful that way.

I flipped through the pages of Terrell's scrapbook, now colored over in bright crayon colors. The first page was a photo of himself as a newborn in the hospital, eyes puffy and sour-faced at the sight of the new world. The next several pages contained old pictures of his mom and dad back when they were still around, before he came to live with Big Mom. There were first- and second-birthday photos, a picture of him holding Taye as a baby, and then all the family stuff stopped. Both Nishia and NeeCee were born addicted to crack—no one takes pictures of events like that. But Terrell had heart: he wrote down their birthdays and put in pictures taken later on at church on Easter and Christmas. As the pages progressed, the family photos began to mix with funeral programs and photos of people holding red flags. In the margins of the pages, now under Nishia's crayon scrawl, he had written the different names or numbers that represented Crip hoods—"30s, 40s, 60s, Hoovers"—and then crossed them out with big red *X*'s. He'd written "BIP" (Blood in Peace) under pictures of Bloods who had been shot. In one picture, Terrell stood in front of the school with two other boys, his thumb and pointer finger forming a circle while the other three fingers stood straight up to make the letter *b*.

"That's what they do," Tiffany had once explained, demonstrating with her fingers. "That's how you know they a Blood." I looked at the pictures of Terrell. Then, as I turned the pages I saw a picture of Terrell, Taye, and me sitting on a bench at the park, and in the margin he had written, "Me, lil bro, an sis." I just stared at it, reading the words over and over again.

Finally Taye tapped me on the knee.

"What we finna do?"

"I dunno," I said, flipping back through the pages.

Taye stood and picked Nishia up. We contemplated our different options while Nishia, who didn't understand but knew she had done *something* wrong, said she was sorry over and over.

"Sorry for what?" Big Mom had suddenly appeared in the doorway.

I tucked the book under my arm and stood up. I knew that if Big Mom saw these recent pages—the pictures, the writing, the red bandanas and hand signs—there would be no more pretending that red was simply Terrell's favorite color. I knew she was going to yell and that they were going to fight.

"Nothin, Momma," I said, pushing the book further behind my back and then leaning up against the wall to hide it completely from her sight. "I got it."

Big Mom looked back and forth between me and Taye, trying to decide if she believed me.

Her gaze was one we all knew. Nishia clung tight to Taye, her little fingers gripping at his shoulders. "Don't be mad."

Big Mom held her hand out toward me.

I said nothing. I was supposed to have been watching Nishia. This was largely my fault. I looked down at the floor and held the book out toward Big Mom. I didn't want to see her face as she looked through it. Why hadn't I gone right in and checked on Nishia when Big Mom first asked, instead of goofing around with Taye?

A moment passed. I could hear the turning of the pages and then a deep sigh. I looked up as Big Mom shut the book, her face quickly changing from a deep furrowed anguish to a removed calm.

"Well, the damage could be worse. Go tell him. He jus down at the park, I think. All of you, go on together."

I reached up to take the book back from her, but she pulled back. "I'll hold on to it. Go and bring me the baby from her crib. Don't need her napping too long an staying up all night."

I nodded my head and followed her directions. My stomach ached all the way to the park.

I saw Terrell the minute we got into the park. He was playing basketball with some of his homies and even though most of them were older than him, he was scoring. Taye put Nishia down and she ran in a wobbly toddler style over to the courts, clapping her hands together and saying, "Yeah, my brother!"

Terrell looked over and smiled, then gestured for Taye to come play. Taye pulled his shirt off over his head and ran in. I sat down and lifted Nishia onto my lap. Nishia clapped and yelled "Yeah!" every time someone scored a point, regardless of which team it was. "Yeah, my brothers!"

Taye and Terrell were dripping in sweat when the game was over, and as they came over to where Nishia and I were sitting, Nishia jumped up and down, arms stretched up over her head. Terrell wiped his forehead with a white hand towel and reached down to lift her up. She smiled proudly on his shoulders as the other players patted him on the back saying, "Good game."

"Man"—Taye shook his head, as we started the walk home—"you might kould get a skolarship, bro."

"You trippin, lil bro, I ain been ta skool on the regular in a year, how ima go ta kollege? You gotta take all them tests an shyt. That ain me."

"I dunno," Taye kept on it, "you good tho man. I mean GOOD."

The conversation stopped for a moment and I looked over at Terrell. "Hey, Tee," I started. His comment on ditching school had reminded me of the confrontation waiting for him at home. I couldn't stand not telling him anymore. "Nishia, she colored in ure photo book. And then Big Mom looked through it"—I stumbled with my words for a minute—"but, I mean . . . it's my fault. I was supposed ta be watchin her."

Terrell's eyes changed and his mouth slackened slightly. Nishia, on his shoulders, started to cry, and then Terrell's expression changed again. The muscles in his jaw tensed and his eyes cleared of emotion.

"Ain no thing," Terrell said, though I could tell he didn't mean it. "Don't kry, Nishia." He lifted her off his shoulders and held her against his chest, and she buried her little head against him. We walked the rest of the way home in silence.

Big Mom met us on the porch. "Dinner's ready, go wash up. You all been playin ball?"

"Yea, Momma," Taye said.

"Who won?"

Taye tossed the ball to Momma, who caught it like a pro. "Terrell's team always win, Momma, you kno that."

"Go inside and wash up, let me talk to Terrell a minute." I hesitated, but finally obeyed, the screen door banging against its crooked frame behind me.

The yelling started instantly.

"You think you a gangsta now? Is that it? I seen all the pictures. Yea, that's right. I seen the red Chucks, the bandanas, the gang signs. You one of these gangbangers now?"

Taye and I each stood looking hopelessly at each other on opposite sides of the door frame, listening.

Terrell would try to talk, but a soft, defeated-sounding "Momma, look . . ." was as far as he could get. There was really nothing he could say, anyway, and Big Mom's rage came from that very knowledge.

We lived in a place where gangs recruited with the same intensity as the NFL did, and Terrell, with his natural athleticism, sense of loyalty, and rage against the cards that life had handed him, was the equivalent of a first-round draft pick. We all knew, too, that once that ball started rolling, there was no turning back.

I looked over at Taye, who had shifted his gaze from me to the street outside. The room had grown noticeably darker as the sun set over the city. I gazed out at the power lines, the palm trees, the reddening sky, and the street that led away from our house out toward the park, and thought about something I'd overheard one of Terrell's friends say once. "A nigga didn't choose this, it chose me. It ain't my fault the streets was kalling."

GOD'S FAVORITES

SIX MONTHS LATER, Terrell became "official" and got jumped into the gang. He had the good sense to stay out of Big Mom's sight for a week while word spread and the cuts and bruises faded. No one called the police to file a missing-persons report. The next morning's graffiti told us what we had suspected, that he had been initiated into the neighborhood Blood set and made an official active member. After a few days, Big Mom confirmed it, walking up to a little Blood who was sitting on the hood of her car and asking him, with surprising street flair, "Who's ure G?" He pointed across the street. Big Mom breathed in heavy and approached him. She wrung her hands together as they talked. After a few minutes, she reached out and shook his hand, walked back across the street into the house, and shut herself in her room.

Little did Big Mom know, she needn't have gone to the G, she could have asked me. Some classmates and I had witnessed the initiation, fully aware of what it was and what it meant. The homies were testing Terrell to see if he had heart. If he didn't fight back hard enough, or if he gave up or cried when the homies were coming at him, it guaranteed he would be useless against the enemy. No matter how bad this fight seemed, the homies wouldn't kill him, but the enemy would. So five grown men beat thirteen-year-old Terrell for two minutes in the street. He fought back, but they still left him with two black eyes and a raw, swollen nose. When it was over, the biggest one reached out a hand to help him sit up, patted him on the back, and he and the others walked away. We went over and sat next to Terrell. He looked like a monster. He couldn't come home like that. He spit a mouthful of blood into the street and we parted ways.

Ever since then, Terrell had been hitting the streets at night after Big Mom had left for her night job cleaning office buildings across town. He would often take Taye out with him. They both had dreams of ghetto fortune and fame. They were out to get their names known and earn their stripes. In the morning, as Taye walked me to school, I listened wide-eyed as he recapped their adventures. Then, in November of 1983, Terrell was picked up by the police on robbery and assault charges. He was fourteen.

I wasn't a good sleeper, and although I had gotten used to the constant noises that came from outside, every little sound within the house woke me up and kept me up for hours. Doctors said my insomnia was a symptom of post-traumatic stress disorder, an actual chemical reprogramming of my brain. They could medicate the symptom, but there was no fixing the problem. I hated the way the pills they prescribed left me feeling tired and groggy all day, so on weeknights when Big Mom worked and wasn't home to enforce things, I took the pill out of the orange container and pushed it down the sink drain.

I spent a lot of the time lying awake and thinking about what my brothers were doing, or getting up and watching what went on outside my bedroom window. People do dirt on about every street of Los Angeles and ours was no exception. So at night, for something to do, I would study the business of it all.

Sometimes I would watch my sisters sleep. Nishia, now almost four, tossed and turned restlessly all night, while almost-two-year-old NeeCee, who at the doctor's suggestion had slept with her arms bound up against her at night for the first year of her life, slept solidly in one place, hardly moving. She still slept as though swaddled, but those in the know could see the jerky movements, traces of her rocky start.

I was awake that night when the phone rang. I looked at the red digital numbers of the alarm clock glowing in the almost darkness: 3:15. I got out of bed and crept to the door, cracking it open so that it wouldn't squeak. I looked out and down the hall. Momma usually got home from her second job about that time and she was standing, her back to me, in the kitchen. Her pink robe was drawn tightly around her. Her dinner sat, half eaten, on the table beside her.

"Oh dear. Yes, yes. I understand. Am-am I supposed to come get you?" Her voice cracked and she stumbled over her words. "Okay, you say you got an arraignment Monday, then? Yea, I'll call an find out the time. Terrell?" She paused, running one hand over the top of her head. "I love you, boy."

Momma's hands must've been shaking because she couldn't get the phone back onto the receiver. She attempted and failed a few times and then just let it hit the floor. Big Mom's tears were always silent and whatever words followed them were always directed toward God. *There's only two people you can truly depend on in life, she would tell us, yourself and God, and please believe, God is whole lot smarter, so whenever you find yourself in a situation an you're upset, you betta ask him for some guidance.* She lived by those words as surely as she asked us to.

"Lord"—she started pacing the kitchen floor back and forth, hitting her palm against the counter as she walked—"I kno you don't give me more than I can handle, but please, sweet Jesus, help me with these youngstas." She fell silent for a minute, as though listening for the answer, and then her usually confident voice changed.

"Lord," she said again, this time as though pleading, "I don't think I understand the world anymore. My own daughter off doin drugs when she got babies hungry at home, no sign they daddies. Now them boys actin up on me. I need help, Lord. I need help. This ain the world I knew." She shook her head slowly in disbelief, wiping at her eyes with a kerchief. "I don't kno what ta do. Please, Lord, guide me."

Momma's shoulders collapsed under her burdens and she started to cry hard, head down on the table, one hand held up to God. I pushed the door closed, not caring this time if it made noise. She wouldn't notice.

I walked over to Nishia's bed. She had kicked most of her blankets and her stuffed dog off onto the floor; one of her arms hung over the side of the bed, threatening to pull her down on top of them. It was nothing for Nishia to fall out of the bed. Taye had found a large, somewhat flat, green and purple stuffed dog at the swap meet and thought to bring him home to block the side of the bed, thus keeping her from rolling out. Before that, it had been an almost nightly event, Nishia waking up, panicked and screaming half the time. The other half of the time she'd hit the floor without noticing, staying there until morning.

I scooted her over away from the edge toward the wall. Her brow tightened and furrowed, and she mumbled something inaudible.

"What, baby?" I hoped my voice would wake her up the rest of the way so I would have some company, but she just mumbled something else, rolled over onto her side, and faded back into sleep. If she woke up on her own, I would take the flashlight from under the bed and we would read or play Candyland, but I had learned my lesson about waking her up: she would only wake up crabby and cry until she fell back asleep. It was cold, dipping down into the fifties at night. I picked up her blankets and piled them back on top of her. I placed Boodle, as she called her giant dog, back next to her and gave him a pat on the head.

"Stay, Boodle. Good dog." It was our joke, and I repeated it even though she was asleep. I reached up above her and knocked on the wall twice. Taye knocked back once. I had heard him sneak in the door just before Momma got home.

I slid open the closet door, and sat down inside. We had punched out a small hole in the wall between the two rooms in the back of the closet so that we could conference when we had to. The idea had come one day when Momma had left us at Auntie's house while she went to the grocery store. Big Mom didn't like that Denise lived in the projects, the men she dated, or that she sometimes stayed out late at night when she had a kid at home, but leaving us in her care was still easier than trying to do the shopping with us and all our requests, and it was only for an hour or so. We sat on the sofa and watched TV as Auntie had another fight with her boyfriend. Then he pushed her so hard her head left a hole in the wall where it hit. Later, at home that night, Terrell took a hammer into the closet, pushed the clothes to the side, and swung five times before it went all the way through the Sheetrock partition.

"You hear what happen on the phone?"

"Naw, jus heard it ring." In the darkness, I could see the outline of Taye's face.

"It was Terrell. He in jail."

"Aww, daymn, you kno fo what?"

"Naw, jus heard Momma say he had, umm, arraignment? What's that?"

"Oh," Taye said, his voice steady and knowledgeable, "that's when they set bail and give you ure charges an shyt. Well, daymn, that means it's fo mo than spray paint on the walls, I'll tell you that much. Ay, I got some Pop-Tarts from the store. Want one?"

"What kind?"

"Them brown suga ones."

"Those my favorites."

"I already know." Taye handed me one through the hole. "That's why I got them, sucka."

I ripped open the foil and pulled out one of the pastries. Surely there was no better food on earth then the frosting-covered Pop-Tarts. I bit off the corner and let the filling melt in my mouth.

"Daymn, that shyt's good."

"Yup. Well, lil sis, might as well get some sleep, ain nothing ta do but wait an see what happens in the morning. You kool, though?"

"Yea, I'm aiight, jus hope Tee straight."

"He straight, lil momma, don't trip. You always worry too much." Taye stuck his hand through the hole and we shook.

"Love you, lil sis."

"Love you, too."

I got up and walked over to the window. Outside, smokers walked around, piling recyclables into carts, anticipating the money they would get for their morning fix. I thought about Terrell. I bet he wasn't sleeping, either. I wondered if he was going to be taken away because of this, or if we all were. Who knew what kind of reason they needed to come and snatch you up. I rested my head on the window ledge and watched a white woman in a tight short black dress and spikey heels approach the Chevy that stayed parked all night on the corner, and hand some money to the man inside. The height of the heels gave her walk a certain stagger and sway that I knew was enhanced by the visit she had made to Terrell's friend Ryder, who stood out on the corner, sleepy-eyed, slangin' dope all night long, rain or shine. A few minutes later a different woman in similar attire did the same thing. I watched them disappear all night long in different men's cars and then reappear, get out and divide up the bills in hand. They would pocket some, take some to the Chevy and some to the dope dealer. The ritual repeated over and over, and my brain half focused on them and half focused on my life, my losses, and what was possibly to come.

I saw two men pull up in a lowered Regal and step out to talk to Ryder. They were wearing red—gang members. From the way Ryder nodded and let them talk I knew they were OGs. The two big homies finished talking and for the first time I saw Ryder's mouth move, saying some short acknowledgment, then the two men put their pointer fingers and thumbs together and held up the *b*, and got back into the car. Ryder stepped out off the curb and into the street and held up the *b* as the car pulled away. He remained there for a minute after they'd gone, as though saluting, and then came running diagonally across the street and up to Taye's window. Since that window was next to mine and the old walls did nothing to block out sound, I heard everything.

"Aye, yo, Taye, you up, lil homie?" At first there was no answer, so he tapped on the window, "Aye, dawg . . ."

"Yea, wassup? What happen wit my brother?" Taye's voice sounded more tired than eager, but I knew he wanted to know what happened as badly as I did. He just couldn't sound like a bitch about it.

"Yea, was fukked up, Blood. Guess he was up off Exposition an this nigga had this thick gold chain on. So the homie told Tee, ima go ask this nigga some shit and when he start talking to me, yank homie chain an take off. Easy kome up, feel me? Pawn shop'll buy it an ain really traceable. So homie walk up to the nigga an ask him some bullish, you seen my sister, she got in a fight wit her boyfriend an ask me kome pick her up, that kinda shyt, and then Tee he run up an grab that chain an take off, but this nigga . . . I dunno, mothafukka musta run track in the day or some shyt kause he take off after him and katches him. Jus grabs Tee, and Tee start swingin on him and jus then, mothafukkin one-time kome round the korner. Tee try ta get away, but nigga has his arms lokked round his chest. Then when the police looked, Tee still had that chain in his pocket."

"Daymn." Taye's voice sounded shaken. Terrell had recently been caught by the police on tagging crew and let off with a warning. The chances of a second warning weren't too good. The robbery didn't so much matter, but assault would be considered a violent offense. I didn't want to hear any more. I walked away from the window and lay down on my bed, pushing my pillow over my head to block out the conversation. I didn't want to think about Terrell not coming home tomorrow, about my new family being broken up. I knew Big

Mom couldn't sleep either because I'd heard the TV through the living room wall, fake laughter at fake people living their happy made-up lives. Eventually, I pulled the pillow from my head and waited for morning; watching the room grow slowly lighter.

I must have fallen asleep at some point, because suddenly I bolted up in bed to the sound of voices in the living room, only this time it wasn't the happy voices of TV land, it was Momma and Taye fighting. I looked at the alarm clock, it was still before seven. I pushed my ear against the paper-thin wall to make out the words. Momma was laying into him, asking him what had happened, if he had been there.

"What is wrong wit y'all? Don't you see how hard I work to make sure y'all have something? An what you do? You run around, actin a fool, willin to jus throw it all away like it ain nothin. What them streets done fo you? I'm waitin . . ."

At first Taye said nothing. He knew better. There was nothing to say that Momma could understand. The gap had grown too great. It was true what Momma was saying. She did work hard, too hard, and that was part of the problem. It didn't feel good to watch her come and go from cleaning other people's homes and businesses and then come home and clean ours. We did have a roof over our heads, clothes, food, but the price seemed so high, and outside our door was a whole other world. The reality was, she couldn't understand it and she certainly couldn't protect us from it, and for all her hard work she couldn't buy us the material things we craved, or give my brothers the fathers they needed.

"That's what I thought," she started up again. "What ure big homies done for you, Taye? I just hope you seein all this, I mean really seein this. I hope you seein what Terrell's big homies done for him. An now guess who it's on? Who he call when it all falls down? Yea, that's right, me. Ain no one care but your family an God."

Then I heard Taye's voice. He spoke quietly enough that I had to strain to make out the words.

"Yea, Momma? Really? Where exactly is ure God?" Taye's voice changed, growing from a scared twelve-year-old boy's to that of a strong young man with a lifetime of experience. "You talk all this shyt bout God's favorites an how we have a hard time but God never give us nothing we kan't handle. Look the fukk around. Look at this. Know what I think?"

It was dead silent in the house for a moment. I squeezed my eyes shut, and dug my nails deeply into my palm, knowing what was coming.

"God is jus like everyone else. He jus don't give a fukk. I didn't ask fo this shyt. Fukk, Momma, what if I ain like you? What if I ain that strong? What if I don't want to be one of God's favorites an have to overcome, work two, three jobs and jus trust that my life is harder than otha people's kause God thinks I'm strong?"

Then came the sound of flesh being struck. Whatever she hit him with, she hit him hard because I could hear the impact of the blows through the wall. Between the blows came Momma's voice, begging the Lord to help her, to help Taye, to protect him, to keep him from harm. She begged Taye, too, asking him to understand why she did what she did, because she loved him, because she needed him to understand how serious things were. Taye didn't make a sound, though. He didn't cry or beg or scream or answer Momma's voice. When it was over, I heard the door open.

"Where you goin?"

"Out."

"Oh ta hang out with ure street punk homies? What bout church?"

"Fukk ure God, Momma. He ain got no love fo me, and I don't give a fukk bout him, neither."

The door slammed shut and I could hear Momma crying. I sat up and pulled the covers down. Nishia and NeeCee were still sleeping soundly. Those two would sleep through just about anything. I reached down and grabbed my slippers. A few months earlier, Momma had let each of us reach into her big knitting bag and choose the yarn that we liked best and with it made us each a pair of slippers. I had fallen in love with the soft pink, and since there wasn't enough of it to make two slippers, Momma had put a thick purple stripe in the middle.

I walked out into the living room and Momma swiped at the tears on her face and tightened her robe around her thick middle.

I don't know if it is true, but I've since read that the tradition of beating children in the black community may be a psychological scar inherited from slavery. A child allowed to misbehave at home might misbehave in front of an overseer or the master, calling down a punishment far worse than anything a parent would ever do. Historians also say that the constant upheaval of slave families, the selling of children away from their parents, instilled a fear of loving their children too much. How different was it in modern-day South Central, where the odds were stacked against a male child living to see twenty-five? Insurance men went door to door selling life-insurance policies, reminding parents of the statistics on a regular basis. In the hood, as in slavery, physical discipline was the only thing that kept parents from feeling powerless. It was something they could do to protect. It left an impression.

"I didn't know you were up already. The two lil ones still sleepin?"

I nodded my head and sat down on the sofa next to her, putting my hand on her leg. I wanted her to know that I wasn't fooled, that I knew she'd been crying.

"Why you upset, Momma, cause a Terrell bein in jail?"

She looked at me, surprised. I held her gaze steady.

She shook her head and faked a smile, tears still forming in her eyes. "You jus gettin so big, aren't chu? I be forgettin sometimes, ain no hidin nothing from you no more."

I smiled and Momma put her hand on my back.

"Yea, I'm upset bout Terrell bein in jail, an bout both them boys runnin round on the streets like they ain got no sense in they heads."

It was silent for a moment and I tried to think of what comfort I could offer.

"It's like we livin in a war zone, Bree. It's jus hard ta keep y'all safe and keep the nonsense outside that door." She pointed at the front door and I knew that we were both thinking about Taye and what he had left to do.

"Well, Momma, they say God's favorites have a hard time, right?" I didn't really believe it. My own beliefs were trapped somewhere in between hers and Taye's, but I said it because I knew she needed to hear it.

Momma smiled again, this time a big heartfelt smile. She took my face in her hands, leaning in first to kiss my forehead and then hugging me hard, so hard she practically squeezed the breath out of me. The alarm went off in the bedroom.

"Momma," I whispered. She was still hugging me tightly. "Momma, the alarm."

She released me, told me she loved me, and sent me off to get the little ones up while she ironed our dresses and shined our shoes. Usually she made pancakes or some other big breakfast on Sunday mornings, but today Big Mom was moving slowly; I had to feed my sisters cereal so we wouldn't be late for services. The house was chaos for half an hour, and then we were in the car, heading down into West Adams and onto South Harvard to the First AME Church.

AME stands for African Methodist Episcopal. The First AME— or FAME, as it is known—is one of the biggest and most influential forces in South Los Angeles. Historically, it was the first black congregation in the city, founded in 1872 by a former slave woman named Biddy Mason, who, years before, had walked from Mississippi to California, where she was able to gain her freedom.

Momma had been going to the church since before the pastor, Chip Murray, arrived in 1977. Back when the congregation was about 300 members she was sitting in the pews, and she stayed sitting there, every Sunday rain or shine, in sickness or in health as the church grew up to several thousand members in 1983. (It now has 18,000 members.) She understood Pastor Murray's vision and watched as he built the church up, starting all sorts of community-development programs. She said it was an honor to sit there and watch him preach, and it was, even if we now had to get there thirty minutes early to get a seat. When we walked in, Momma scanned the place and then led us toward the front, where our neighbor from across the street waved, patting at the pew next to her. Sonya Snow was an older woman who often watched NeeCee and Nishia during the day. She had a warm and casual nature, and laughed when the kids called her Mrs. Snow. "Call me Sonya," she would say. " 'Mrs. Snow' sounds like I owe you money."

Nishia went a step further and called her her "otha gramma."

We slid into the pew with Momma on one end and Sonya on the other. NeeCee climbed onto her lap and hugged her. Sonya smiled and then tightened her brow, noticing something on NeeCee's cheek. Sonya licked her finger and rubbed at NeeCee's face while Big Mom held court with all those who came to talk to her about life or the various church committees she served on.

"Where are the boys?" they would often ask, and Momma would shake her head.

This morning her response was, "Terrell got arrested last night and the otha one took off early this morning upset." There was no need to explain further. Anyone who lived where we did understood. They would shake their heads or lean over and take Momma's hand.

"I'll pray for em, sister, and for you."

Momma looked each of them in the eye and nodded, sincerely grateful for their support.

It must have worked, because by the grace of God, about five minutes before services started, I saw Taye walk in the door with Ryder and one of the big homies I'd seen last night talking with Ryder. The church was crowded, but as they walked down the aisle some boys and men in red waved and scooted over and they took a seat across the aisle, a few rows back from where we sat with Momma.

"Momma," I said in a whisper, reaching across NeeCee and tapping Big Mom on the leg.

"Don't interrupt."

I knew better than to keep talking, but I kept tapping her on the leg and staring back and forth at Taye in case he changed his mind and left or moved. Taye mouthed at me to knock it off and pointed at the front of the church. I looked at the pulpit, its flowers and candles and the gleaming gold cross, but couldn't help but keep turning back to look at him and see what he was doing, who he was with.

"Excuse me, sister," Momma said sternly and turned to give me a look that could kill. "What is it, Bree?"

I looked up in her face and pointed to where Taye sat, then watched as her expression changed. Taye's did, too. He sank down in his seat and held his program up to cover his face. Momma pushed me back against the pew.

"Don't look at them. It's bout ta start." I knew the company he was with bothered her, but I also knew that Momma was relieved that Taye had shown up. It was one thing to know that her boys were out there running the streets doing bad, it was another altogether to think they were doing bad and had given up on the Lord, because then if anything did happen, they might not get their souls. That was the worst possible thought.

Once the choir started singing, Momma's guard dropped. Momma sang loudly and raised her hands up to the Lord. When they were done singing, Pastor Murray began preaching. He knew the area and all its issues well. It was common to see Pastor Murray out among the people; he was the kind of leader who got out and talked to everyone, not just church members. In the hood, you never know who is related to whom. The junkie on the corner might be the mom of the star Sunday school student. The pastor was well aware of the interconnectedness of the community's people, and it was reflected in his sermon, which seemed to speak directly to me and the things going on in our family.

When it was time for the collection, Nishia tapped me on the shoulder excitedly. Momma had bought us each a little purse, and each week she put in a crisp dollar for the collection. I reached in and took out my bill and as I turned toward the aisle, I caught sight again of Taye. I watched him for a minute as he talked with his homies. They were close enough that I could see their every detail, down to the big homie's tattoo tear, inked in a prison blue-green under his eye. Nishia's daddy had a prison tattoo on his arm. It was the same blue-green color. I asked him about it once.

"Oh, that. Well, it ain something I'm proud of, shorty. I got that back in the pen. You can always tell a prison tat cause they gonna be that blue-green color from pen ink. I got that a lifetime ago. The person I was then is dead." His eyes looked sad. I knew there was more that he wanted to say, but I didn't know how to ask, and he didn't know how to explain.

He came by about twice a year: drove in from Fontana to see Nishia, bringing with him his new wife, kid, and a trunk full of shoes and clothes for all of us, including Big Mom. We all looked forward to his visit. Somehow, the excitement of new kicks was enough to lessen the blow for Nishia that her daddy had moved on with a new family and left her behind.

I looked around the church and watched the big homie in the pew next to Taye, the tear rising and lowering in the corner of his eye when he smiled. The tattoo tear can mean a few things, but usually it's that the wearer killed someone in prison or lost a loved one while in prison. If it's the latter it is supposed to be symbolic of the tears one cannot cry when locked up. Either way, a lot of people in South Central have them.

When the plate came to them, the big homie reached in his

pocket and pulled out a roll of bills, peeled a hundred-dollar bill off the top and added it to the collection like it was nothing.

"Bree." Momma placed her hand on my back, giving a slight nudge. I looked again at my dollar bill and then dropped it onto the plate.

At the end of the service, I tried to dash across the aisle, but Momma grabbed the back of my dress at the collar.

"Stay right here."

I looked up at Momma, who was talking to several of the church sisters, then sank back down onto the pew, turning my head so that I could watch Taye sneak out the double doors of the church.

"Momma," I said, not caring that I was again interrupting her. My voice was a whisper, almost inaudible even to me. I looked up at my momma's face; she was smiling and talking, but I knew it was a fake smile.

"Momma." I said it again, but loudly this time. She looked down at me and, before I could say anything, responded:

"I know, Bree. He done made his own choice. Let it go and don't be interuptin when grown folk talk. You know better."

NeeCee scooted closer to me on the pew and with a jerky motion took my hand. I squeezed it, warm and sweaty in my own, and watched as Momma stroked the back of Nishia's head where she stood, arms around Momma's legs, laughing whenever anyone else did.

After a while, Momma leaned toward the oldest of the group and laid her hand atop her arm, which held a bent cane.

"Mother," she said loudly so that she was sure that the old woman could hear, "can we carry you home? It's on our way anyhow." The old woman had been around the church so long that peo-

ple addressed her only as Mother Evans or Mother. The woman nodded and shifted her dentures in her mouth, her face suddenly shifting shape in a way that was grotesque, but fascinating.

"Bree," Momma called to me, motioning for me to take the
woman's purse and Bible for her. The woman smiled and handed
them to me. Her Bible was covered in a thick handmade cover. She
put one arm through Momma's and leaned heavily on her and her
cane as we all walked slowly toward the door.

Mother Evans lived in Baldwin Village in the southwest section of
South Central, in other words, the projects. The area was commonly
referred to as "the jungle," or "the jays." People said that back in the
day the name had referred to the many trees that grew there. But
things change with time, and now when people mention "the jungle," it's never the green of trees that comes to mind, it's the red of
violence, bloodshed, and the Blood gang.

Momma helped Mother Evans into the front seat while the rest
of us loaded into the back of the comically small brown Datsun
hatchback. Momma drove down South Western, deep into the heart
of the 30s, where Crips walked the streets and hung out on corners,
down past Denker and then MLK Park, and turned right onto MLK
Boulevard, past Arlington and then Crenshaw. Crenshaw is the
boundary line for the jays. Entering the jungle, everything has a different feel to it. The houses disappear and a maze of apartments
crowd every street. Momma turned in and out of side streets and
apartment alleys until she stopped in front of one building.

"Bree, walk Mother Evans to her door."

I climbed out of the crowded backseat and lifted the old woman's bag and Bible off her lap. When I offered my hand to help her up, she took it and gave a hard pull while at the same time pushing up off the seat with her other hand. For a moment I was sure we would both fall over, but then she was on her feet, reaching behind her for her cane, and when she had that, along with her balance and composure, she reached for her bag.

"I got it," I said confidently. She smiled at me and then reached again for her bag. I wondered if she had heard me, so I repeated myself, only louder this time. "Don't worry, I got it."

"It's okay, baby, I betta get it from here."

I looked back at Momma, hoping she wouldn't be mad as Mother Evans took her bag and slung it over her shoulder. People came in and out of apartments and stood hanging out everywhere, in the courtyards, on the walkways, and sitting out against the cars that lined the streets. I walked beside Mother Evans, carrying her Bible. She lived in the last apartment on the bottom floor. When we finally reached it, it took her a minute to get the key into the lock.

"My eyes ain what they were, I tell you what." She looked me in the eye, laughing hoarsely as she said it. I smiled back, but then, before I could say anything, a man came around the corner of the building and grabbed Mother Evans by the arm.

"Gimme the purse, ol lady." His head looked nervously from side to side. "And the diamond ring, too."

Mother Evans shook her head. Her face looked sad beyond explanation. Suddenly I understood why she didn't want me to carry her bag. She reached slowly toward her bag, but then, instead of taking the bag from her shoulder, she reached into her coat and pulled out a small pistol and turned back on the man.

"Punk ass mothafukka," she said, pointing the pistol in his face.

"Git up on outta here, you ain takin shyt. Punk mothafukka." The man looked shocked for a minute and then took off, running back around the side of the building.

Mother Evans tucked the pistol back into her jacket and opened her door as though nothing had happened. She turned back to me where I stood, still in a state of semi-shock, and took the Bible from my hands.

"Tell ure mom again I said thank you."

I nodded. It was all I could do. And then I stood there as she shut the door, staring up around the corner where the man had run off, until Momma sounded the horn. I ran back to the car as fast as I could and got into the now vacant front seat. Momma hummed hymns as she turned back in and out of apartment alleys and side streets and up onto Rodeo, back past the church and back toward the house. I looked out the window, suddenly aware all over again of the dangers surrounding me.

At home we ate together, and then Momma sent us to wash up and get pajamas on. Nishia and NeeCee said their good nights and got tucked in, first by Momma and then by me. Taye still hadn't come home. I watched TV with Momma a while, hoping that every squeak of the house was the door opening, but it never was. At nine o'clock, Momma gave me my sleeping pill and sent me to bed, too, reminding me to pray for Terrell's situation. As I started off down the hallway, she called me back.

"Bree, don't forget, pray for Taye, too. When they ain here with us, that's when they need the prayers more." I nodded my head.

"I know, Momma." She held her arms out to me and I hugged her. I knew by the way she held on for an extra minute that she was scared. "Terrell's gonna be aiight, Momma."

"I know, baby," she said, still holding me close.

"You know what they say bout God's favorites, right?" Momma stopped hugging me and instead placed a hand on each side of my face.

"Bless ure heart, Bree. I jus don't know what I would do without chu. You really are such a comfort to me." It felt good to hear. I smiled and then headed back down the hall to the room. I stood and stared out the window, watching for Taye until I couldn't stay awake any longer.

In the morning we all went off to school and Momma stayed home from work to make phone calls. I tried calling home three different times, but the phone stayed busy. When I got home, Momma explained that she had been on the phone, first with someone from the Juvenile Court who said Terrell wasn't on the docket to be arraigned, then trying to get in touch with Terrell's public defender who failed to call her back, then was at lunch, and then left for the day at two o'clock. Finally, Momma had called the jail where Terrell was being held, only to be told that he had been arraigned that morning and would go before the judge the following Tuesday. When I asked if Taye had come home, she shook her head. Momma looked tired, but not the kind of tired that came from not sleeping enough. She made us some tea with sugar and we waited for the Head Start bus to drop the little ones off.

The rest of that Monday dragged by. Taye still didn't come home that evening, but he was there at Eastlake Juvenile Courthouse on Tuesday morning when Terrell went before the judge. Momma had taken her savings from the Folgers jar in the back of the cabinet and bought Terrell a new suit. When his public defender finally called Momma back Monday afternoon, he said that sort of thing really didn't make a difference, but that she could meet him when he planned to arrive, fifteen minutes before Tee was to go before the judge, if it would make her feel better. Momma had sent the two little girls off to their Head Start program that Tuesday morning, but perhaps for company, or perhaps as a warning, she had allowed me to miss school and come with her. I sat alone on a wooden bench with a stiff back, watching Taye as Momma paced the hall, waiting for Terrell's lawyer. After a while, Taye came over and sat down next to me, neither of us saying a word. I looked him over; he was wearing his black jacket over a red T-shirt and red Chuck Taylor tennis shoes. His khaki pants were freshly pressed. His eye was slightly darkened, the last traces of a black eye fading. I knew that was why he hadn't come home. Momma never gave us black eyes when she hit us; this was from a beating just like the one Tee had gotten when he was jumped in. I wasn't surprised, and even though I knew Big Mom would be disappointed in him, I knew she had expected it, too.

When the judge came in, the court services officer motioned for all of us to stand, and when the CSO announced that we should be seated and we sat back down, Taye put his arm around my shoulders.

"Figures, Momma didn't kome back in," he whispered in my ear. He sounded hurt and mad and his words came out somewhere between a question and a statement.

"Naw," I whispered back, "she bought him a suit. She waitin in the hall to meet his lawyer."

Taye smiled first, but then stiffened in his seat. He knew that when Momma came through the door and saw him, she would assault him with questions. And she would know by looking at his clothes and his eye what had happened, and in her knowing, things would never be the same. Elsewhere in the world, twelve-year-old boys were playing with Transformers and Ninja Turtles, but my brothers were becoming soldiers. Momma knew she couldn't stop it, but she still wanted them to be good Atari-playing, church-going boys.

The judge had been plugging away at the court docket for twenty minutes by the time Momma finally slipped in the door. She did a double take when she saw Taye next to me, her face fading from shock and anger to relief. She sat down beside her youngest grandson and reached over and placed her hand on top of his. Tall for twelve, he was already taller than she was, and his hands, though leaner, were larger, with long, tapered fingers and a wide palm. He turned his hand over and grasped hers. We all sat, and waited, each tick of the clock seeming to take forever.

Finally they called out Terrell's name. I moved to the edge of my seat. We listened as Terrell and his lawyer spoke, back and forth. Then it was the judge's turn. He spoke for a few moments about the path that Terrell seemed to be choosing and then said, "Young man, I don't know where your family is, but even if no one else in this world cares that you are headed toward a dark future, you can rest assured that I do. I don't want to see you in my court again." I snuck my eyes over to Big Mom, who looked as if she had been struck.

Then the white judge sentenced Terrell to six months and they took him toward the back door. As they led him out, he looked over his shoulder at us. He knew that Momma had put her savings into the suit so that when the judge looked at him he would see him as a refined young man, someone whose family cared enough to buy him nice clothes. He knew that what the judge said hurt Momma, and I knew that hurt him. It hurt all of us.

"K'mon, Momma," Taye said, putting an arm around her shoulders. "Let's go home." I followed his cue and took Momma's hand, and she leaned down and kissed the top of my head. I wanted so badly to cry, but I didn't want Big Mom to see me cry. I bit down on my lip as we walked to the parking lot.

The ride home was silent and when we got there, Momma said she thought she would go lie down.

"Will you still be here when I get up?" she asked, looking at Taye.

"Yea, Momma, I will. I'll wait for the lil ones, too, an make dinner."

"Thank you, baby," Momma said, her tired eyes starting to tear. She kissed Taye on the cheek and then went into her room and shut the door. She didn't come out at dinnertime and we didn't wake her; instead we ate together and then got NeeCee and Nishia off to bed.

Nishia's fourth birthday was on November 20. It was hard to imagine Terrell missing that. And Christmas. Unless he got out early, he would miss NeeCee's third birthday, too. Taye and I watched TV for a while, trying to lose ourselves in *Diff'rent Strokes*.

At the end of the show, Taye rose to turn the TV off and then sat back down next to me. After minutes of silence he placed his hand on my knee with a slap.

"You aiight?"

I nodded my head. "Yea, you?"

He nodded his head back, and then after a few more minutes he stood up.

"Aiight, then, ima get some sleep."

I sat there for a while in the dark, then got up and made sure that the door and the dead bolt were locked and the chain was fastened. Back in my room I lay in bed, listening to Nishia's tiny snores. I thought about my brothers and I thought about Momma. I thought about *Diff'rent Strokes* and how it was really an idealized foster-care story. In the show, two orphaned black kids, Arnold and Willis, are adopted by a rich white family, the Drummonds, who live in a penthouse. No one tries to rob them, no one judges them. I thought about what the judge said about Momma and wondered if he would have said the same thing about Mr. Drummond. I fell asleep for a while, but then woke to the sound of things being moved in the living room. I bolted up, scared of the worst, but when I opened the door I knew there was no way we were getting robbed because all the lights were on.

When I turned the hallway I saw Momma was making piles of clothes and dishes, filling trash bags and boxes.

"What chu doin, Big Mom?"

Momma looked up and held my gaze for several seconds, then let her head drop back down. Her hands shuffled through the pile in front of her.

"We movin, Bree." She looked back up at me. "I ain a bad mom, an I ain gonna jus let this neighborhood take my kids under. We movin. That's it."

And that was it. I went back to bed. By the time we all got home from school the next day, Big Mom had gotten more boxes and packed up most of the house. Two weeks later, we started loading stuff into the car and made trip after trip away from South Gramercy Place over to the other side of town. A week after that, we celebrated Nishia's birthday at our new house.

They say nothing ever changes in South Central except the date and the time. I guess that's true. In our new house, we had the same small three bedrooms, the same broken porch steps, and the same falling-over fence. Now, instead of having three locks on our door, we had four, but the grass in the yard was green, and even though Terrell was still locked up and Taye ran back to the old neighborhood daily, Big Mom had a dream that the gang's appeal would blow over and eventually we would all be there together as a family.

BITCH

"STAY AWAY FROM that fence. Fa real, that ain no friendly dog."

Our new neighbor was infamous on the L.A. streets, a gangster known simply as Big Rodney. After six months living next door to him, though, I knew not to be afraid. I ignored his warning and stretched my gangly, dust-covered arms over the chain-link as far as they could reach toward the beefy pit bull inside, tail sticking out from her wooden doghouse.

"Oh, okay. Aiight. I know you hear me. You think u a bad ass now, huh?" The words may sound harsh, but the tone, even in its loud low boom, was all love.

Shaking his head, he continued walking toward his car, then stopped short and pointed a fat finger in my direction. "Wait, why ain chu at skool, anyway?"

I looked up, squinting to make him out through the blinding Southern California sun. By May, the sun reflected off the cement and the heat and glare were relentless, even at nine in the morning. Lawns dried up and passing cars added dust to the already smog-filled air. South Central in summer looks and feels like a wasteland.

"Shyt, Auntie ain kome home again lass night. Big Mom had ta go ta work so it ain nobody ta watch the babies," I said, pointing at NeeCee, who sat pulling up newly dead grass and throwing it up into the air. In her concentration, drool hung off her lip and fell onto her arm, making shiny spots on her ashy skin. A faded fuschia bougainvillea blossom we'd found across the street was stuck in her hair. She looked like a wild child. Big Rodney already knew everything I was telling him and more.

With Terrell in jail and Taye usually missing in action, Big Mom needed more help caring for Nishia and NeeCee. She had used the move as an opportunity to try to get Denise out of the projects. Big Mom had worked hard on converting our new garage into a livable space with the idea that Denise could have it free rent in exchange for watching her nieces in the morning and making sure they got off to Head Start. In Big Mom's head, that left Denise the rest of the day and the weekends to work—and with no expenses, she could save a nice chunk of change while Tiffany was staying with her dad, enough to move to a nicer area before the school year started up again. It worked great for about a month, but lately Denise had become almost as worthless and unreliable as her sister—and so the responsibility fell to me.

"Where the other one at?" Rodney asked, referring to Nishia.

"She aiight. She watchin TV."

Rodney walked back up the cement path that led from the street to our house. I was the smallest in my fifth-grade class; most of the other kids towered above me. To me, Rodney was a giant: six feet five, probably 300 pounds, and always decked out in a freshly creased khaki suit and polished Stacy Adams shoes. If there was one thing about Big Rodney that everyone noticed, it was his style. Everyone knew that he was selling dope—"slangin kane," the gangstas would say—to get that roll of bills he carried around in his pocket, but since he was the person helping to put food in our mouths I wasn't about to care. In fact, Big Rodney had become one of my heroes.

"Aiight," Rodney said, kneeling down to meet my eyes, "you take this an you go up ta Dave's. Get some food: bread, milk, an sandwich meat. You're a smart kid, whatever's left over get some apples, peanut butter, that kinda stuff. Don't be wastin on no junk. That's first." He pushed a twenty-dollar food-stamp voucher into my hand and patted my cheek.

"Then," he continued, shifting back into his most businesslike tone, "go down the laundry an wash some clothes, do some in the sink an lay it out first if you ain got nothing ta put on the shorties. Don be havin CPS kreepin an peekin round here again, that ain good for nobody." He handed me a five spot, but pulled it back as I reached for it. "Wash them off an do both they hair fore you take em anywhere, you hear me?"

"I kno, Rodney." He let me grab the five as he stood back up.

"Youze a good girl, Bree Bree." He put his fist out and I slammed mine down on top of it with all my might.

"Oooowieee," Rodney said as he started down the path, "youze strong, lil bit. Ima watch out fo you." He rubbed his hand as though I really hurt him. "Might mess up get you mad, then you finna beat me up." I couldn't see his face but I knew he was smiling at the impossibility of it. Amused and proud, I was, too.

"An stay away from that dog," he added over his shoulder. Within seconds the big engine of his '73 El Camino was turning over with a loud thump, kicking exhaust and dust up into the gray sky as Big

Rodney spun off on gold Daytons. I drifted down to our sagging front gate and grasped its twisted top, watching as the dust settled and the shiny car faded off in the distance.

Away from the shade of the porch the dirt was hot, even under my calloused feet. I lifted my foot and examined the leather-like skin, half an inch thick and ugly. I turned, looked at NeeCee, and sighed.

Big Mom had a favorite story about me that she liked to tell from that time. In it the school social worker puts a glass of milk in front of me on the table and says, "This is a glass of milk. Now, some people will say that it is half full and some will say that it's half empty. What do you think?"

I remember it, too. I looked over at her clean skin and pretty pink nails as she pushed the glass toward me and replied, "Well, I think it's a half glass ah milk an if that's what chu got, chu might as well drink it." Life had taught me well. What I knew was that I was tired and it was still morning, and with a whole long day ahead and no sense of when or if Auntie might show up, it was all on me so I'd better get things started.

Over in Rodney's yard, his pit bull walked out of her doghouse and lay down where her heavy chain's length ended. Next to her was a butchered half of an old metal keg that served as her water dish, but only when Rodney remembered to fill it. She peered down into it, found it barren, and, defeated, lay down panting in the shade of the yard's only tree.

"What up, Bitch?" I said, calling her by name and throwing up my arms like I'd seen Rodney do each day upon coming home. The pit bull turned a scarred and massive head toward me, neither barking nor wagging her tail, just panting as before. We'd been taking each other in for a while already. We weren't strangers; we just weren't sure if we were allies yet either. After a few moments, she grew bored of watching me watch her; she ran a large pink tongue over a disfigured upper lip and laid her head down in the dirt.

I walked back to NeeCee, who threw grass at me and smiled. I took her hand and pulled her up to her feet. We crossed the living room, with its distorted sounds of *Roadrunner* playing loudly on our old TV, and stepped over Nishia, who was lying on her stomach in a pile of dirty laundry and watching intently.

In the kitchen, I closed my eyes as I opened the refrigerator, hoping that maybe its contents had changed. Please, please, please . . . I opened my eyes. No milk, no juice, no nothing that I could feed the babies. Half a bottle of ketchup, generic chocolate syrup, and strawberry daiquiri mix.

"Dammit," I said as I set NeeCee down on the kitchen floor.

"Ooooo, bad werd," she said and laughed before running off to watch cartoons with Nishia.

I pushed a chair to the counter, climbed up to the cupboard, and pulled down an open pouch of Kool-Aid and a bag of sugar: ants. Slowly I poured the sugar into the trash till I didn't see ants anymore. I mixed up a pitcher of Kool-Aid, dug through the overflowing sink of dishes until I found a cup and a bottle, washed them out, filled them up, and took them into the living room. "Yeah!" screamed NeeCee and Nishia, eyes wide, clapping their hands as though I were Jesus turning water into wine.

Back in the kitchen, I grabbed a glass of Kool-Aid for myself (underflavored and oversugared) and slipped a comb, a handful of rubber bands, and the jar of Comb-Thru grease into my pocket. Walking back into the living room, I sat down behind Nishia, who, thankfully, was too caught up in Wile E. Coyote's endless quest for the Roadrunner to notice the bulge in my pocket. By the time she did realize what was going on it was too late.

"NOOOOO!" she screamed in protest. "You hurtin me!"

"That's cause you movin all ova. If u jus sit still it'll be fastah an it won't pull so much. Anyways, ain like I like doin this." Nishia, who did not care if I liked it or not, continued crying, pushing, and shoving, trying to break free from my grasp.

"Look, I got sum monies. If you let me braid it, I'll buy you a piece of kandy at Dave's." With that, all squirming ceased and she spun around, then wiped the collected tears from her cheek with her forearm.

"Just four braids. Real quick, I promise."

"Lemme see the monies."

I pulled the food-stamp voucher from my sock and held it before her.

"Okay," she said and turned back around, sitting as straight and still as I had ever seen her. I parted her hair into four sections, greased the parts, brushed them out and braided them.

"Go wash ure face, knees, an elbows," I instructed her, aware of my new powers, and then started on NeeCee. In the wide spectrum of hair, NeeCee's was easy. Hers was fine and fell in loose curls that Momma kept short. Little pieces of twigs and bougainvilleas had wound their way into her curls and needed to be picked out, but at least her hair required little actual brushing, braiding, or styling. I got a washcloth and scrubbed her little face till it shined. She wasn't three yet, and she was still way behind developmentally, small for her age, and stubborn to boot. The easiest way to get around with her was to use a stroller. I strapped her in and went to check on Nishia's progress. Within minutes we were on our way to Dave's.

"Candy, candy, candy . . ." Nishia repeated with every step the entire way to the store, stomping her sandals hard against the ground to add to the impact of her words. When we got to Dave's and the door opened with its familiar convenience-store ding-dong, she said it again, a little too loud. "CANDY!"

The Korean storeowner was on it. "You no touch, you no touch. You got money? Show me money." I pulled the food-stamp voucher out of my sock and held it up. She put her glasses on and leaned down to scrutinize it. "Go put on counter." I felt humiliated, but I did what she said. We made our way around the small store grabbing two loaves of Wonder Bread, peanut butter, a can of grape juice, a bag of sugar, Kool-Aid, bologna, milk, and a box of Pop-Tarts. I thought about the laundry money. I needed it for laundry, but we needed diapers more, and they won't let you buy those with food stamps. If need be, we could hand-wash some clothes in the sink, so I grabbed the pack of diapers. Nishia kept tugging at the hem of my shorts. "Candy?"

"Aiight, Nishia, go git it, but don let NeeCee see it." She pounded down the candy aisle, the Korean shopkeeper glaring at me. Nishia returned, seconds later, with her fist clenched. Opening it in front of me, she revealed a quarter-sized grape Jolly Rancher. I nodded my head. The shopkeeper rang up the groceries and took the voucher. I had to ask for the change, which she then promptly slammed down on the counter.

"Go," she said.

I started to pile the bread and other groceries into the back of the stroller, but they didn't all fit. "Go," she said again. "You must go." Nishia was already pushing on the door, which dinged each time she got it open a little bit, and each time it fell back closed again. Ding-dong. Ding-dong. Ding-dong. "Go." Ding-dong.

"Nishia," I called to her, "carry the milk. And be careful." She ran back to the counter, tucked her candy into her pocket, and grabbed the milk off the counter, all the while smiling at the lady.

"Tank you," Nishia said to her.

"Go," said the storekeeper as she gestured with her hand for us to shoo. We made it out the door, me struggling with the overfull stroller and Nishia straining to carry the milk. We made it almost halfway home before she dropped it. The cardboard busted open and the milk streamed into the gutter.

"Don't be mad. Please, don't be mad, Bee Bee," Nishia said as she burst into tears. She tried to pick up the carton and scrape the milk back into it.

"It's gone, jus leave it." I started walking again toward home. After a few steps I looked over my shoulder to see Nishia still kneeling on the cement with the milk carton.

"I said *leave it,* Nishia." She dropped the empty carton and ran after me, drops of milk and dirt dotting her legs. We walked the rest of the way home in silence.

At home I took NeeCee out of the stroller and carried her into the living room. I went back out for the groceries. With the milk gone there was only the bologna that would spoil in the heat and sun. Nishia was standing on the bottom step, still silent, eyes looking down at her feet.

"I ain mad," I said. But I was mad. A half-gallon of milk wasted. Two dollars gone. Really, I didn't know whom I should be mad at. I should've given her the bread to carry. It was light and couldn't break. She was four years old. I was mad at myself. I was mad at the Korean lady for getting me flustered enough to make a bad decision. Whoever's fault it was, though, there was less than a dollar left and no milk. It didn't matter whose fault it was now. Nishia reached out her hand and held her candy out to me.

"Here," she said. "I'm sorry."

"I said I ain mad, Nishia. Jus go inside." She placed the candy at my feet and scurried inside, turning the TV back on. She'd had about enough of reality for the morning. I picked up the candy and put it in my pocket. I took the bologna out of the stroller bag and walked to the fence.

"Bitch."

She opened one eye, looked at me, and then closed it again.

"K'mon, gurl." I held out a piece of bologna. Nothing. I climbed up on the chain-link and jumped over. For a moment, as my feet hit the dirt, I was scared. I knew I was not supposed to mess with the dog. But, to my relief, she didn't charge at me. Hell, she didn't even get up. I ripped the circle of processed meat in two and threw the smaller piece to her. She caught it in the air with one snap of her huge jaw and ate it without moving her body. I started to worry again. Bitch sniffed at the air, then stretched and walked toward me. I held the other half out, my hand shaking a little. She gently took the meat and ate it, then licked my hand. Her tongue felt surprisingly coarse against my skin. I ran my free hand over her head. You could not only see but feel all her scars. Some formed deep ridges in her skull, a roadmap of a life that somewhere along the way had gone bad. Her eyes, though, looking up at me shone a warm, golden brown. There was a kindness and beauty in those eyes, despite all the ugliness that they had seen. I scratched behind her right ear, trying to imagine what she looked like before she lost the left one, before the scars, before the mangled lip.

"Good gurl," I said. Her big head leaned back against my chest as she tried to lick my face. I was in love.

I left Bitch long enough to put away the groceries, then filled a pitcher with water and returned to her. When she saw me she thumped her tail against the ground. Thud, thud, thud. They say that the tail of a pit bull is as strong as that of a beaver. I filled her keg water dish and watched as she happily lapped and splashed it up. Then we sat under the tree, her head in my lap, and I told her everything. I told her about Nishia, about the milk, and the Korean lady. I told her how the baby wouldn't have milk that night and how it was probably my fault. I told her how tired I was, but I didn't mean tired. I meant depressed. I told her that I hated doing the laundry. I took the candy out of my pocket and unwrapped it. Again she sniffed at the air. I placed it in my hand and held it out to her. I didn't know if dogs liked candy, but in that moment, I wanted her to have it as badly as Nishia wanted me to have it. She sniffed it thoughtfully and looked at me confused. Then she stood up, tilted her head, first to one side, then the other, and barked twice. It was a loud bark, but I wasn't scared anymore. I would never be scared of her again.

"Okay," I said. "You right. Plus I still gotta do the laundry." I popped the candy into my mouth, petted her head, jumped the fence back into my own yard, and went back inside.

When I walked in the door Taye was sitting on the couch flamed up: red shirt, red Dickies pants, red shoes and fitted cap, smiling from ear to ear.

"Taye!" I tried to hug him, but Nishia and the baby were both already in his lap so he clapped his hand against my shoulder and nodded his head at me.

"West brakkin, gurl? How you holdin up?" He took off his cap and put it on my head, turning the brim to the right.

"Yea, that's it right there, gurl, dats da BLOOD side. Rep it, rep it. Where's Auntie at?"

"Shyt, dunno." I pulled the hat down a little so that the brim covered my forehead.

"That better?" I asked as I tilted my head back a little so that I could see him.

"Daymn, same shyt different day, huh?" He shook his head and looked around at the house, some things still in piles from the move. "An yea, hat looks tight. You holdin it down, tho, right? I mean the babies looking aiight, even got they hair done."

"Yea, I got it on lock, bro." I sat down next to him and he put his arm around me. It felt good to see him; it had been almost a month this time since he had been home. Since being made "official," before we left our old neighborhood, he had more or less stayed behind. Gang was his family now more than we were. Looking around at the dilapidated house and then at my brother, with his shiny watch and fat chain, it was pretty clear who had more to offer him.

"Taye, kan I tell you sunnthin?"

"Anything, babygurl, you kno that."

"Big Rodney gave me food stamps. I took em to the store and the Korean lady . . ." Nishia started to cry.

"I fuckin hate them people," my brother said. "Why they even open stores in here if they hate us so much. Look baby, don't cry. Nishia, don't cry. Bree Bree"—my brother pushed a fifty-dollar bill into my hand—"look, I'm leavin money for Big Mom, too. You hold this, tho. Don't tell no one you got it, but use it when you all need anything."

I nodded earnestly, understanding with a sudden thrill that my brother was still watching out for us. I knew where the money came from, but I didn't think about it. I took the crisp new bill into the bedroom I shared with my sisters. I had never seen a fifty-dollar bill before, at least not a real one. I hoisted the corner of the mattress and stuffed the bill into a small hole, pushing it in as deep as I could with my finger.

When I rejoined the others in the living room, Taye wasn't smiling anymore. It seemed to pain him not to be able to do more for us. We sat on the couch a while, not talking, and then he got up, taped an envelope on Big Mom's door, and said goodbye.

Big Mom came home after we'd gone to bed that night, but when I heard her I snuck to the crack in the door to watch her find the envelope. She stopped in her tracks and counted through the money, counting out loud, over and over again.

"Twenty, forty, sixty, eighty, one hundred. Twenty, forty, sixty, eighty, two hundred. Twenty, forty, sixty, eighty, three hundred." She'd sigh and then start over. "Twenty, forty, sixty, eighty, one hundred. Twenty, forty, sixty, eighty, two hundred. Twenty, forty, sixty, eighty, three hundred." Three hundred dollars, in 1984, in that house, in that neighborhood, was a lot of money. Did she think about where the money came from? I think she did, and I think it bothered her more than she could say. I think it bothered her even more that we needed it so badly she had no choice but to take it. She tucked the money into her pocketbook and went into her room.

I climbed back into bed and closed my eyes. Big Mom always said if you worried it made no sense to pray and that if you prayed it made no sense to worry. I prayed, but I still worried, too.

Since moving to South Central, I'd gotten used to walking past homeless people and their shopping-cart recycling trains every day. One woman had her shopping carts tied together two-wide and five-long, each cart holding a different kind of recycling. I had tried to talk to her a few times, asking where she took the stuff in and things like that, but all her answers were nonsense. I walked by her, the crackheads, the home bums, and the winos. I bet when they were my age none of them thought they would be sleeping on the streets or in MacArthur Park when they grew up, but here they were now. Sometimes people just get broken in ways that cannot be fixed. I understood. That night, I lay awake for hours, hoping I wasn't getting broken, too.

It was almost ten when I woke up the next morning. The house was already hopping. Big Mom was mixing up a pitcher of Kool-Aid. She held the pitcher up for me to see.

"You know what happen to this? The neighbor brung it over this morning. Was in his yard." I just looked at her. "Stay away from that dog."

"Yes, Big Mom."

"You seen ure brother yesterday?"

"Yea, I seen him. He come by for a minute. He looked aiight. All flamed up in red an got a nice new watch an stuff. He steady talking that Blood talk, everything *b*'s. Bickin back, bein bool, an all that."

Big Mom was quiet for a minute. Her silence said more than anything.

"I'm sorry about the pitcher, Big Mom. I got a couple dollars saved. You kan get a new one wit it if you want." Ten A.M. and I'd already failed her.

"No, this one work jus fine still. It looks a lil worn is all. Shoot, I look a lil worn, too." She patted at her hair under its kerchief, smiled at me and started humming her favorite song, "When Jesus Woke Me Up This Morning." It nicely summed up her approach to life, that you should take each day as its own blessing. I loved when she sang that song. When Big Mom was in a singing mood, I'd walk out the door singing, too, as if nothing else mattered. The world seemed an okay place, and even if it wasn't, it seemed we might all overcome it together.

"Nishia hair look real nice, by the way," she added as I started to leave the room. I turned and hugged her, my arms not quite reaching around her hips.

"I love you, Big Mom."

"Goodness, child, where that come from?" She patted my back and then rested her hand atop my head. "I love you, too. An Bree Bree, that's why I'm telling you: stay away from that dog. I ain mad, but people an dogs, you jus neva know what they might do."

"Naw, Momma, she aiight. She nice to me. I swear ta God."

"Ta God? Oooo, child, go wash ure mouth. You'd rather die than listen to a person, is that it? Sweet Jesus," she said throwing her hands skyward toward the broken ceiling fan with its one working light-bulb, "please watch out ova this child fore the devil come get her." She leaned down, kissed the top my head, and patted me on the back, the sign that our talk was over.

"Big Mom?" I paused at the doorway. "Do I really have to wash my mouth out?" She started laughing, so I smiled, even though I had been serious about the question, since she'd made me do it several times before.

"No, child. Now go check on your sisters." The air filled with the smell of bleach as Big Mom started her cleaning. Her singing carried through the room, competing with *The Smurfs* as I jumped onto the sofa, where Nishia and NeeCee sat, as always, watching TV. The money helped, even if Taye was doing something bad to get it. Just knowing that the bills were covered for now had turned everyone's mood around. I rubbed my face on NeeCee's stomach and she laughed and clapped her hands against my cheeks.

She pulled her shirt up, her movements stiff and jerky: she still suffered from muscle weakness in one of her arms, and she fought to keep hold of her T-shirt.

"K'mon, let's wrestle," I said, lifting her arms up over her head and then pulling them out toward me. It was a game her doctor had invented, the "wrestle game." She was supposed to build up strength and coordination by trying to get away.

NeeCee was behind in everything. I'd look at other kids her age, and it made me deeply sad in a way that I couldn't completely un-derstand. I loved her, but I hadn't always. Taye and Terrell said that she had been born small and gray and crying and that it seemed like all she did those first months was cry. When I first met her, at eight months, she wasn't that different. I'd put the pillow over my head and hate myself for hating her while Big Mom and Terrell took turns walking the hallway holding the baby as she shook with the inten-sity of her inconsolable screaming. None of the neighbors or relatives ever said she was a beautiful baby and I couldn't remember one time that any of them asked to hold her. Her obvious problems were just another thing left unsaid.

It wasn't NeeCee's fault, Big Mom would tell us. She never said whose fault it *was,* but I knew. We all knew. When she was born she got some of her momma's sickness, too. Terrell, who understood what was going on better than the rest of us, threw fits, hit walls. But it didn't change his mom, didn't make her come around or stop getting high, and it didn't change what had happened to the baby.

"The doctors say she'll catch up, Terrell," Big Mom would say, appeasing him.

Then one day, he just said it: "Fukk that bitch." Big Mom slapped him.

"That's your momma, boy. Don't you ever disrespect your momma. You hear me, Terrell?"

"Please, she ain my momma, she ain done shit for me. I don't need her and I don't need you, either." We all watched Terrell walk out the door that night. That was just before he caught the robbery charge.

I pulled on NeeCee's arms and legs, stretching her tight limbs out until she again figured out that most of the game consisted of me making her do things she didn't want to do and got angry with me. The third time she told me to go, I went ahead and left to play with Rodney's dog.

I stuffed a rag in my shirt to play tug with and eased out the front door. In our house if you didn't announce your departure, nobody was gonna notice you weren't around until they needed something from you. I knew I had a good hour. I hopped over the fence and stuck my head inside the doghouse. No one home.

"Bitch?" I called loud enough for her to hear, but soft enough that Big Mom couldn't hear me by accident. No response. I walked around the back of the doghouse and heard a whimper, then a shriek. Her chain had caught up on a branch and was hanging down from the tree. She stood on her back legs, toes barely touching the ground, almost hanging. I panicked.

Options, options, I thought as I looked at her. She was whimpering, unable to move without hanging herself. Stretched up like that, she was almost as tall as I was, and definitely bigger and stronger. Every minute she'd toss her head as though maybe she could shake the chain free, but she could only move about three inches before her legs threatened to swing out from under her. Her collar was choking her and her breaths were hoarse gasps.

Her eyes stayed focused on me, but they looked different than usual. They were not the same kind, gentle, loving eyes. They were panicked and wild. Still, I didn't think to be afraid of her. I was her only hope, the way I saw it, so she couldn't possibly hurt me.

I had no idea what the dog would do if I unchained her. Maybe she would run away. I couldn't go get Big Mom, because as many times as she had told me not to mess with the dog, I knew she wouldn't touch her, and Rodney wasn't home. I looked at Bitch, her eyes strained. I reached up to undo the chain, but her weight was pulling it so tight that I couldn't get it unhooked from her collar. I needed more height.

"Hold up, gurl," I told her.

I looked around the yard quickly. Weight bench. I went over and tried to move it. Bitch started yelping wildly when I got out of her sight. I yelled to her that I'd be right there, forgetting by now about Big Mom and being heard, about trying to be quiet. I shoved the bench with all my strength, but it was too heavy. I couldn't even budge it. I looked around again, but there was nothing but trash, beer bottles, and the water keg, empty yet again, next to the tree. I went and tipped it over. It was rounded, but I could stand on it. It was heavy, but not impossible. I strained as I pushed it over to the tree, kicking up dirt with my feet, Bitch still yelping. Out of breath, I climbed the keg, reached up, untwisted the connecter, and pried it loose from the chain. Bitch's body crashed to the dirt, knocking into the keg and sending me sprawling next to her. My elbow broke my fall. At first it stung, then it bled, a little at first then more and more. I took the rag out of my pocket and put it where it was bleeding like Big Mom would do. My head ached and my body felt hot. I crawled into the doghouse and held the rag, watching as it turned from white to red. I started to cry. Poor Bitch still lay outside the doghouse, panting, trying to catch her breath. Upon hearing my tears, though, her one good ear perked up. She dragged herself to the opening of her house, laid her head on my leg.

When I woke up, Rodney was shining a flashlight into my eyes. Around him was nothing but darkness.

"Big Mom trippin. She got everyone lookin for you. You best get ure lil ass home."

"She was kaught, Rodney. I didn't . . . I . . . I didn't . . ."

Rodney shined his flashlight onto Bitch and instantly saw the deep marks in her neck where the chain had cut her as she hung.

"Daymn," he said, sinking down to his knees and falling silent. He put a hand on Bitch's head and began to look around, noticing the turned-over keg, and my bloody elbow. After a minute, he started speaking again. "I ain mad. Cept I did tell you not ta mess wit that dog. You saved her life, tho, Bree Bree. I seen a dog hang like that before, too. Straight fucked up." Rodney stumbled for his words. "I kno you love that dog, babygurl."

I stood, looking at him. He was sitting next to the doghouse now, flashlight in his lap. Bitch was between us, her head still on my leg.

"I love that dog, too, shorty. Daymn, I dunno. If I'd come home seen that . . . *mannn*." He looked like I felt, and in that moment Rodney wasn't so big. "Sometime it seem like a dog be a better friend than most ure best homies. You kno that, too. Huh, shorty?"

I nodded. I felt like I should say something, but I couldn't think of anything that would make sense or help. Rodney lay a big hand atop my foot, rested it there a minute.

"You want me tell Big Mom what happen?" I shook my head no. "Well, then you want me ta walk you ova there, or you wanna go alone?"

"Naw, I got this, Rodney." He lifted his hand and patted Bitch on her side.

"Aiight, then, you best go handle that. Like I say, she worried." He stood up and Bitch looked from him back to me. "K'mon, gurl," he said, and she slowly stood up, still looking at me. She bent her head down, licked my leg, and followed him. I sat in the darkness a minute, getting my thoughts together, and then got up to go home.

THE LAST THREADS
OF INNOCENCE

IN JULY OF 1986 I turned twelve. "Twelve, that's big time," I told Big Mom over and over as the day approached. "Next year ima be a teenager."

In South Central L.A., adolescence is when a lot of kids start having babies and dying in shootings. It's also the prime age for joining a gang. Momma would nod her head as though she had only half heard me, but I noticed she'd started praying a whole lot more recently.

Momma had tried to reason with Terrell and then with Taye, done the whole lecture, sit down, and talk thing, but when Taye joined Terrell in juvie for possession of a controlled substance in 1985, there was a part of her that in some small way gave up on all of us. She loved us, no doubt. One time, in fact, she told me that her biggest fault in life had been that she loved us too much, so much that at times she failed to realize what was impossible. After Terrell and then Taye, she just couldn't waste her breath on the lectures and talks, or cry over damage done anymore. Our house was one of love, but above all else it was one of survival, and that left little room to talk about feelings. Feelings are messy and painful, so Big Mom worked and prayed and the rest of us did what we had to do. In the inner city, there are lots of different ways to lose and hold on to hope.

In those days, I was learning how to navigate the city, how to make its sicknesses work for me. I was stuck in summer school due to my poor attendance during the year, and on the rare occasion that I actually made it there, I noticed that the boys were nicer to me and the teachers meaner. One new math teacher was completely scared of us. His voice was a permanent quiver and when he turned to write on the chalkboard he would repeatedly look over his shoulder to make sure we weren't plotting his death. Some of the bolder students started spitting in his coffee or hiding his glasses when he stepped into the hall, but to say that we enjoyed this new power over our teacher would be incorrect. We used the opportunity to entertain ourselves at his expense, but the knowledge that his fear came from some deep-rooted belief that we were bad, beyond help, and somehow less human than him kept us from really enjoying ourselves. We understood that he was judging us. In some ways I guess we figured we might as well just go ahead and prove him right, give him something to talk about.

The L.A. Unified School District had a hard time getting anyone who knew the area and accompanying risks to accept positions there. Only the new, young teachers armed with the necessary optimism and little to no practical classroom experience or knowledge of the conditions could be lured to our neighborhoods to teach. More-experienced teachers knew to go elsewhere. Some of the inner-city high schools came complete with their own LAPD homicide divisions. Our schools, like our streets, were war zones, divided by race and bandana colors. Everyone in L.A. must always respect the laws that are set by the different gangs, upon penalty of death.

The new teachers came in with visions of saving us from ourselves, but in doing so they failed to see what we already knew: that sometimes what seems like the problem isn't really the problem at all. Most of us were struggling on a daily basis to save ourselves from things much greater than our own misperceptions and weaknesses. So, after a while, we learned to nod when they held us after class to talk about our problems, and to snicker at each other during their inspirational speeches. We played with their paranoia and fear of us, and learned, most importantly, never to expect much.

Somewhere down the line, in a day or a week or in six months, the new crop of teachers, still trying to make a good impression in their coordinated outfits, would walk out to find their cars gone or stripped; they'd see a shooting in front of the school or read an article in the *Los Angeles Times* about a bystander getting shot; and then they'd pack their bags and leave us. Each time, I couldn't help but wonder what they said to their friends and families when they returned home early. Did they tell people that we had failed *them*: we truly were the thugs and psychopaths that the newspaper articles claimed, and deserved the conditions we lived in? Or did they tell them that they had failed us: it was just too much, they were afraid every moment of dying, and no one should have to live as we do?

That summer I began to really hate school. The older I got, the more school felt like a prison. They locked us in at 8:30 and opened the gates again at 3:30. L.A. was in the midst of a budget crisis and the schools were bearing the brunt. Despite the fact that they found money for metal detectors and security guards, our books were left over from the dark ages—missing pages, out of date, worthless. Each classroom had a shelf on which the decrepit things were stored. We weren't allowed to remove them from the classroom, though sometimes, just to be bad, we'd fold the once hardback books in half and shove them in a back pocket or under a jacket and smuggle them out into the hallway, where we usually just tore them up or threw them away.

I got picked on almost every day that I went to school, especially now that I was at a new school in a different neighborhood where I didn't know anyone. Unlike most kids, I welcomed the beef and used it as an opportunity to tell everyone who my brothers were and what set they were from. I bought red Chuck Taylors and changed into them as soon as I got out of the house, and out of Big Mom's sight, to remind the other kids of the people I knew. Some days the fights happened before I could even get off the bus. One girl in particular, Vanessa, would sit behind me and poke me in the shoulder until I turned around, and then say, "Neva mind her, she think she all that jus kause she *think* she got good hair." Then everyone would laugh. After a while, I learned to keep petroleum jelly in my bag, and I got pretty good with my hands. In the rare instance that someone landed a blow to my face, the petroleum jelly made their fist slide right off. No cuts, no bruises. My catchphrase became: "Oh yea, you wanna see what light skin kan do?"

Before he had gotten locked up, Taye had introduced me to some people and I had started to sell some weed on the side, just so I could have some ends, make sure the babies had food, and keep a fresh pair of kicks on my feet. Hand-me-downs just gave the other kids like Vanessa more fuel to work with. The only thing school was good for was fighting and finding customers; only generally I didn't find them, they found me. Taye and Terrell were both climbing the ranks in their prospective sets while in juvie. Terrell had earned much respect, as well as additional time, for his constant fighting with Crips. With their names constantly coming from my mouth, I became somebody by default. Even the security guard who locked and unlocked the school's gates would trade a week's worth of free passes in and out for a dime bag.

The truth was, I liked to learn, though not much of that went on in school. For me, learning happened elsewhere. Taye had sent me a long letter from juvie telling me about things he was learning. He said I had to read *Manchild in the Promised Land* by Claude Brown. He said it was about a kid growing up in the hood and in juvie and told me to go get it out the library, but I didn't know where the library was, or even if my junior high school had one. I asked Big Mom if she would buy it for me for my birthday.

"What? Manchild in the what? What kind of book is that, anyway?"

"I dunno, Momma. Taye said it real good, tho."

"Taye?" Her face went from curious to serious. "No, nothing he suggests. That boy done messed up his life already. I ain helpin him take you down with him. If you want it, you go out an get it."

That was that. Big Mom was just one of those people; there was no sense in explaining or asking more than once. You couldn't change her mind.

"Aiight, Big Mom. I understand. I'm jus finna go outside a while, get me some air."

"I'm sorry, child," she said as I stepped out onto the porch. "One day you'll understand."

"I said I understood, Momma, but dang, ain like I axed fo no gun. It's a book."

I let the screen door slam shut behind me and walked down the top two steps, then jumped the bottom broken one onto the walkway.

"What up, punks?" I said, kneeling down next to Nishia and NeeCee, who were playing with dusty, naked Barbies.

"*You* da the punk, punk," Nishia said, twisting her fingers into a W, for Westside, and throwing me her best attitude, while NeeCee, not to be excluded, stuck her tongue out.

"Dats it, dats it, west up now?" I said, pushing NeeCee down on her back and tickling her as Nishia jumped on my back. "Oh, you think you tough, huh? Is that right? Show me what you got, lil gurl. I ain scurred of you." I reached back and grabbed her ankle, tugging a little bit. We all laughed and wrestled on the dried-out lawn a while, and then lay back under the summer sun.

"Aiight, y'all, ima bounce." I stood up, reached in my pocket, and tossed a few Tootsie Rolls at each of them, trying to hit them on their bellies. I prided myself now on always being prepared. They squealed as the candies hit them and bounced in all different directions. They scuffled to pick them all up as quickly as possible, already fighting over who had more.

I walked down the path unnoticed and into Rodney's yard. Bitch had had puppies and Rodney was pouring a bag of Puppy Chow onto the ground where the pups bounced about, playing and wagging their tails. Some of them were white with brown or black spots and velvety black noses, like Bitch, others were a light tan with yellow eyes and pink noses. Rodney said that there were eleven of them all together, but it was hard to tell because they never stood still long enough for me to count. I figured he'd know, though.

"What that B like, lil bit?" Rodney smiled.

I plopped down on the ground and the puppies pounced all over me, licking and nipping with sharp little puppy teeth. A few grabbed at the bottom of my T-shirt and began tugging in all directions, shaking their big little heads and growling.

"I seen Terrell today, said you got a birthday komin." Big Rodney would visit juvie sometimes as part of his court-ordered community service, which had him go around to juvenile facilities and schools and talk about gangs, and how crime and violence only landed you in prison or in the funeral home. Everything he said in his presentation was true, but sometimes in L.A. you had to do certain things just to survive, and no matter how logical the community service message was, the gang problem wasn't one that could ever be solved through "scared-straight" tactics.

"Fa sho. I asked Big Mom fo a book fo my B-day, too, but she said no. Fukked up, huh?"

"Depends on the book." Rodney winked at me. Everyone liked Big Mom, so it was hard to find allies sometimes.

"Man, I don't even kno, jus sum book Taye said I should read. It's kalt *Manchild in the Promised Land*. He jus said it's real good."

"Yea, I read that in the pen. That is a good book. Lil Taye reading like that, huh? It might be a lil grown fo you, tho, missy."

"Taye said the kid in it my age."

"Well, maybe in the beginning at least," Rodney laughed. "How's Taye doin, anyway?"

"You mean otha than bein locked up? I dunno, man, he say in the letter he doin aiight."

"Black man's university," Rodney said. "I did all my best learning in juvie and the pen. He prolly mess around an kome out a better person. Wait here."

I pushed the puppies off, trying to pet Bitch, but it was point-less. By the time I pushed one off, another three were on me, jump-ing and nipping, licking and yelping.

Rodney came back outside smoking a blunt and tossed a book at me.

"There, I thought I still had it." He motioned to the blunt. "You blaze? I heard you be sellin some round the skool."

I reached up, took the blunt, even though I barely ever smoked. I took a quick, shallow hit and handed it back as I exhaled. I held the book with both hands now. I'd never owned a grown-up book be-fore. It felt cool to the touch, soft somehow. On the cover was a pic-ture of a boy climbing the fire escape of a tall building, other tall buildings rising up on either side. I immediately opened it, looked at all that small type. I tried to imagine my brother reading the book. I'd never seen him read a book before. This was over 400 pages.

"It's long."

Rodney held out a hand to take it back. "I toldt you it might be too grown fo ya."

"Naw," I tucked it under my arm. "Ima read it. It jus gonna take a while, I guess. Hey, Rodney, how long it take ta read a book like that?"

"Like I said, lil bit, I read it in the pen, wasn't nothing else ta do but sit an read all daymn day. It take however long it take, ain noth-ing wrong wit that." He smiled. "Now, I got otha business ta talk ta you about. You ready?"

"Yea, I'm ready," I said, pushing off one puppy, then another. Rodney laughed.

"Well it's about them anyway, really. Your brother paid me fo two puppies. One fo him an one fo you. He said tell you Happy Birthday if he don't bee you."

"Big Mom would neva let me take one, Rodney." I couldn't even let myself be excited over something so hopeless. "There already too many hungry mouths in the house and if I offered ta buy the food myself I'd have to explain to her how ima get the money. It ain even worth a try. I mean, thanks an all, but it's no way."

"Naw, we already talked bout that." He broke out a big, wide smile. "Terrell's pup gonna stay here till he gets out an you kan keep yours here, too. But you finna take care of it AND feed it. Otha than that, it's between us, ain no one know'n our business. Deal?" He held out his hand so that we could shake on it, but instead I jumped up and hugged him.

"I love you, Rodney."

"Is that so?" he said. I lifted my head to look at him, my arms still wrapped around him. I didn't expect him to say it back. He was a man. Most days my brothers couldn't tell me they loved me. Yet, at the same time, Rodney and Terrell *had* both just told me that they loved me, clear as anything, and I knew it.

"K'mon now, people finna see you huggin me like that, start think'n I gone soft." He patted my back and I let go.

"Now, Terrell, I told him bout all the pups an he picked that black an white female ova there. Ain nobody else made they pick yet. So, Bree Bree, which it gonna be?"

"Which one you think I should take?" It was hard to focus on any one pup in particular. The pups tumbled and jumped, dodging in and out of one another's legs.

"Hard ta say, lil bit. It's ure dog. You want a female or a male?

Now, see, the boys, they nicer. People think it's the opposite, but it ain true. The females, they more protective, an because of that they usually more aggressive. They go inta momma mode an watch out! In a fight, I always put my money on the female." Rodney was feeling the weed, talking all animated. I looked at Bitch, at her scars and missing ear. She was retired from fighting, but it was hard to deny what she had been made to be in the past. I thought about how other dogs had torn into Bitch and made all those scars, how she'd had to have done still worse to them to even survive. I looked at her missing ear and then at the ground, feeling guilty for in that moment loving Rodney less.

"Well, I don't wanna fight my dog." I looked back up at Bitch, then at the puppies, but not at Rodney.

"Aiight, then, how bout one them boys?"

Rodney started pointing out which ones were males, but I was no longer paying attention. I had noticed the smallest puppy, golden with a pink nose and green eyes. All the others were running around, but this one just sat there next to Bitch, watching, one of his giant ears folded over backwards. I bent down and gently scooped it up.

"This one a boy?" Rodney looked at me, nodded his head that it was.

"Yea," he said after a minute with a deep sigh, "but you don't want that one. That's the runt." I looked at the puppy. His nose had a small scratch on it that was dotted with blood.

"It's my dog, rite?" I looked at Rodney.

"Yea, Bree, it is, but you still don't want the runt. You got ure choice outta all them. That one, he jus best used as a baiter. Pick one the bigger ones. Thems some nice-looking dogs, why pick the one ain worth nothin? You don't wanna have to tell Terrell you picked the runt, do you? He paid good money fo the pup. Sides, lots ah times the runt don't even make it."

"If it's my choice, then I want this one." I handed the puppy to Rodney.

"Aiight, then, babygurl. What chu wanna kall him?" The puppy looked so small in Rodney's hand. Its brow was furrowed, but its eyes were bright. Bitch looked up at her pup, stretched her short, stocky neck up as far as she could, and licked his foot with her long pink tongue.

"How bout Red?"

Rodney laughed and shook his head. "Gurl, half these red pits end up named Red." He scratched the puppy's head and put him down next to Bitch, who licked at his hurt nose. I liked the pup because it always stayed next to Bitch while the others ran around. I liked the idea that because of me they could stay together and always have each other.

"Well, what you think I should name him? What's a good dog name?" Rodney thought a minute, looked down at the tiny puppy, and again shook his head.

"How bout Cinque?"

I looked at him and scrunched my nose.

"Was that mean?"

"Cinque was a brave an honest man, a real man." Rodney smiled again. "It's too bad they don't teach you bout people like him in skool, but of course they don't want y'all ta kno nothing bout real history. You wanna hear a story, Bree Bree, a true one? One they ain finna tell you in skool?" I nodded yes.

"Well, it was right bout the time when the Alantik slave trade was goin on. It was twisted evil an complicated shyt. One ship, it was kalled the *Amistad,* it was a Spanish ship. They used it ta transport slaves from Africa an on it was this man named Cinque. In 1839 he led a slave revolt on it an killed the kaptin and took the boat over. Well, they captured that ship outside of New York. It became a big battle. The Spanish authorities wanted the ship and the slaves back, an even ol President Van Buren wanted ta give the slaves back to Spain, but it was two years later an some judge from the Supreme Court looked at all the evidence an deemed all the men on it free persons. See Cinque, he was one ah the few. Over fifteen million African people got brought to this country, stolen from they lands and families, but Cinque was the one who showed that some resisted. Some fought for what was right, despite the odds. You feel? Maybe ure lil runt will surprise us, too."

I looked at the little dog with his wrinkly head, hurt nose, and big feet.

"Aiight, Cinque seem like a good name," I said and reached out, shook Rodney's hand. Rodney was one of the smartest people I knew. He was always droppin' his wisdom. "The magik knowledge sprinkler," he called it. "Gotta let it trickle down."

"I'm ghost, man. Ima go buy sum dog food. And hey, Rodney, you right, we ain learned *that* in skool."

"Sho nuff," Rodney said, shaking my hand and making it official. I took off down the walk and he checked his pager. It had gone off a few times while we were talking, but Rodney was cool like that. He always gave you his full attention. It made me feel like I was important, not just some stupid kid. He treated me like I mattered, at least as much as anyone else, if not more. "Make sure that gate good an shut, don't wanna lose none these pups," he called after me.

I latched the gate and gave it a tug to make sure. In the next yard, my sisters were still playing with Barbies and chewing on Tootsie Rolls. I needed to head down to the park for a while, make some cash and bring Big Rodney the dog food like I said. Keeping my word was important. Word is bond, the OGs always said. I ran inside to let Big Mom know I was going down to the park.

Big Mom was at the sink, doing dishes, when I came in. As I pulled open a package of generic Pop-Tarts, I vaguely heard a neighborhood crackhead outside arguing with her pimp. Various screamed and slurred insults were traded, ending with a loud slap. By now, I was familiar with this sort of exchange, and we didn't pay much attention, unless one of us recognized one of the voices, or if it was followed by gunshots.

But this time it stirred something in Big Mom. Suddenly she was behind me, grabbing me by the shoulders, spinning me around to face her. There were tears in her eyes, not running down her cheeks, but small beads clinging to the corners of her eyes and on the tips of her dark lashes.

"Bree, promise me. Promise me."

My breath stuck in my chest.

"I kno, Momma. K'mon now, you raised me betta than that bullish." I smiled at her nervously. She was hurting and I knew it. I reached my arms around and hugged her. She threw her thick arms around me and squeezed so tightly it scared me. I couldn't move, speak, or breathe. When she let go of me she turned so I couldn't see her face. I knew she was fighting hard to keep from crying. She leaned forward onto the counter, her shoulders sagging.

"Go on now."

I knew the last thing she wanted was for me or the babies to see her cry. She had her pride. I started to walk out of the kitchen, looking back from the doorway. She hadn't moved and was still hunched, crying now into the uncaring dishes.

"Momma, ima take the babies down ta the park, too." No answer. "You kno, I'll be careful an all that." Still no answer. I grabbed their shoes and went outside. I figured she'd be grateful for the break.

"K'ome on, y'all, let's get out this dusty ass yard. Ima take you down ta the park." Nishia scurried to put her shoes on while I helped NeeCee with hers.

"These the right feet?" Nishia asked, the toes of her shoes pointing outward, clearly on the wrong feet.

"Naw, Nishia, I done told you a million times, buckles on the outside. Daymn . . ." I sat down next to her and undid her shoes.

"Don't be mad. I'll do it," she said in a firm tone, pulling her feet out of my grasp and shoving my hand away. "Jus lemme do it myself." Her brow was furrowed. She looked up at me and her eyes narrowed a little. I could tell she was thinking about whether or not to say something.

"What, Nishia? Jus say it."

"You ain so big, you kno."

"Well, I'm hella bigger than you, I kno that." I grabbed her wrist and pulled her up to her feet. I did it harder than I should have. Not hard enough to hurt, but harder than I should have. "Let's go."

Nishia jerked her hand away from me and took NeeCee's hand. It surprised me; Nishia had always been my partner. The whole interaction surprised me; she had never given me any attitude before. But here we were. I guess I wasn't the only one getting older and becoming aware of the world around us.

"Nishia, you better stop wit the attitude fore y'all don't get ta go nowhere. I ain takin you down there ta act a foo in front my friends.

What's it gonna be, then?" She stood looking at me, saying nothing, still holding NeeCee's hand. After one of those minutes that seemed way longer, she had still said nothing.

"Fine, then," I said grabbing NeeCee's other hand and pulling her behind me toward the gate, "Fine. Say nothin, but then *stay* sayin nothin."

We walked down the street toward the park, first silently, me walking faster than my sisters, pulling them slightly. Halfway there, Nishia started to pipe up again.

"What friends you got at the park?"

"I got friends, Nishia."

"Why you wearin them red shoes like that. You ain no gangsta."

"Maybe I jus like red, Nishia."

"Ain nobody wear red jus cause they like it."

"I'm wearin red kause I like it, Nishia, so you wrong. I told you, you jus a baby, stop talkin like you kno what you talkin about, okay? Kause fa real, on some real shyt, you don't kno nothin bout it."

I knew she just had unanswered questions, like we all did. She'd watched Terrell and Taye leave the house, get locked up, and none of it made sense to her. I knew that none of her defiance or attitude was meant as disrespect, but somehow it felt like it was and I lacked the patience to take it, or to explain things to her.

"Bree Bree." She stopped walking. I turned around and she looked so small, standing by herself on the sidewalk, that I felt bad for fighting with her. She wasn't particularly short, just thin with knobby knees and big round cheeks. Looking at her, I couldn't be annoyed anymore.

"What is it, Nishia?"

"You finna leave like Terrell and Taye did, aren't you? I don't want you ta leave. Who finna take care of us?" Tears started to roll down her cheeks. Nishia quickly pressed her hands over her eyes to stop the tears, but they just came streaming down her arms. NeeCee ran over and hugged her, and then she started to cry, too.

I sat down on the curb. The girls looked so small and young and helpless standing there, crying, yet their lives lacked the simplicity and innocence of childhood. No kid should have to beg someone to take care of her. And what if I did leave? What if my social worker moved me or I got locked up? Nishia was right. Who would take care of them? Nishia and NeeCee stopped crying and now stood waiting for a response from me. Somehow I was supposed to make everything okay. Nishia was still holding her hands over her eyes. The city bustled on around us, not noticing or caring.

In South Central, the city literally closes you in on all sides. It's a fortress of raised freeways protected by sound-dulling, bullet-shielding walls. Beyond all these obstructions, blocked from our view, are the suburbs, with their private walls and gates. When they first went up, the city government tried to say that the walls were to protect us from the noise of the cars, but they had never shown such consideration toward us before, and who were they fooling when they started building them right after an "innocent person" was hit with a stray bullet. Of course, we all knew "innocent" meant white, because in the hood innocent people get hit by strays all the time.

I studied the buildings and freeways rising behind my sisters, trapping us, holding us and our futures in. Big Mom cleaned one of the tall downtown buildings starting from its five o'clock closing well into the night, going from office to office, making every corner shine. She probably spent at least as much time in it as the CEOs and their white secretaries, but at the end of the day they took the 10 West home to their gated communities, and she took it south to the ghetto. She came home exhausted, smelling of bleach; then, on her days off, she cleaned our house. In the two years she had been working there her knees had grown rough and leathery from kneeling. I hated her working there. Thinking about it created a desperation within me. I knew that that life wasn't for me, working an hour to get six bucks. I got more than that already, and I knew how I could make more.

I kneeled down on the cement, hot against my knees, and wrapped my arms around my sisters.

"So long as I kan help it, Nishia, I ain goin nowhere. Okay?"

She threw her thin arms around me and I touched the back of her neck with my hand. It hurt. I hoped that what I'd just said wasn't a lie. I bit my lip hard and the pain stopped the tears from coming.

In the park Nishia and NeeCee immediately took off toward the swings. I saw some of Taye's friends that I knew, sitting over on picnic tables with some of the bigger homies from the neighborhood. One of them, Allen, waved at me to come over. With both my brothers in juvie, a few of their homies had taken it upon themselves to look out for me. It made me feel important to have the older kids and gang members know who I was.

"Nishia, ima go over at the benches," I yelled toward the swings. She looked up and I pointed to the corner of the park. She followed my finger to where the homies sat and frowned.

The park was all sorts of chaos at any given moment. On one side was the basketball courts, the loudest part of the park. The ball pounded against the asphalt and everyone cheered, rooted, and sometimes fought. If you sat and watched long enough you would see at least one fight on the court. On the other side was your typical kids' playground scenario, with swings and a slide. Then you had people low-riding around, checking things out, seeing who was at the park, and the people gangbanging, just hanging out to show their colors, hear the latest gossip, and sell their drugs. And, as always, you had crackheads walking around, acting desperate. I scanned the park and the surrounding streets as I walked toward the picnic tables.

If you want to survive in South Central L.A. you must always scan the park, figure out who is where and the best escape route from each direction. It's a common-enough thing for a park to get shot up. You never know who in the park has beef with whom and who might show up busting.

"West brakkin?" I said. Allen put his hand out toward me, palm up and I gave it a hard slap as I sat down next to him.

"Not much, not much. What that B like?"

I shrugged and he turned to his homies.

"Y'all kno Bree Bree? She Taye's lil sister." His statement was met with a few snickers and jokes about us not looking alike and then with apologies and questions as to how Taye was doing and if I'd seen him.

"Yea, I seen him the other day," I lied. "He doin aiight, konsidering, ya kno what I mean? Anyway," I said looking them all in the eyes, "I'm looking ta make sum ends, anyone got sum deliveries they need made or what?"

One of the big homies gave me a good long look up and down then laughed, "What you kno bout makin no deliveries, lil gurl?"

I didn't let his words sting me; I expected it. Really, I didn't know much about making deliveries, except that it paid better than selling weed. I took a step closer to him and looked right at him. That's what my brothers had taught me. Always make people take you seriously. "What you mean, homie? I'm perfect. Who would ever suspect me?"

He thought about it for a minute, then laughed again. "Aiight, sho nuff, you right. Ima take a chance on you. You meet me here tomorrow morning befo skool. You go ta skool, right?"

"Sometimes." I shrugged my shoulders and gave him a half smile. He laughed again. The high school graduation rate, though it varies somewhat from neighborhood to neighborhood in South Central, hovers somewhere around fifty percent.

"Okay, I hear that, I was the same way. But peep it, ima be here early. You git here early, too, aiight, B?"

"Fa sho," I said and reached out to shake his hand. "You won't regret it."

"I hope not," he said. "Name is Slikk." I shook his hand, a good firm shake so he knew I meant it. I knew I was making a move, becoming more like Terrell, Taye, and Rodney, and less like Big Mom and the kids.

I turned to Allen and reached my hand out. "Ima bounce, homie. I'll katch ya later on." He slapped my hand and then hit his chest over his heart, formed his hand into the *b* and held it up to the sun. I did the same.

I started back toward my sisters and Nishia met me halfway. I knew she'd been watching me the whole time, her eyes had caught every interaction, every gang sign. She threw her arms around me and I swung her around in a big circle till she was dizzy.

"Now ima walk." She tried but teetered, then fell onto the grass. NeeCee jumped on top of her, and Nishia, in response, pretended to throw up. We all laughed. I jumped into the pile and we all wrestled there in the summer sun, tugging and pushing and screaming and, in NeeCee's case, biting. It was nice to act like kids together for a minute, forget about everything else. I sat up and held my sisters in headlocks.

"Whoeva wants a soda from Dave's, stand up!" They struggled, but of course couldn't get to their feet with me holding them. "What, y'all don't like soda? Daymnnn." Then Nishia's eyes lit up. She started tickling me until I released my grasp and she was free. She and NeeCee darted off toward the store while I sat on the grass, watching them run.

"Hey, Bree Bree!" Nishia turned around and smiled her huge smile at me. "The last one there pays!" Within seconds she was standing, grinning, and waiting for me on the same curb where she had been crying earlier that day.

I jumped up and caught up to my sisters. We walked into Dave's holding hands and I bought three sodas and a bag of peanut M&M's from the mean Korean lady, then went out and sat down again on the same curb. Might as well make a good memory here today, I thought to myself; that way, tomorrow, when I walk past here to meet Slikk, I will be able to remember my sisters sitting on the curb, laughing and drinking soda. I watched them carefully, sitting there having fun, because I knew I'd never be able to forget them standing there crying.

FRESH OUT

IT HAD BEEN just three months short of three years since Terrell had begun his six-month sentence in juvie on the robbery charge. Before the initial six months were up, Tee had gotten into a fight with a Crip at his group session that had bloodied both their faces, landed each of them in segregation, and extended my brother's sentence by thirty more months. More important to him though, it had earned him some stripes. One of the surest ways to earn respect and rise up in the ranks toward becoming OG was to put in some serious work in Juvenile Hall or the CYA (California Youth Authority). It was such an effective way, in fact, that some kids who hadn't made the set yet and YGs who were new on the set were actually *trying* to get to juvie.

Terrell stayed at Eastlake, the same place he'd had court. I guess it had to do with either the pettiness of his crime or his generally cool temper that he got to stay there, while Taye was sent all the way up to Preston, a CYA facility almost six hours north of Los Angeles. One homie told me that if you caught a crime that was drug related you were always transferred up to a CYA facility instead of staying at juvie because you were required to go through their rehab program. It seemed stupid. If you were selling drugs, rule number one was: Never get high off your own supply. If you violated that rule, it was just a question of time before you used up your supply and ended up broke, begging for a bump like the rest of the smokers. Most people like Taye who were in for selling had never even thought about using the stuff.

Though Eastlake was less strict than some of the other detention centers, they only allowed parents and guardians to visit. When it became apparent that Terrell was going to be in for years rather than months, I called and was told that siblings could also visit—if they were approved by the juvenile's probation or supervising officer, and even then they were only allowed to visit once.

"Excuse me, but what days are visiting?" I asked into the phone, my pen and paper ready.

"Sunday afternoons only, one to four," said the rushed, muffled voice on the other end of the phone. It was possible. I knew Momma wouldn't go if it meant missing church, but since visiting didn't get started until one o'clock, it was completely possible to do both if we made the early service. Eastlake was local, too, just minutes from our house and the church.

I devised a plan. I spent the rest of the day cleaning the house and making dinner. I didn't just make any dinner, either. There was a lady, a crack smoker, who was always selling meat on the street, meat she either bought with food stamps or stole out of her relatives' refrigerators. She had two packs of T-bones; one had two steaks in it, the other had three. I bought both of them. With the money I was earning making deliveries it was nothing. It had been so long since we had steak that I couldn't even remember what it tasted like or how to cook it. On Sundays and special occasions Big Mom made chicken instead of the typical red beans and rice, turkey necks, or black-eyed peas. I put four big brown russet potatoes in the oven and ran across the street to the liquor store for milk, cornmeal, and a box of Nilla Wafers.

"Oh, hold up a second, homie," I said to the man at the register. I went and got a liter of warm Coke out of the cooler and, walking back toward the register, picked out two red Jolly Ranchers for my sisters, checking quickly to make sure they were watermelon and not the hot cinnamon ones.

"Thanks." I looked the man in the eye as I added the items to the ones already on the counter. He caught my gaze for a second and then looked down quickly.

"I have other customers," he said angrily, suggesting, I guess, that I needed to both hurry up and not make him wait next time. I did a quick recon of the store and, seeing no one inside except for him and me, laughed.

"Aiight, homie," I said, smiling at the ridiculousness of what he was saying. "Why don't you hurry up and ring that shyt up, then?" I was no longer the little kid spilling milk outside and I wanted it known. I had my own real money instead of food stamps, and I had enough to buy any of the extras I wanted. Besides, I knew that no matter how rude I was, he wasn't about to refuse to sell to me.

"I don't want no problems," he said, hurriedly ringing in the three remaining items.

"No, noo problems," I said slowly, enunciating every letter. "No problems." No problems sounded pretty good really, but if he really wanted no problems, then he had opened his store in the wrong neighborhood.

I wasn't in the door two minutes before Nishia was telling me that she was hungry. Hearing my commotion in the kitchen, the girls had shut off the television and come to investigate, peering into the bag and asking questions.

I smiled, still trying to shake the interaction with the Korean storeowner from my thoughts, measuring out the cornmeal, flour, milk, and baking powder into a bowl.

"Okay, then, Nishia, let's make some banana pudding. Grab two eggs out the fridge and mix all that together, till there ain no lumps or dry part. NeeCee, get out a pan fo kornbread an grease it wit the oil."

NeeCee watched me over her shoulder, confused, but excited. "It's Momma's birthday?"

I laughed. "Naw, baby."

She scrunched up her forehead. "It's ure birthday?"

Now Nishia was laughing, too. "Naw, baby, ain nobody birthday." NeeCee made a face and then shrugged her shoulders and joined in the laughter. "Ure a fool," I said, smiling from ear to ear.

NeeCee smiled back and then started singing, "I am special, I am special, yes I am. You wanna be jus like me. You wanna be jus like me. Yes you do . . ."

"I'm done," Nishia said and pushed the bowl toward me.

I handed them each a Jolly Rancher and sent them back to watch TV while I poured the slightly lumpy cornbread batter into the pan and put it in the oven with the potatoes. I then cut one of the steaks into pieces for Bitch and Cinque, who was now six months old, and rubbed the rest with pepper and spices.

I was pulling all the food out of the oven when Big Mom walked in. The aroma had filled the house with sweet warmth. Momma smiled and sniffed at the air as she hung her coat up by the door.

"Well," she started, lifting her head and shutting her eyes in an exaggerated gesture, "what on God's great earth is goin on in here."

"We made the cornbread!" NeeCee shouted out with pride, almost cutting off Momma's sentence. "Me an Nishia. All by ourselves. An Bree made banana pudding."

"My goodness." Momma clapped her hands together in feigned amazement. "Well, I guess you betta go wash up, then, cause I'm starved." The two girls ran off and Momma kissed me on the cheek. "Thank you, baby, it sure smells good."

With all the food I'd made, plus yesterday's leftover collard greens, it looked like a feast. Nishia and NeeCee sat down and stared at it wide-eyed.

"Good Lord," Momma said, looking at the food and then at us, "I feel like a queen."

"You are a queen, Momma," I said. "You do a lot for us. I wanted to do something fo you, too. An Momma," I took my opportunity, "I kalled to Eastlake today and they say we kan get it kleared an go visit Terrell on a Sunday afta church."

Momma's demeanor changed. "No." She stood up and turned her back to us, wiping her palms against her hips. She took a few steps, back and forth across the small kitchen trying to regain her composure. "Cups." She changed the subject. "We need cups."

"Momma, don't . . . don't you miss him? Don't you wanna see him?"

"Well, of course I miss him. What kinda question is that?" Her voice sounded angry. "What kinda person do you think I am?"

I didn't know what to say. "The best kind, Momma."

"Well, let's enjoy this food, then," she said, grabbing a spoon and heaping some greens onto her plate. Nishia looked at me as Momma buttered a potato and took a bite. She'd forgotten to say grace. I shrugged my shoulders and grabbed a steak off the plate. We ate in silence. Even NeeCee said nothing until her plate was empty, and then she just asked to be excused.

A full month of begging later, we found ourselves sitting in reception on a Sunday afternoon, still in our church clothes, waiting to be led to visiting. Momma looked nervous and played with her hands while Nishia and NeeCee checked out the vending machine, making mental notes.

"What's wrong, Big Mom?" I whispered. She shook her head as I reached over and took her hand.

She leaned in and whispered back, "I feel like everyone's lookin at me, like they think I'm a bad mom."

"Momma, they all got kids in here, too." Momma laughed, she knew I was right.

Then they called out Terrell's name and we all went through the metal detector and sat down in the visiting room.

But Terrell wasn't there. NeeCee asked every minute where was Terrell and when he was coming. Momma finally quieted her with quarters for the vending machines. Momma tapped her foot and her hands shook, but when Terrell, now seventeen, came walking in, all her nervousness disappeared. Terrell looked different than he had at fourteen. Any trace of skinniness was gone, and even though he was now close to six feet, he had developed an athletic build. His face had narrowed some and his hair, which he wore in tight neat cornrows, was long.

"My baby," she said, jumping up and hugging him tight.

"Momma," Terrell smiled, all his teeth showing. "I kan't breathe, Momma." NeeCee and Nishia threw their packages of Skittles and potato chips onto the table and hugged his legs. Terrell stood there immobilized between Momma and the two girls. I wasn't his mom or a little kid so I couldn't get away with a dramatic gesture, but I think he knew I was as happy as they were to see him.

"West up, Bree Bree?"

The guard came over and informed us that excessive physical contact was grounds to terminate a visit. Momma and the girls let go quickly and we sat down. Momma talked animatedly, telling Terrell what a superior service the pastor had led that morning. "I hope you plan on goin back ta church when you get out," she added.

"Actually"—Terrell was all smiles, looking at Big Mom—"that's finna be soon. Ain had no write-ups, finished all my klasses. Looks like ima get up outta here in a few weeks, or so they say." Momma gasped. "Momma, don't cry." Terrell took her hands in his. "It's gonna be aiight. Ima do things right this time. Shyt"—he straightened in his chair—"look at me. I'm a grown ass man. I gotta get it together."

For the next two hours we talked and ate vending machine snacks and enjoyed being a family. Terrell let NeeCee beat him in checkers, and Momma beat everyone in spades. When they announced that only five minutes remained, Big Mom turned to Terrell. "They said the kids couldn't come back, but I can come next week if you want. After church."

"I'd like that," Terrell said, standing to give final hugs goodbye. "You be good," he pointed to NeeCee. "No troublemaking, missy." She laughed and Momma started gathering the wrappers off the table and throwing them away.

"Bree." Terrell's was face was serious as he turned to me, "Everythang aiight at the krib?" I did my best to assure him and he smiled, relieved, I think, and gave a final wave as we went out different doors to face different problems. It didn't feel so bad leaving because we all had visions of life back together in the near future. Of course, we wouldn't be complete without Taye, but I knew he wouldn't be home for a long, long while.

Taye was a victim of the harsh drug policy that came into prominence in the 1980s. While Nancy Reagan was telling schoolchildren across the country to "Just Say No to Drugs," her husband was championing highly discriminatory drug laws, making it more of a war on the poor than a war on drugs. The drug laws targeted drugs like crack that were rampant in the ghettos, mandating stiff sentences for offenders, while meting out far more lenient punishments for the powder cocaine used in more affluent, white neighborhoods. The new laws also gave the police free rein in the ghettos, where gang and drug task forces could now search or detain you with no warrant.

The whole way home, Momma talked of nothing but the homecoming party she was going to throw for Terrell.

Everything had to be perfect, Momma kept saying. She was going to make gumbo and cornbread, since "Everyone likes gumbo and cornbread, right?" She looked at me, seeking approval. I nodded. "I'll make fried chicken too." She nodded, thinking it over. Then she started in on who she would invite, who she thought would actually come, and who she hoped wouldn't hear about it and show up at the house uninvited. I leaned back in the front seat, listening halfheartedly, my thoughts flitting back and forth between Taye and Terrell as I watched the city change one square block section at a time, and read the graffiti to get the latest news.

The next few weeks, while Big Mom prepared the house and prayed that Terrell would finally get his life together, I spread the word around the neighborhood that my brother was coming home.

Momma had been singing all morning as she cleaned and cooked. I'd never seen so much food in my life, and the people showing up were carrying even more. Big Rodney had helped Momma move the kitchen table outside and then brought an extra card table over from his house, and quickly both of them were covered with pots and bowls of rice, gumbo, potato salad, and collard greens.

"Baby," Big Mom called to me, "go get the rest of the chicken, an that big platter for the barbecue." I walked in the back door, past Auntie and her newest boyfriend. Cousins, uncles, and friends I hadn't seen in months or years ran in and out of the house. When I entered the kitchen, Nishia was standing there in her Sunday dress, mixing up a pitcher of Kool-Aid.

"Momma tell you ta make that?"

"Yea," she said, using a wooden spoon to stir the sugar at the bottom until it dissolved into the red liquid. "I made some already, but we out. She said ta make this an then go ask Sista Cynthia if she got an extra pitcher." Nishia looked at me and rolled her eyes.

Cynthia lived across the street. She was about sixty years old and was Momma's sister in Christ. She didn't actually go to *our* church, but she went to church religiously, and that was good enough for Momma. She also delivered monologues that had no end and no escape.

"Jus take that pitcher out. I'll ask Rodney instead. Don't even trip, Nishia." She smiled and walked out slowly, careful not to spill.

Momma had fried four whole chickens' worth of wings, thighs, legs, and breasts, placing the biggest piece to the side for the guest of honor. Uncle Clayton, the oldest of Big Mom's kids, had driven down from the Bay Area for the event. He stood by the barbecue, fanning the coals and unpacking a bag of pork ribs and hot links that he had stopped and bought along the way. I stacked the fried chicken on top of the big barbecue platter and headed back outside, our cousins Kaleb and Kristy grabbing pieces off before I made it out the door.

"Right here," Momma said, hurrying over to help set the chicken between a basket of some unidentifiable muffins that Auntie had brought and a brown sugar bundt cake with white icing. When she straightened up, she gave the yard a quick once-over.

"It's perfect, ain it?"

"Yea, Momma, it really is."

"The Welcome Home sign ain crooked, is it?"

"Naw, Momma," I assured her, even though it was, "it's all perfect. Tee gonna be real happy."

About an hour later, a car pulled up and Terrell got out, holding a box of his possessions. He was wearing a pair of jeans and a button-down shirt that Big Mom had dropped off for him to be released in.

"Daaaymmn," he said, seeing all the people. "Oh," he looked over at Big Mom, realizing he had cussed, "sorry, Momma."

Momma patted his shoulder. "Go an put that box down and say hello to ure family." Terrell kissed her cheek, then rounded the hallway, getting stopped every inch of the way by excited relatives. Momma's face brimmed with pride and optimism. She had visited Terrell the last three Sundays after church, discussing how things would be when he came home. Afterward, she would come home and recap everything he said. How he was going to go back to church, get a job, and maybe even take some classes at the junior college now that he had earned his GED. The future looked good and she hoped that his new approach to life would teach me to pull away from the activities she rightly suspected me of. Maybe it would even motivate Taye to change his ways. Now her eyes stayed fixed on Tee's every action as he greeted everyone and assured them all that now that he was out he was never going back.

The evening, for the most part, was as Momma hoped, perfect. Momma kept refilling the platter of chicken and Uncle Clay ran out to the store to buy more links and ribs. The little ones ran around outside and got dirty; NeeCee all but ruined her good dress, but somehow, for that one day only, that was perfect, too.

As the sun started to set and the clouds and smog turned crimson, people started to leave. Uncle Clayton was packing the cousins into the car and saying his goodbyes when a big silver Caprice pulled up, music blaring. Momma's eyes deadened.

"Aye, what up, mah nigga?" Freddy jumped out of the passenger seat and threw his arms around Terrell. Slikk killed the ignition and walked slowly around the car, the three homies in the backseat piling out behind him.

"Dizzam!" Slikk said, holding his fist up over his mouth. Terrell, once a head shorter than his peers now towered over Freddy. "You got big."

"Mah lil nigga is my bigga nigga now," Freddy laughed as Terrell smiled and took turns greeting each of the homies.

Momma said nothing. After saying goodbye to Clayton, she walked in the house, slamming the front door shut behind her.

"Bye, Terrell," Uncle Clay said and waved.

"Bye," Terrell waved back. "Thanks fo komin down, man, I appreciate it."

"Fa sho," Clayton said, opening the door of his car. "Keep ure head up an stay outta trouble." Terrell nodded in agreement, waving again as the car pulled away.

Freddy pulled a bottle of Hennessey out of the car and held it up. "Hell, yea," Terrell said, drifting closer to him. "You kno I missed that shyt right there."

Within minutes, all six of them had a cup in their hands. Terrell leaned against Slikk's car while everyone else talked, interrupting one another to give him a rundown of what was going on in the neighborhood.

"Someone been steady askin bout chu, too, mah nigga," Freddy added, raising an eyebrow and giving Tee a quick elbow jab.

"Oh, Shawna?" Terrell asked and the homies all laughed. He nodded. "Yea, she flew me a few kytes when I was in there, even threw a dawg a few bones, put money on my account."

"You already knowin," Freddy said. "Keep it pimpin, huh homie?"

"You kno how we do," Slikk chimed in. "Keep the pimpin klean an the makkin' mean."

"Naw, fa real tho, she gonna be at this party tonight. You done here? Wanna bounce, go ova there?"

"Hell, yea," Tee said. "Let's go." He looked at me. "Wanna go, Bree Bree? You big nuff."

I looked at my brother and then at the car, already full before him. "Naw, ima stay an help Momma klean up. She . . ." I paused for a minute, not sure how to express to Tee how important all this was to her and how much weight she was putting on him. "She really put a lot into this."

"I'm already knowin, sis. Moms an I is real kool right now. Don't even trip." Everyone was already loading into the car, piling four homies into the back to leave the passenger seat for Terrell. He climbed in and threw the *b* up at me out the window. I watched as they drove off, then went into the house.

Momma was scrubbing away at the piles of dishes that she had rounded up and set on the counter. "He leave with them?" she asked without turning around.

"Yea," I said. "You want some help, Momma?"

"No," she said, still scrubbing. "I think I'd like to be alone. Jus get ure sisters into bed fo me, if you could do that."

"Sure, Momma, I'll do that." I started to walk down the hall, then paused. "I love you, Momma."

"I love you, too, baby. Good night."

I sent Nishia and NeeCee into the bathroom to brush their teeth and wash their faces as I pulled on my pajamas. When they came back, I kissed them good night and shut off the lights. I wanted to give Momma her space. I lay down on my bed and stared at the ceiling for a while. I started out thinking about Terrell and Momma, torn in different directions by their different realities, but I ended up thinking about Taye.

When I was sure that both of my sisters were asleep, I turned on the small light on the nightstand, took out some paper and started to write Taye. I wrote for hours. I told him all the details of the day and how happy Momma had been. I told him about Uncle Clayton driving down and all the food Momma had made. Then I wrote about how confusing it was. How Momma had all these high hopes for us and how I appreciated her belief that if we prayed and worked hard we could accomplish anything we wanted, but it just wasn't true. I couldn't understand how she could live here and not see that. It was as if she thought Tee would give up all his friends, his past, and just become some preppy college kid like the USC students we'd sometimes see walking around by the movie theaters. She had to know that even if that was what he wanted to do on some level, that wasn't how it worked.

That was when I heard a car pull up outside for the second time tonight. Slikk's car. I looked out the window and watched Terrell walk up the steps, stumbling slightly. Momma's voice came right after that.

"Right back ta the same ol shyt, huh?" she yelled at him. "Ain nothing changed."

"Momma, I jus went ta see some friends. We weren't doin nothin, I swear to you. Plus, I'm home early, ain I?"

"Friends? Those ain ure friends. They the ones who got you landed up in there, and that's right where they gonna get you all ova again."

"Momma," Terrell tried to calm her, "you gonna wake the lil ones up."

"Good," she said, "maybe they need to hear it so they don't grow up thinking this is an okay way ta act. Lemme ask you something, Terrell." She paused for a moment. "Do you really think you settin a good example fo the rest of them? Are you proud of what they see you doin? Hangin out wit gangbangers an goin ta juvie? Robbin people?"

Terrell didn't say anything, but I heard him shut the door behind him as he left and I watched as he walked down the stairs onto the street and away from the house. It was quiet in the living room for a while as Momma waited to see if he would come back. Then I heard her walk into her room and shut the door. I put my pen and paper down and went back to lying awake, staring at the ceiling, waiting for morning to come.

THE STATISTIKS WE LIVE

TERRELL DIDN'T STAY at the house anymore after that night, and he and Momma never really mended their post-homecoming falling-out. He still came by the house sometimes, and he always told Momma he loved her. She said she loved him, too, but there was something different about how it sounded. The tone was more reserved, and they never looked each other in the eye when they spoke.

I still saw Terrell around the neighborhood a lot, though, and he always had plenty to say. He talked about how unrealistic Momma was, how she was blind to the way things worked. I knew that Momma wasn't as blind to how things worked as she let on, and I knew Tee knew that, too, but he was hurt.

Being able to see Tee, if only briefly and sporadically as it was, made me miss Taye even more than I already did. Taye had been in CYA for about two years at this point, and there was no telling how much longer they'd keep delaying his release. Finally, I convinced the woman in the gray jacket to take me there to visit him. Even with my childhood of moving around, this would be my first time outside of L.A. County. I was shocked at how quickly the city ended. In my mind L.A. stretched out almost forever: I couldn't imagine a world beyond it. Nervous and excited, I sat up on the edge of the seat in that giant Cadillac sedan to take it all in. It reminded me of the game I used to play when the woman in the gray jacket took me to new placements. And now it also reminded me of Taye's friend Marcus.

In Taye's absence, Marcus had taken me under his wing. He was from the same Blood set as Taye, but he was higher-ranked. He was lighter-skinned with a square chin and muscular build. At seventeen, he was too old for me romantically, but he filled the place left empty by my brother's absence—giving me advice about school, the neighborhood, and how to handle Big Mom's suspicions—and, in turn, he was able to tell me things he couldn't share with other people. Some days, when I was getting out of school, he would roll up in his silver-pearl Monte Carlo and lean across from the driver's seat to open the passenger door. I'd smile and hop in. He was the only person I knew who shared my love of driving aimlessly through the city.

"Come on," he'd say as I threw my backpack onto the backseat, "ima go on a mental huddle. You down to ride with me?"

He always said it like it was something important, like we were about to go out on some mission, to put in work and earn our stripes.

"Fa sho, Blood," I'd say, flattered and grateful that of all the girls always hanging around him, Marcus had picked me. "Let's roll."

We'd grab some food and drive to the beach to look out over the cliffs at the waves, or drive out toward Torrance and up above the city, where we would sit and talk and wait for the sun to set so we could see the city lights and, sometimes, if the smog wasn't too bad, the stars. Still, in our adventures we never went far. Everything both of us loved and understood was nearby. We only really knew how to navigate within the city and only knew how to live by its rules.

Sometimes we would go to this one park just outside of Torrance, where we'd be surrounded by suburban white people who sat talking, walking their dogs, or watching their kids play. Marcus would always tense up. His eyes would narrow and fill with a hatred and pain so deep that it became hard to meet his gaze. He'd look around, sizing up the park, his eyes darting back and forth in the same way they did when we were driving through an enemy's neighborhood.

Sitting there, he said to me, "You're too white-looking."

"What?"

"Look at all these mothafukkas lookin at us. You too white-lookin, they ain feelin that. Look at all them. Like they finna kall one time and report a kidnappin."

"Naw," I laughed, "only black people think I look white. White people always think I'm Mexican." I looked at Marcus. He wore brown Gucci shades, the sides of which almost covered a deep scar that ran from his eye to his ear. I reached up and touched it with my finger. "What happened?" The question broke his chain of thought for a minute and his eyes relaxed and the hatred faded as he turned to face me. He lowered his head and shook it quickly from side to side twice.

"Ahh shyt, that's a old one. Rips kaught me slippin in the wrong hood, beat me up real bad." He looked up quick and met my eye. "I mean, that's only kause it was four ah them an jus me, tho. This one nigga, the littlest one, I wasn't payin attention to him kause I figured if I took down the biggest one, then the rest them would back off, but this lil skinny nigga kome from the side an Bam! Hit me right there with the butt of a .357. Knocked my ass out. I'm lucky he didn't shoot me." He lifted his hand and ran his fingers over the scar, as if he could read it like Braille, then he smiled at me.

"People always talk this an that. 'I got shot five times an I'm still here,' or 'I ain scurred.' But we both know people shot ten times and still walkin round and othas shot once and restin in peace. Find yourself in a moment like that an if you ain scurred to die, somethins wrong wit ya." It was silent for a moment, both of us staring out over the cliff.

"Look at that, ma," he said, finally pointing out over the cliff's edge. The sun was setting and all the lights were beginning to show. "Look at all those lights. It's so many, it's like they don't end." I nodded in agreement. Marcus lit up a blunt and took a drag before offering it to me.

"What do you think is out there, ma? I mean, way out there, beyond all them lights?"

I shook my head. "I dunno, what you think?"

Marcus shook his head again and reached over and took the blunt back. He took another deep drag and then after a minute, slowly let the smoke out. "Maybe quiet, or peace or sunthin." I looked out at the city lights and wondered if people killed each other out there where the lights ended like they did in the city. I looked at all the people walking their dogs and all the kids playing on the nice new playgrounds. It was crazy how this park wasn't even fenced in to keep the homeless people and loiterers out at night. I thought of Second Avenue Park, Loren Miller Park, and Mount Carmel Park, and how different they looked, full of outdated, broken-down play equipment, dotted with trash. I wondered if these people, with their picnics and kids on tricycles, knew what it was like to love someone as much as I loved Marcus or my brothers, to love someone with the full knowledge that they might die or be taken away from you at any moment without warning.

After a few minutes, Marcus slapped his hand on my knee. "Let's bounce." As we got up, Marcus tucked the last quarter of the blunt behind his ear and pulled down his Boston Red Sox cap, with its B—for Blood—to cover it. He took one last look out over the lights and sighed.

"Peace out," he said toward the lights as he shaped his hand into a *b* and held it out over the edge of the cliff.

We walked back toward the car in silence, which seemed strange. Marcus might get lost in thought in a deeper moment, but he usually turned it around quickly with some sort of thought or joke to share with me.

I knew a lot about Marcus. He would clown and tell me that I knew him better than anyone: better than his own momma. But there is both a good and bad side to understanding someone so well. It's beautiful to have someone to know and love unconditionally, but it also makes it impossible not to see their pain: you know it, and they know it.

"You hungry?" I asked as we neared the car. "I got some food stamps." He shook his head again: no. That seemed even more unusual. Marcus not hungry? I wondered what it was that was so heavy on his mind.

"What's goin on, Marcus?" Again he shook his head. I listened as he fumbled around in the dark with his keys, trying to find the right one. After several attempts, I heard the key slip into the car's lock and the door click. Then, instead of opening the door, Marcus reached up and rested both his arms on top of the car and looked across at me.

"One day," he said slowly, carefully, thinking about what he was about to say and the best way to say it, "I jus hope I find out what's out there. An I sure the fuck hope I do it leavin this bitch fo sunthin better, an not on a goddamn prison bus."

I was thinking about that night as I looked out the window of the woman in the gray jacket's car, finally seeing what was beyond the lights. I thought of Marcus. I thought about what he'd said, that he wanted to leave L.A. for something better, and what that meant. I thought of Taye. I thought about his one trip out of L.A. on the CYA van and what he must have been thinking. I watched as the buildings and cars and people disappeared, and then there was nothing but dusty dry earth and brush.

The car climbed uphill, losing speed and lagging behind the newer, smaller cars. The freeway twisted and turned through the mountains and every once in a while a small cul-de-sac development would pop up on one side or the other, but mostly out my window was a dry, vast nothing. I looked over at the woman in the gray jacket and suddenly felt grateful. A month ago when I was in her office, begging her to drive me up, I hadn't realized how far it really was. She was going well out of her way for me.

"Thanks for drivin, you kno?" They were probably the first words either of us had spoken in three hours.

She glanced sideways at me and sighed. With that, I went back to hating her all over again. It bothered me that she looked at me like I was a child beyond all hope. I suspected she hated me and was just waiting for me to mess up. That way she could be right about me and be justified in hating me. I stared at her emotionless face, which was fixed on the road ahead, and wondered what she was thinking about.

With her pink shimmery lipstick, tan nylons, and white chunky shoes—and a ceramic mug of coffee braced between her knees—nothing about her fit into my understanding of the world. We were two people tied by circumstance and endless lengths of bureaucracy and procedure.

But as I thought again of all the other times I'd been in the car with this woman, my hatred subsided. She was the only person in the world who knew my whole history, had been there as it happened. She knew the good, the bad, even the unmentionable. In that moment, in the middle of nowhere, looking out at all the nothingness, that felt like enough.

I wanted to tell her that. As lucky as I felt now, to be loved by Big Mom and my foster siblings, who really had become my new family, I still felt abandoned by my real family. For all I knew, they never even tried to get me back. If they did, they certainly didn't try hard enough. Foster care is an emotional limbo, you never really know what's going on. Maybe your "real" family visits you, maybe not. If and when they do, you might hear their version, but what parents could look in their child's face and *not* say we are trying to get you back, regardless of the truth? Meanwhile your foster family knows only what your caseworker tells them. The only person who knows the true facts of your life is the caseworker.

I looked at mine and suddenly wanted her to like me, just because she was the only person in my life who'd known me back when I had a real family. I tried to think of something I could offer, some gesture or peace offering. I stared at the road and thought. She had mentioned once that a drawing I'd done was good and that she thought I had some talent. Still, I couldn't think of anything she might like that I knew how to draw. I drew pictures of my sisters sitting at the park, of pit bulls and lowriders. Drawing something for her that she didn't like was just awkward because she would have to pretend she liked it anyway. Then I thought of something I could offer her. It was a really small something, but it was all I had. In order to convince her to bring me up here to see my brother I had promised not to ditch school anymore. I turned to her now, an almost satisfied smile on my face.

"You know," I started, "I really won't ditch skool anymore. I mean, I know you think that was all game I spit to get you to bring me up here, but I promised, and my word is good. Plus, daymn, I really didn't know it was this far."

At first she didn't say anything, but I figured it was probably a shock to her. All I usually offered her was bad attitude. She lifted the mug of coffee to her mouth and took a sip, the pink print of her lips staying behind on the cup. Then she sighed again. The discontented sigh was her trademark. I felt stupid, and instantly regretted having spoken. I braced myself for what she would say.

"I don't actually expect that to be true, but you sure enough better watch out or you'll be making the drive up here again. Only next time you'll be in the CYA van, and you won't be leaving the same day."

I looked down at my hands, twisting my fingers nervously. In some ways I knew she wasn't wrong. I didn't really doubt that juvie might be in my future, but her words hurt just the same. I twisted sideways to stare out the window so she wouldn't read my hurt. Nothing, and then cows, and then nothing again.

"And Bree, I would appreciate if you didn't curse, at least in front of me."

I leaned my head back against the seat and closed my eyes.

The California Youth Authority is a system of detention centers that comprise the largest youth correction agencies in the nation. Of its inmates, slightly less than half are committed for violent criminal offenses and about two-thirds have some sort of background in gangs or gang activities. In short, it generally houses the more problem "problem youth," the violent and chronic offenders, the murderers.

Within the CYA there are different levels and different locations that a juvenile offender gets sent to, based on his or her history of violence, the number of violations or write-ups they have received, and how serious their initial crime was. Taye was currently housed at the Preston Youth Correction Facility, in Ione. When he was first charged he had been sent to El Paso de Robles Youth Correction Facility, in Paso Robles, but that hadn't lasted long. One of the tenets of the CYA is to integrate disparate gang members, to prove to the youths that they can all coexist. It's a nice, though unrealistic, idea. With all these different groups in the mix, juvie quickly becomes a proving ground for Nazi skinheads, Mexican Norturos, Sureños and Bulldogs, 415s, Bloods and Crips. Statistically, if you are a Blood, you probably have the worst odds of all because Bloods have the most enemies of anyone in there. In the system, as in L.A., there are about ten Crips to every one Blood. If you are a Blood in juvie, you better prove yourself right off the bat, and that's exactly what my brother had done.

After a few incidents at El Paso de Robles, Taye, now sixteen, got put on the van and taken up to Preston. The Ironwood Unit at Preston is the only location in CYA that has solitary units. A month ago Taye had been released from solitary back into the dorms. He wrote us letting us know where he was, and told us not to visit because it was so far. We hadn't heard from him since. He hadn't included any description of the facility, or of Ironwood, but asking around the hood I had learned more than I ever wanted to know about its rumored abuses.

Communication with Taye had been trailing off for months now. Back when he'd first gone away, we'd stayed in constant contact. He wrote me about everything that happened, telling me about people I knew who were locked up with him, who was getting into fights, and who was acting "real weenie-like." He told me about books he was reading and how nasty the food was. In turn, I wrote him about what was going on at home. Since his transfer to Ione three months ago, the weekly letters had stopped. He seemed to have drifted away from the family. The only recent information I had was from calling up to the CYA to check his status. All they were willing to offer was which facility he was being held at, if he was in Ironwood or some other disciplinary setting, and, if action was being taken as a result, what the charges were and when and where his hearing would be. To them Taye was just a number on a computer screen. I'd called again that morning before we left, as the woman in the gray jacket had requested.

"Don't want to make the drive for nothing," she said, "just to get there and be told he wasn't allowed visits and have to come straight back." It was a valid point. I had managed not to tell her that we hadn't heard from Taye since he'd been there, that although I was sure he could have visits, I did not know whether he wanted or would accept them. I had written him a quick note some weeks prior letting him know I had talked the woman in the gray jacket into driving me up, but had again heard no reply.

The facility, when we arrived, looked exactly the way I had expected from what I'd heard. A brick castle on a sprawling campus. I took a deep breath as we parked in the visitors' lot and tried to gather my courage. A sign clearly stated what could and couldn't be brought inside. I moved my dollar bills from my bag to my back pocket. I'd been told how bad the food was and that at visiting you could get things out of the vending machines. I had brought fourteen singles, just in case my brother was hungry.

"You ready?" I asked the social worker anxiously. She nodded, took a last drag of her cigarette, and ground it out on the bottom of her shoe. In the waiting room, I filled out a form with a stubby pencil that desperately needed sharpening. As I entered Taye's name and number along with my name I had to turn the pencil at different angles in order to expose the lead. When I was done, I handed it to the woman in the gray jacket to sign where it said "legal guardian." She signed quickly and returned to the *Reader's Digest* she had picked up.

"It didn't show up," I said as she handed the pencil back to me. She looked briefly at the paper, took the pencil back and tried again, then went back to her magazine. I stifled a laugh and pushed the paper over the magazine.

"It, umm, still didn't show up." She looked at me like I was crazy, then looked at the paper. She held the pencil up and took a good look at it.

"Oh, for Pete's sake," she said and laughed. It was the first time I remembered seeing her laugh. She shook her head and smiled again. "Their budget must be even worse then ours." She used her

fingernails to break back one small piece of the pencil's wood to expose the lead and signed the paper.

"There you go," she said and handed it to me, eyes completely
focused on me now instead of the magazine. I smiled at her. A real
smile. And as her hand reached toward mine, extending the paper,
she also extended her other hand and patted me on the arm. I looked
down at the floor, confused by the gesture, what it meant, and how
to respond. I took the paper and stood up to take it to the desk.
When I returned she was again fixated on the magazine. I sat down
and waited. When they called Taye's last name I walked over to the
corrections officer, who ran a metal detector wand up and down my
front, and then my back. I put my money in a small plastic container and walked through yet another metal detector. The CO motioned at the woman in the gray jacket.

"Oh, she good. She all into that *Reader's Digest.*"

"Well," the CO said with a look that let me know she was not
amused, "you're under eighteen, so either she goes, or you don't go."

I walked back over to the woman in the gray jacket and told her
the news. She shook her head and rose. When she got through the
metal detector, the CO handed her back the contents of her pockets, minus the *Reader's Digest.* The woman in the gray jacket didn't
miss a beat, she simply extended her hand as though commanding
the CO to hand the magazine over.

"Sorry," the CO said, "you can't take it in with you."

The woman in the gray jacket looked at me and shook her head.
"Ridiculous." Again she smiled and put her hand on my shoulder.
"Let's go."

We walked out the door and into another building, where we
found a room full of tables, chairs, and the anticipated vending ma-

chines. Some kids stood or sat in their CYA-provided clothing, looking for their loved ones, but none of them was Taye. I looked back
at the woman in the gray jacket. She smiled, nodded, and pointed toward a table.

"Might as well take a seat while we're waiting. And I need to go
find a new magazine or book, or something." She walked up to the
front to dig through a pile of outdated and battered magazines—
Reader's Digest, Highlights, People, Newsweek—and when she returned, a stack of reading material in hand, she sat not next to me
but at the next table. She began to shuffle through her pile and then
looked up at me. I'd been looking at her, but quickly lowered my
gaze. She leaned across and patted me on the arm.

"He'll be here, just relax."

I scanned the room again. Still no Taye. The door opened every
few minutes and every time I strained to see if he was one of the people walking in, but each time it was someone else, and he walked over
to a different table where people were waiting. I noticed that some
of the people had come in after us. I started to panic. And then, as if
on cue, the door opened and in walked Taye. I had to smile. Taye was
one of those people who never changed much. He was slightly taller
and slightly lighter from constantly being inside, but overall he
looked exactly as he did almost two years earlier. He kept his eyes
down on the floor and walked directly to the desk where the CO sat.
Taye said something to the guard and then shook his head. The guard
said something back and then scanned the room and pointed in my
direction. Taye looked over with the most stunned look I'd ever seen
cross his face, his already round eyes widening. For a second I feared
that he was mad, but then he broke out in the biggest smile and ran
across the floor toward me.

"Jontaye," the guard called out, "No running, man." It was too late. Taye had already reached me, wrapped his arms around me and swung me around in a complete circle.

"Daymn, babygurl. I didn't know you was here." He had released me from his arms but still held tightly to both my hands as if to keep me from getting away. He kept laughing and shaking his head. "They done called my name for the visit, right?" he started laughing and shook his head again. He motioned toward the table and we sat down. He still held my hands. His hands were warm and strong on mine.

"Taye—"

"No, wait, check it. Anyways, I tell the CO naw, I ain got no visit. It's a mistake. My family is real far, and Moms kouldn't take off work if she wanted to." He stared at my hands the whole time he was talking. Then he looked up and smiled. "Plus, that ol whip Moms be drivin"—he laughed a loud, carefree laugh—"Neva woulda made it."

"Taye."

"No, wait, so the CO leaves, right? But then he kome back. I'm like, look man, it's a mistake. But he say naw, I double, triple checked. You got a visit. So I put on my shoes, right? I kome down here, walk right up to the desk, like, yo, it's a mistake. An then he point over at you, say, well, that young lady been here a while." Taye raised his voice two octaves and tried to talk all proper when he imitated the white CO.

"Taye."

"Daymn, babygurl, I'm so sorry. I didn't know or I neva woulda left you waitin like that. You know that, right?"

"Yea," I looked at my brother. He looked so happy and so sad all at the same time. "I know, Taye, but, umm, Taye?" He leaned in to

get closer to me as though what I was about to say was the most important thing in the world. "Um," I said again, wishing that I did have
something important to tell him, something that could take all the
hurt away, but then I started to laugh. I laughed because I didn't
know what to say, because what I did have to say seemed so stupid,
because my brother was happy to see me, because I knew beyond any
doubt that he loved me.

He scrunched his nose up and his look quickly turned from serious to curious: "What?"

"I kan't feel my fingers. You're squeezing, really, REALLY tight."
Taye started to laugh, hard. He released my hands and banged the
table with his fist twice.

"Sorry, Bee, that's my bad. Shyt, I been in the ad seg, you know?
No kontact." He wiped his hands on his jeans and then laid them out,
palms up, on the table. He cocked his head to the side and raised his
eyebrows. Then he nodded his chin toward his hands, directing me
to again put mine into them. I smiled and cracked my knuckles. "I'll
be nice this time. I'm jus outta practice."

I reached out and put my hands into his. My brother. It was
silent for a minute. We just sat there, my hands on top of his. He
made no effort to grasp at them, or even to wrap his fingers around
mine. Then, after a minute he took one of my hands and placed it
on top of the other and then placed his on top of that.

"Daymn, it's good to bee you." He shook his head.

I looked at my brother; I'd never known him to be at a loss for
words. We both were, though. Taye just stared at my hands between
his. Every once in a while, he picked up his hand and then patted the
top of mine. Finally, he looked up. He wasn't crying; he'd never allow
that, especially not in a public place, but there were tears in his eyes.

Taye was a master of control, a master of his environment. He knew exactly how far he could go without crossing the line.

"How'd you get here, B?"

At least thirty minutes had passed since Taye had walked in and I hadn't even looked over at my caseworker. I quickly glanced at the table next to us where she sat, still flipping through magazines. Taye followed my gaze and then looked back at me confused.

"Who dat?"

"You don't remember my caseworker?" I asked him, surprised. It was true, she didn't come around a lot, but we all lived in fear of the times she did, so her visits were, to say the least, noteworthy. On scheduled visit days, Big Mom would have us cleaning the house, down to the smallest nook and cranny. We scrubbed walls and polished doorknobs. We did the laundry and neatly folded all the clothes and organized them carefully within closets and drawers.

Taye looked over at her and then back at me.

"Who'da thunk, huh?" He stood up and walked over to her. When she looked up at him, he extended his hand.

"Thanks, I appreciate you drivin my sister all the way up here. That's above and beyond, fa sho." She reached out and took his hand, giving it a firm shake, clearly impressed by the gesture. It must have struck her as odd that a thug could act so courteously. The L.A. papers were full of stories about car-jackings, shootings, robberies, and the ways in which its urban inhabitants had no regard for human life. To judge him by his charges alone, my brother, a dope dealer and gang member, was one of those heartless criminals, yet looking at him, she knew he was more complicated than that. I watched her face as she took him in and saw that he was getting through to her—by being human, by being himself.

For the rest of the visit she barely turned another page, and I knew she had begun to listen in as Taye and I spoke: he wanted all the details of what was going on at home. He asked how Nishia was wearing her hair (braids) and what toys she and NeeCee were into (Barbie and Pound Puppies). He asked if Momma was still working the night job and if I was making sure she ate when she came home.

"Sometimes she jus forget ta eat, man, you gotta stay up an make sure she eats, you kno?" He looked down at the table, shaking his head. "I don't like that shyt. It shouldn't be like that, man."

I understood what he meant. But he knew I either got up or stayed up until she got home. He'd seen me do it. He just wanted to make sure, to remind me, to set his own mind at ease. I felt bad that Momma had to work like that, too, but there was no solution in sight. It was true that she was too old for that kind of work, but we were barely making ends meet. I didn't bother to tell Taye that since he'd been locked up, Denise had started in on smoking crack, and now her two kids had been staying at the house with us as well. It would only make him feel bad. Plus, I knew that the woman in the gray jacket was listening and I wasn't sure it was anything she should hear. The house was small, even for us, without adding two more hungry kids into the equation.

Sometimes, the little ones squabbled over toys and space. Two of them would go after the same thing at the same time and get to fighting, flapping arms in the air, trying to hit the other. The littler you are, the harder those tensions can be. At my age I could just leave, go to the park, get away and clear my head. Nishia and NeeCee, and now Pam and Kaleb, were dependent on me or Big Mom to referee.

I looked at Taye as he stared down at the table, his shoulders sagging. For the first time since I met him, Taye looked vulnerable, help-less. "Hey," I said as I gave his hand a shake. I swallowed hard and lied to him: "Everything's kool at home, don't give it anotha worry."

He looked up and smiled at me. I wasn't sure if he believed me or not. I hated lying to him, but that lie was the one gift I could give him. I knew it killed him, sitting up in there, not being able to help us, not knowing if we were okay, if the lights were shut off, if there was food in the cupboard or on the table. The least I could do was tell him that we were getting by, because even if we weren't there wasn't anything he could do about it.

I tried to lift the mood by turning the subject away from the family. I told him all the latest happenings of the hood, most of which he seemed to know through the prison grapevine. It was good to see his mood lighten, and then, just as I was doing my impression of one of the neighborhood winos, a guard announced that there was only five minutes left for visiting. Taye turned his head to look at the clock, and his face visibly changed.

"Daymn, that went fast, huh?" He began to flood me with all the questions he had put off asking earlier in the visit. Yea, I was going to school; naw, wasn't smoking too much weed; yea, tryin to stay outta trouble. Then they sounded the two-minute warning.

"Aye, yo, look, Bree. I'm sorry I kame in late, aiight?" I tried to assure him it didn't matter, but he cut me off before I could say anything. "Look, it's not a lot ah time left an it's somethin I need ta tell you, need ta explain ta you. I need ta make sure you understand." Taye took his hands off of mine and rested them on the table in front of his chest. He looked down at them as though they held some answers.

"I know it's real far up here, an man, when I first got put up in here I was real heated, you kno? Kause I knew no one kould kome to visit me. It tore me up knowin I wasn't gonna get ta see you or Moms or my gurl or them bad ass lil ones, but see, what's krazy is this. Then I realized that it was actually easier that way." He gave me a look that was a mix of pain and sheer cold survival. Even if I couldn't understand his situation, his look communicated everything he was feeling. The desperation and keen self-discipline of it scared me a little. I looked away from him and down at the table.

"Bree, I ain mad, and I ain tryin ta hurt you, but look, when you leave today, don't kome back here again." His voice was hushed and I had to strain to hear it. We both looked down at our hands. "It's jus, when I was back in L.A.—man, I'd sit up in there every day waitin on a letter or a visit, an it was killin me. I'd sit there all night an make myself sick thinkin about y'all, wondering all kinda krazy shyt. Then when I got here I jus had ta resolve myself I wasn't gonna bee y'all or even find out what was up wit y'all."

My brother looked up at me. I could feel his gaze upon me, but I couldn't look up. I knew if I did I would cry, and I couldn't do that to him. He reached out and touched my hand.

"Bree, look at me." I looked up slowly, fighting back the tears. When my line of sight reached his face I saw that he wasn't fighting his tears back anymore. A small stream ran down each of his cheeks and landed on the table.

"I wish I was that person, babygurl," my brother said, gripping my hand. "I wish I was that strong, but I'm not. I gotta do this time solo." He held my gaze for a minute, then took his hand away and looked back down at the table. "If I don't," he said softly, almost as a whisper, "I ain gonna make it."

"Okay, let's go. Time's up." The guards started walking around the room, tapping all the kids on the back or shoulder. Taye stood up and started to gather all the soda cans, candy, and chip wrappers. "Just leave it," the guard said, pushing him a little. "It's time to go. Say goodbye."

"Tell Momma I love her, aiight?" I nodded my head. Taye started to walk away, but then turned back to face me. "Hey, I love you, too, gurl." With that, the guard put his hand on Taye's back and led him out through the door.

I wanted to cry, to just break down and let the flood of tears flow free. I pulled my hands down into my lap and dug my fingernails into my palms. I concentrated on the pain. The woman in the gray jacket stood up and walked over to the table.

"You all right?" I nodded my head yes and she finished the job that Taye had started, taking the trash over to the trash can. When she turned her back, I reached across the table and stuck my finger in the tears that had fallen on the table. My brother's tears. I'd seen my brother get robbed by bigger kids in the neighborhood; seen him get beat down to where we had to help him up out of the street, but I'd never, ever seen him cry. I touched my finger to my lips as though I could kiss the pain away, but I knew I couldn't.

I walked over to the woman in the gray jacket and she surprised me by putting her arm around my shoulder. We walked like that out the door, down the path, and to the car.

WORLD GONE KOLD

I WATCHED OUT the window as we pulled out of Preston, the car's tinted windows adding a haze to the already dreary view of the facility. I tried to take in all the details as the car took me farther and farther away, watching as the CYA sign faded into the distance. I watched until I couldn't make out anything anymore, the last traces of the visit fading away in front of me. It broke my heart to think of not seeing Taye for the two years he had left to serve; but no matter how bad the heartbreak was, it could be turned into a numbness that I knew how to handle. It was just one more scar that I would wear on the inside, and I knew that no matter how hard it hurt me, it hurt Taye worse. But we were warriors, and warriors have to take their scars as they come.

I could tell that the social worker wanted to talk to me about what she had seen, but our relationship didn't give her the words to start that conversation. I felt for her. During the course of a single day we both had been forced to reevaluate our assumptions and see each other in a new light. The sign, the buildings, the castle now out of sight I switched my position in the seat, facing forward. I looked over at her and she smiled at me. I gave her a half smile back. I wanted to do better, show her that I felt the change, too, but I was tired, worn down. I leaned back in the seat.

"Jontaye," she said and waited for me to look at her or say something, and when I didn't, she continued, searching for the right words to open up the conversation. "It . . . really seems like he loves you a lot."

"Yea, he do." I turned my head back to look out the passenger-side window. What I didn't want to do on the ride home was debate whether my brother loved me or not, or, for that matter, whether my family, the family she had given me, loved me or not. I didn't want to talk about it, especially not with her. I knew that on some level it was her job, but we had never discussed it before. And now I had let her cross the line between the professional and the personal, and I regretted it. I had let her see something too precious. Something that left me vulnerable.

"That must feel good."

I looked directly at her. Her eyes shifted between me and the road ahead. "Well," I said, back to my hardest, most defiant tone, "ain to the end the road yet, are we? You jus said on the way up how the next time I'm makin this drive I'll prolly be on *my* way ta juvie, right?"

"I'm sorry for that," she sighed. "You're just hard to reach sometimes."

The files in her office said I had RAD (radical attachment disorder). That meant that I was unable to bond with other human beings, and she had believed it, until now. It angered me that after all the years, after all the placements, all the things that she knew had happened, all the things I told her, it took her witnessing my brother's grief for her to see my humanness.

They make you take all these classes as a foster kid, especially once you start to get older and it becomes clear that you'll never get adopted. Once they realize that it's up to the state to teach you all the basic survival skills of life, you find yourself in countless classes and group sessions on the path to what they call "aging out." They teach you all sorts of different things, from how to buy a car, find an apartment, and keep a job to how to deal with anger and emotions. In these classes and group sessions, they take every opportunity to tell you that anger isn't really an emotion, it's just a reaction to emotions—a mask. I guess that's true, because as I sat back in the Cadillac and let my mind run, my anger faded and instead I felt a deep sorrow about my life and my lack of control in it.

"I was jus a kid," I said, somewhere between the anger and the sadness, both still clearly audible in my voice. "You can't be hard to reach as a kid." I said it, but I knew I was wrong. From the very first day, with the pink and white cookies, I had deemed her the enemy, blamed her for everything.

"Well," she continued, "some kids are more reachable than others. But the first time I met you, you made it pretty clear that no matter what I did or how hard I tried, you didn't want my help. You know how with any job there are certain truths? Certain things that even though you may not like them, they just are?"

I didn't say anything. I guess I understood on some level, but if she thought I was going to tell her that it was okay that she signed my life away at five, she had lost her mind.

"The thing of it is, my job, it's a hard job. A lot of people start out trying to do what I do and it just gets to them, and within the first year they quit because every time they can't reach a kid it breaks their heart and makes them feel like a failure. But I had this professor in graduate school who told me, 'Count the successes, not the failures.' So I always knew the only way I could do what I do is if I concentrated on the kids I *could* reach." Her voice trailed off there as she became aware of what she was saying and how it sounded.

"So I wasn't worth it." I said it under my breath to myself. I said it not as an accusation, just an observation, an explanation to myself.

"What did you say?" The car swerved slightly to the right as she looked at me, her hands instinctively following her vision.

I shook my head. No. No way.

"Tell me." After a few minutes of silence she sighed deeply. "Look, it's been a long day. I'm hungry, let's stop and get something to eat, okay? On me, anything you want. What'll it be?"

"Don't matter."

She busied herself looking at the signs and reading off town names, exit numbers, and fast-food options. She exaggerated each word and gesture in an effort to include me and draw me in. Finally she stopped at a McDonald's.

It was deadly quiet once the engine shut off. After a long moment of silence,, I reached for the door and started to pull the handle. Then, quickly, her hand reached across and rested on my turned back.

"Wait."

I froze, my hand still gripping the handle, the door slightly ajar, the warning bell chiming.

"Please tell me what you said before. I really would like to know."

"What? Now you kare?" It was my turn to pause. I knew that for the first time and maybe for the last, in that one moment I had power over her. I seized it. I looked at her as she watched me, uncomfortable, and knew that she was feeling what I had felt at every interaction I ever had with her. Then I started to feel bad for making anyone else feel that way, even her.

I dropped my gaze and looked down at my shoes, one inside the car and the other out the door. "Look, I jus said I guess I wasn't worth it, but it wasn't no question. It was just a statement, you kno? Like suddenly"—I shook my head—"like suddenly, everything made sense."

I opened the door the rest of the way and stepped out before she could say anything. She followed my cue and did the same. Inside the McDonald's we ordered burgers, fries, and milk shakes. I made sure to over-order so I could take something home to split between my sisters.

Over lunch we talked. I figured that was her whole reason for stopping. She felt bad about what she'd said. I didn't really care anymore. My anger and hurt had passed almost as quickly as my stomach had filled up. She asked me questions about my moms, about if we ate well, if she took care of us, when the last time I had been to a dentist was. I kind of knew what she might be getting at so I just went ahead and answered her questions with the proper answers and assured her at every point that my mom was the closest thing to a saint that I had ever come across. She smiled at that. When she had run out of questions, I looked up at her over my cheeseburger, quickly swallowing my mouthful, and smiled.

"Aiight, my turn." I could see that I had shocked her with that one. She pulled herself up straight and her brow furrowed. She was actually kind of pretty, even with that too-pink lipstick. She had light-green eyes, the color of new leaves, and light-brown hair the tips of which had been bleached blond by the sun.

"I don't know what you mean."

"Well, it's jus, I was thinking. You know, it's a lot you know bout me. Everything, really. But I don't know nothin bout you."

"What do you want to know?" She pushed her food forward and folded her hands in front of her. I suppose she did that to show me that I had her full attention and approval, but it just seemed a waste of food to me. I picked up a french fry and gestured toward her food with it.

"You done eatin?"

"I guess so."

I shook my head and put the french fry in my mouth; then I wrapped up the rest of my food, put it in the bag with the extra burger and slid her tray in front of me and started in on her leftover fries and half a burger.

"You sure she feeds you well?" she asked again. If it had been anyone else, anyone from my neighborhood, I would have told them to shut their mouth about my momma and mind their own business, but I knew I couldn't talk to her that way.

"Like I said," I said with my mouth full, "don't even trip, my moms a saint. Fa real, plus she feed us good, buys us clothes, *an* listens to our problems even though she prolly got bigger ones ah her own. She feed us, just not necessarily McDonald's.

"So, movin on. What does everyone kall you? Seem like that's a good start, rite?"

"Anna."

Figured, didn't even have a nickname. Seemed like about as suburban, white a name as you could get, too. With a name like that I
couldn't even get mad that she didn't understand half of what I told
her. It wasn't even really her fault. Sure, somewhere along the way,
through her work, she had been exposed to some things, but seeing
and living are separated by a big, maybe even uncrossable divide. I
was beginning to regret giving her such a hard time; although it was
a little late, she was trying to reach me.

"Kool. So, Anna, where you keep trash at?"

"What?" Again, confused, not her fault.

"My bad, I was tryin to be funny. Where you stay at, rite? Kause,
that's where you keep ure trash." I looked up and met her gaze and
smiled to ease things.

"I'm over in Glendale."

"That's by Pasadena?" I asked, trying to place it. She nodded her
head yes, it was. I sat for a minute, just smiling and nodding my
head, trying to think of something else to ask. I looked up and
shrugged my shoulders. "Married? Kids? Got a dog?"

She laughed and took a sip of her milk shake. "Not married, no
kids. I work a lot, sometimes fifty or more hours a week. It doesn't
leave a lot of time for all that. I do have a dog, though. Unlike kids,
you can just leave them in the yard. He's a little Lhasa apso. He's really cute and he gets all excited to see me every time I come home.
His name is Claude. I don't know why I named him that. It just
seemed like such a good dog name."

I smiled at her. Silly, her dog even had a human name. Momma
worked more hours than she did on any given week and still man-

aged to raise a houseful of kids, and was now on to raising her grand-kids and me, but it seemed a bad idea to point that out. She obviously looked down upon working long hours while raising kids. But she also looked down on not feeding kids. I mean, it had to be one way or the other, right? Outside of her little world, things rarely came "at the right time" or "under ideal circumstances."

"You want kids?" She looked uncomfortable for a minute, so I figured she did. If the answer is no, then it's an easy question: you just say no. But if the answer is yes and the odds are slim that it will ever happen, to confess it is like admitting fear and failure. Maybe dealing with lost kids all day every day made her afraid of failing.

"Kan I ask you somethin?" I looked her directly in the eye so she knew how serious I was. She caught my vibe and nodded. Suddenly we were having a very grown conversation. "When you said I was un-reachable, what did you mean?"

"Well," she started, and then paused. Again, I already knew her answer. That fact that she had to stop and think about it told it all. "It's just that you weren't a baby, and you weren't the most receptive or affectionate child."

"I understand," I said as I stood up, stacked the empty trays on top of each other, and took them over to the trash can. I figured she would follow me, but she didn't, so I had to walk back to the table.

Anna looked upset.

As I came back to the table, she started rambling on about all sorts of details and the downfalls of the system and difficulties that go with it. I knew I should care, but I didn't. It wasn't anything that I understood or could see, and it didn't seem to be anything that could help me. I didn't want to know anything more than what I already knew.

"Look," I interrupted her, "I feel you." She looked unconvinced, so I went on. "I mean, I know." I sighed, realizing I couldn't explain. I sat there for a minute, held her gaze and then leaned forward a bit. "We kool, I swear to GOD." Then I slammed both my palms down on the table, pushed myself up and backwards to standing, and said, "Now, let's roll."

I was happy to see that she stood up with me, and we walked together out to the car. All I wanted was to get home. The closeness of the visiting room was gone. She no longer tried to rest her hand on my back or shoulder, but it wasn't like it had been when we left the house this morning, either. I heard the door click unlocked and I got in. She stuck the key in the ignition, but before she turned it she looked at me.

"You sure you understand?"

"Yup, fa sho." I smiled and then slammed the door shut. I leaned back in my seat and looked out the window as we drove down the street and merged back onto the freeway. We drove the rest of the way home in silence.

As we exited the ten, I watched Anna tense up. At least this time she didn't lean across me to lock my door. I hated that.

When we rolled up in front of Momma's house I was exhausted and relieved to finally be back at home. I got out the car and threw up two fingers. "Peace."

I knew she couldn't hear me. The window was rolled up. I reached to open the door again real quick, but she had already locked it. Daymn, I thought, that was fast. Didn't even see her do that. She leaned over and unlocked it, clearly embarrassed. I opened the door and grabbed my red cap off the dash and reached my hand out to her. She hesitated, then extended hers.

"Thanks again." We shook hands. She had a firm handshake. I didn't know what that meant, but Moms always said it was important. Shake hands like you mean it. I shut the car door and turned toward the house. I heard the click of the lock as I started up the walkway and grabbed NeeCee.

"Sissy, sissy, sissy!" she yelled excitedly.

"Hey," I said, getting all close and up in her face. "Who you kallin a sissy? You lil punk!"

"Noooo," she smiled a huge smile, her dark eyes gleaming. "You *my* sissy."

"Ohhhh," I threw my bag down on the floor and bent down to unzip it. Outside, I heard the woman in the gray jacket's car start to pull away. NeeCee got real close and leaned over my bag, looking down into it, always curious about its contents. I purposely pulled it closer to me and undid the zipper real slow. "Oh, shyt! You want a McDonald's?"

Her little shoulders shook with excitement. From the other room I heard a voice.

"Was that Momma?" I yelled at the top of my lungs.

Momma's face appeared in the doorway. "I saaaid don't curse in the house. An come in here an tell me about ure visit with Taye. I'm doin the dishes."

I handed the bag of food to NeeCee and walked up and gave Big Mom a kiss on the cheek. She put her arm around my shoulder.

"Aiight, Momma, but you sit down. Leave them dishes to me."

Momma smiled and in that moment, standing in that warm

kitchen under my momma's gentle gaze, childish squeals of my sisters coming from the next room, I felt good. I felt loved. I wouldn't have traded my place in the world with anyone or for anything. Sometimes Momma's love was enough to fill the greatest voids, ease the greatest pains. It wasn't something Anna would understand. It's not something that can be explained to others. Either you get it, or you don't.

BORN TO BLEED

THE NEXT MORNING I couldn't wait to call Marcus. I was anxious to tell him about the land that existed out beyond all the lights; about the cactus, the cows, and the dusty small towns. Finally, I had something to report to him that he didn't know anything about.

And I needed to tell him about the visit with Taye, because its conclusion still burned. I needed him to tell me how to handle things. Marcus had enough distance to have some perspective. He would know what to do.

I had thought about talking to Terrell about it, but then thought better of it. Terrell and Taye were brothers, real brothers, with a lifetime of shared history and blood between them, and what Taye had said might hurt Terrell even more than it hurt me, especially since he had helped put Taye on the set and felt responsible for his lockup.

Terrell was still making no effort to go to church or really to do any of the things he and Momma had talked about. Occasionally he would pop up at the house for a short visit, but I hadn't seen him in about two weeks. He called, almost daily, so at least Moms knew he was alive, but he had gone sort of silent lately on the subject of his little brother. I just couldn't tell him how much Taye was struggling inside Preston. I hadn't told Moms, either, though she clung to every word upon my return home and asked me at least ten times if Taye had lost weight. I just kept telling her he looked good, the same, not skinny, that he asked about her and busted up laughing when I told him stories about what the little ones were up to.

It was early morning still, and I lay in bed rehearsing the conversation I'd have with Marcus later today. I thought again about the place where the lights ended. Would Moms cry less if she lived out there?

The girls were asleep, but I couldn't wait any longer. I got up and crept over to the dresser, sneaking open the top drawer and pulling out a clean white tank top and jean shorts. I dressed quickly and grabbed my red Chuck Taylors and an L.A. Dodgers fitted cap. They had started making Dodgers caps in red with the logo stitched in white, instead of the traditional blue-and-white cap. Finally we could represent. We had all laughed when they came out and wondered out loud if they had made them with us in mind. With my hair in a low ponytail, I put the cap on backwards, brim slightly to the right. Then I bent down and retrieved my cigar box from under the bed and dumped its precious contents out on the sheets, grabbed all the change and bus tokens, and left the rest: the bullet shell I'd found when Kraziak was killed, a feather, scraps of paper and napkins with pager and phone numbers on them. At the last minute I pulled the blanket off the floor and smoothed it over the top of the bed, covering the mess.

I scooted past Momma in the kitchen on my way out the front door. "Bye, Momma," I called, the screen door banging shut before she could say anything. I jumped the steps to save the time of navigating the broken one and sprinted down the walkway, out the bro-

ken gate and down the block. I took a deep breath as I turned the corner, knowing that I was too far for Momma to call me back, and
slowed my pace.

When I found a pay phone I fed my coins into it and dialed
Marcus's pager. After the tone I entered the code we had established
for "meet me at the park" and hit "911" after that. I knew he'd be
there quickly, so I headed to the bus stop and caught a bus to the old
neighborhood.

The bus is crazy in L.A., paying no mind to gang boundaries.
Soldiers from different sets will hunt for enemies, waiting for one to
get caught slipping through their neighborhood on the bus. I'd seen
all sorts of crazy things happen on the bus, and even worse happen
to those just getting off. I slumped down in a seat at the back, where
I could clearly see everyone who got on and off.

When the bus finally pulled up across from our old house, I
heaved a sigh of relief and jumped down the step. It felt good to be
on my own turf.

"Aye, yo," I heard as I approached the park.

"Bree, sooooo woooop."

"Soo woop," the universal Blood call. This was a place where
people knew me and where I knew people, where I was someone. I
looked over to see Freddy in the far corner of the park with his hands
up over his head, proudly throwing up the neighborhood with in-
tricate ghetto sign language and signaling for me to come over and
talk to him. I smiled and nodded. I headed across the park, stopping
here and there along the way to exchange greetings with people I
knew or who knew my brothers.

The longer I spent in and around the neighborhood, and the
more entrenched I became in it, the more I loved it.

Everyone had a rank within the neighborhood, and everyone else knew what it was. Some people were so well respected that you had to be careful just how you used their names. Say a name in a way that someone mistook as disrespect, and there would be a grip of little homies eager to whoop your ass just to prove themselves to their big OG homies. Others had failed to prove themselves and were now known as "punks," "marks," and "bustas," unable to raise their names above the ruins they had become. Associate with them and your name would be no better.

Like countless others, all I wanted was to be accepted as a Blood, to find my place among our warriors. Being around the homies in the neighborhood gave me a place where I felt important, a place where I belonged. Like my brothers before me, I watched my superiors, studied and emulated their ways of speaking, dressing, and acting, and while Big Mom prayed at night for God to show me a different path, I prayed for the opportunity to prove myself in the path of the flame and earn the respect of my neighborhood. If I could do that, if I could become official, it wouldn't matter anymore that I had no real family of my own. I would no longer have to feel like an orphan and it wouldn't matter who or where my parents were. I would have all the family and identity I needed within the set. No one would even ask about my family. I would simply be Bree, Bree from the Neighborhood. The older I got, the more I truly saw that as my best, most appealing option.

As a female, you always had to be careful. The hood was full of pimps and hustlers, and, male or female, there was a fine balance to always making sure that no one ever pimped you harder than you were pimping them. For a female, however, there were more ways you could go wrong, more avenues of exploitation. As I'd seen so well out my bedroom window, many women found themselves caught up in prostitution, and then turned to drugs to ease the pain of what they were doing. The cycles fed each other and in the end, they ended up tricking just to feed their habits. "Baseheads," "strawberries," "smokers," we called them. When the pain grew too great for the drugs they had become dependent on, most of them ended up over-dosing or killing themselves. There weren't many that came back from a crack habit. Under the grips of the drug, they became desperate, lost souls. They had their own look and style to them, if you could call it that. There was no way to hide what they were. More than once, on her way to school Nishia had walked past her mom begging on the street. What was worse, her mom would break into the house and steal anything she could get money for. She didn't care if her kids went without, if we had no TV or toaster. Once she even stole the food out of the refrigerator.

When it came down to it, really, I couldn't find too many female role models or examples of futures I wanted for myself. A lot of the women I saw were just the chickenheads and hoodrats a lot of the homies hung out with. They were girls who looked good enough to hit, but were plainly after money or whatever else they could get from a man. There was no shortage of them in the hood. The minute a homie got sick of one or saw her for what she was, he could throw her away and get another. To me, they didn't seem much above prostitutes. They slept with the homies just to get status, or to get them to pay for their hair and nails. I once pointed this out to Terrell and he defended them, but when I said the same thing to Marcus he laughed and shook his head.

"I kan't even argue, B. You got a point there." Then he shook his head and laughed some more. I figured the truth of it was probably somewhere in the middle. Personally, though, I didn't want to mess around in the gray area with my own life. I'd long ago promised myself I'd never again let a man—or anyone—take something from me that I didn't freely want to give.

And that was the other reason I wanted to be a Blood.

If my brothers' and Marcus's loyalties were any indication of how things worked, I could find safety inside the gang. A wrong committed against one member was a wrong against everyone in the set, and it would be righted.

There was one homegirl on the set whom I did look up to. She was a caramel-complected woman in her twenties, trim, and pretty by anyone's standards. Everyone called her simply Sis, or Big Sis. Sis had a humble, easygoing way about her, despite the respect she had earned or the beauty the good Lord had blessed her with. She was always well dressed, with her hair and nails done, but she never flaunted it.

Rather, she stood on her own two and had no problem calling any of the homeboys on their shit, even threatening to beat them down if she had to. She had had just about everyone's back at some point, so when she got to talking like that, most of the homies would laugh it off or wave their hand at her instead of getting up in her face, disrespecting her. On the odd chance that one did say something back, one of the others would pipe in and say, "Oh, jus let her be, dawg, you know how she be when she gets mad. Thinks she turn six feet tall and green." There were all sorts of rumors about how she beat this or that homeboy down in the street.

In a world full of chickenheads, smokers, whores, and prissy bitches, Sis, to me, was kindness, beauty, and honor. The highest-caliber Blood female I had met. I respected all the church mothers like Big Mom, but I felt in my heart that I was a sinner, that after all the things that had happened in the darkness and all the things I had seen on the street, I was beyond God's love and forgiveness.

"Ayye, yo!" A hand reached out and grabbed my shoulder, jolting me from my thoughts.

"Fuck is wrong wit chu, B? Daymn, you gonna get ureself kapped doin that shyt. You know you gotta be always lookin out round here. Crabs, one time, baseheads. People mean you harm."

I shrugged my shoulders and Marcus shook his head at me and we made our way over and sat down on the bench in the Southern California sun.

"Keep an eye out fo wolves in Damu clothing, too, Blood. Trust no one, really. Sometimes your own homies are the ones to do you harm." Damu was the Swahili word for blood. The homies who were locked up often used the foreign language to communicate in front of the guards, and it had now begun to leak out onto the streets as people came and went, in and out of the prison system.

Marcus held his arm out in front of him and admired his new gold nugget ring. I hated when he told me things that I already knew, like I was a little kid.

"I jus got a lot on my mind, an besides, I'm already knowin all that," I said defensively and then changed my tone. "Nice ring, though, baller." I leaned against him and gave him a sharp nudge with my shoulder.

"Oh, you like that, huh?" He cracked a smile, couldn't help but be proud. "Well, babygurl, you know how we do, gotta get that shine on. I put gas in the whip, too, wanna go fo a ride?"

Marcus stood up and extended his hand out to help pull me off the bench. I put my hand in his and let him yank me up.

Marcus put his arm around me.

"We kan pick up a few tall kans and bick back, be bool, talk. You kan tell me what's goin on in that head of ures, aiight?"

My mood lightened and the sun shone through the tall palm trees. We made our way through the park, laughing and throwing up the hood or saying soo woop to the homies we passed along the way.

Once outside the park and in the Monte Carlo, Marcus carefully sorted through cassette tapes until he found one he approved of, his face lighting up. He popped it into the tape deck and looked at me, waiting for the song to come on. The tape clicked from the B side back to the A side and after a scratchy suspenseful moment, Marvin Gaye's voice filled the car and carried out into the street.

"Mother, Mother, there's too many of you crying . . ."

As the engine came to life, Marcus reached across me into the glove compartment and produced a blunt and a lighter and handed them to me.

"Grown-folk musik, Blood. I borrowed it from Moms. Hit that, ease ure head."

I did what he said, grateful for the relief that I knew would come, and then handed them back to him. He hit them and navigated the giant car onto the narrow side street, I leaned back in the seat and watched as the red flag tied to the mirror flapped in the wind.

Marcus pulled in front of the liquor store and killed the engine, but not the music.

"You komin in or waitin?"

"Ima wait." I looked at him through heavy-lidded eyes, my body feeling too slow to move.

"What chu want, then?"

I shrugged my shoulders.

"Kome on, I know that kronik got you hungry." He smiled, proud of having good-quality smoke and not shake or that brown dirt weed.

Again I shrugged my shoulders.

"Aiight, I'll surprise you, then, Miss Lady." He nodded toward the stereo. "You like'n that ol skool?"

I smiled and nodded. I did like it. It reminded me of Momma. She listened to Marvin sometimes when she cleaned the house, dancing around while she dusted and straightened, scoured and scrubbed until our humble, crowded little house shone like something to be proud of.

As Marcus ran into the store, I hit reverse on the cassette player and backed the tape up to "Inner City Blues." It was already halfway through the song, but I left it, leaned back again in my seat, feeling gravity's pull, and watched the neighborhood as I listened.

A crackhead ran back and forth between begging a dealer a half block up and begging passersby for change, desperate beyond anything I could imagine. The dealer yelled at him to stop drawing attention or else he wouldn't sell to him anymore.

"An don't bring me no change, either," the dealer added, yelling out after him. "Bills only!"

Meanwhile Marvin's voice went out, deep and true.

As it came to an end and Marvin sang his last lines, Marcus emerged from the store with a brown bag. The crackhead hit him up as soon as he was out the door and Marcus, to my surprise, stopped and talked with the man, balancing the bag in one arm while he reached into his pocket and handed the man a bill. The crackhead talked to him a minute more and then turned to walk away. Marcus reached out and touched his arm, stopping him and then, as the man turned around, Marcus removed a tall can from the bag and handed it to him.

As Marcus crossed the street back toward the car, the crackhead called after him. "Thanks again, dawg."

Marcus threw the *b* up toward the sky, then reached down and opened the door. He placed the bag in between us and started the car up again.

"Yea yea, we got us some beers, I got some Fritos, got some punch ta drink, kause it's hot as a mothafukka. We'll hit up the drive-thru, get a lil chicken . . ." He stopped talking when he caught my eye. "What? Why you lookin at me like that?"

"What you give that basehead money? You kno he jus gonna buy rock with it."

Marcus sighed and reached forward to turn the stereo down.

"Man, he usta be OG from the set. Had madd respect, too, but he went ta the pen for, daymn, a good minute. I dunno, five, seven years. He got hooked on the shyt in there and when he got out, he jus neva got right again." Marcus stopped for a minute and looked down at his hands as they rested on the steering wheel. I wasn't sure if he was thinking about what he was about to say or reflecting on the fall of the former soldier.

"Bree," he started finally, "life is hard. I mean, you jus kan't judge another's choices or prescribe another's medicines for them."

I looked at the crackhead again. No surprise there. He'd quickly made his way over to the man who was slangin' rocks and was making his purchase in bills and change, minutes away from that next high. It was hard to imagine someone like that being a soldier. I couldn't imagine having worked so hard for so long to earn stripes, and then being willing to give them up. I watched the hands of the two men make the exchange and I thought about prison and what it must mean to lose years of your life, while all your friends and loved ones are moving on, outside. I thought about Taye again, about what he had said about wishing he was that strong. I thought about Rodney and how much I respected him. I couldn't help but wonder how I would feel about him and what I would do if I saw him on a corner as a basehead.

I looked over at Marcus, his eyes following as the crackhead took off down the street at top speed, his business done for now. He watched until his fallen hero disappeared down the alley and then Marcus put the Monte Carlo in drive and sped off, the tires screeching as he pulled away from the curb. We drove in silence for several minutes.

Turning left onto Crenshaw, Marcus looked over his shoulder at me and pointed toward the Chicken Shack. I nodded. He quickly got into the right lane and pulled up to the drive-thru. When the old half-deaf woman opened the bulletproof window, he ordered the half-chicken plate and paid.

"You get two sides," she said in a loud but almost unintelligible raspy voice.

Marcus looked at me.

"Kollards?" I suggested. "Westeva you want, really."

"Yea," he said, leaning slightly out the car window, "Lemme get kollards and mak an cheese."

"Aiight, babies," she said and smiled as she shut the window, going off to fix the plate.

"Where we goin, ma?"

"Park?"

Marcus uncapped a black Sharpie marker and reached out to

write the setup on the drive-thru window's ledge in thick letters. The restaurant was on the street that served as a border between our neighborhood and the enemy Crip one. It was always good to be clear that we had no intention of letting that line get pushed. He looked tired. It was the first I'd noticed it. After what seemed like for- ever, the lady returned and opened the thick bulletproof glass win- dow, handing out the Styrofoam container tied up in a plastic bag.

"Y'all be careful out there," the lady said and quickly shut the heavy window.

"Guess she tryin be safe in there," Marcus said and laughed, even though we both knew the Chicken Shack had been shot up more then once and robbed more times than the LAPD could count. He pulled slowly forward, stopping at the exit, "How bout the beach?" I nodded and he pulled back onto Crenshaw heading toward the 10 freeway.

At the beach, Marcus spread out a blanket he kept in the trunk of the car. We cracked open the first beers and Marcus untied the plastic bag and smiled and laughed as he opened the Styrofoam up.

"What's funny?" I asked, and he turned the container to face me. Instead of collard greens and mac and cheese, the old woman had given us cheese grits and black-eyed peas.

"I got this theory"—Marcus raised his eyebrows up—"that that woman hears perfect. She jus only makes two or three sides a day an that's how she pulls it off."

I told Marcus all about my visit with Taye. Mostly he just listened as I told him about how hard Taye squeezed my hands and what he said. I knew that in the back of his mind, as in the back of mine, was that fallen OG, broken down by the system.

"What time ure momma expectin you home?" Marcus said when I finished off the last details. It was already sunset.

"Oh," I started, disappointed. I wanted him to tell me something. I wanted him to make it okay, to tell me my brother was fine. "She didn't say really. I kinda ran out the door fore she kould tell me anything."

"Ah," he said, pausing. "Fa sho." A few minutes went by and neither of us said anything, we just watched the sky as it faded to black and then, in the darkness, Marcus stood up and extended his hand to me.

"Kome on, let's go."

I took his hand and he pulled me up. We rode the 10 back into L.A. in silence. When we pulled in front of Momma's house, Marcus killed the engine and turned to face me. His face looked sad, stressed in the street's half-light.

"Bree, you did the right thing. I mean, you kan't blame a nigga fo what he said, but it's good you went anyway. I'm sure it felt good ta him to know you kared enough ta do that. That mighta been all he needed ta make it thru, an now knowin' that, he kan shut down an do his time. Jus, write him, even if he don't write chu bakk. He'll read it. He jus don't wanna set himself up ta get hurt, that's all. Ain personal, you already knowin Blood loves you."

"Yea," I said, digging my nails into my hand. "I know."

"Kryin like a lil bitch, huh?" Marcus shook his head and for a minute I was sorry I'd told him, mad that he could say something like that about my brother. "Thas aiight, Bree Bree, you allowed ta kry, but only for your momma or your sister."

Marcus shrugged his shoulders. "As long as you ain kryin ova no random bitch, it's aiight." He looked me in the eye and smiled. It was a fake smile, a forced one. "I wouldn't tell Terrell none of that. Jus tell him Taye's koo."

I looked down at my lap and tried not to cry, digging my fingernails deeper and deeper into my palms.

"You ain kryin, are you?"

I shook my head no, but I could feel the tears streaming hot down my cheeks.

"Ah, naw," Marcus scooted closer to me in his seat and leaned across and put his arms around me. I held my body straight, refusing to lean into him, refusing to let him comfort me.

"It's aiight, Bree," he said, lifting a hand up and stroking my hair. After a minute he leaned back and placed his hands on my shoulders, holding me steady and forcing me to look at him.

"Bree, look, I kno it hurts, okay? But peep game, Taye gonna be aiight, and so are you. What's pain to a warrior is a privilege. Pain, and handling pain, are measures of a warrior, kause to know victory is to know defeat."

I nodded and reached around Marcus, hugging him. Over his shoulder I could see Momma looking out the window, watching. I knew from the way she stood, arms crossed, shoulders square and head straight that she was mad. I kissed Marcus on the cheek and pulled away.

"Marcus, guess what? I forgot to tell you! I seen what's out there beyond the lights ah the city when we was drivin up. It was hella far."

"Oh, yea? What?" He smiled, a real smile this time.

"Ain shyt really," I laughed. "Lots ah cows, a few lil places here an there. It's jus peace, man."

Marcus nodded, thinking it over for a minute and then shook his head. "Naw, fukk all that. Fukk errything. I am L.A. Ima live an die in this bitch."

I reached on the door and fumbled for a minute with the handle.

"Aye, Bree, tell me bout it tomorrow, aiight?"

"Fa sho," I said, opening the door and stepping out. "I'll kall you when I get up."

Marcus started the engine and I slammed the door shut, and walked around the back of the car. He stuck his arm out the window, waving bye to me and Moms all at the same time before taking off. Mom held the door open now, watching me as I came up the walkway.

"Why you all hugged up wit that boy?" she demanded as I crossed the threshold. Her voice was stern. Big Mom had become paranoid. At thirteen, I was only a year younger than Terrell's mom had been when she got pregnant with him.

"Momma, ain nothing like that, you kno that. We was jus talking."

"Oh, is that what you call it?" She turned and walked toward the kitchen, but I knew she wasn't done yet. I watched her back as she walked over and opened a drawer.

"C'mon ova here, child," she said, slamming it shut, right hand clutching an extension cord. I looked down at the floor as I slowly walked over.

"Yes, Momma."

"You hangin out with them gangbangers? You think that's cool?"

"Naw, Momma, it ain like that."

"Look at me when you talk to me, child. Show grown people that much respect. I try an show you how ta act. And you runnin round all day with gangbangers."

I looked up at Big Mom's face. There were tears in her eyes.

"I'm sorry, Momma."

She clenched her jaw tightly and swallowed. "Turn around, then," she said, "turn round and grab the counter."

"Yes, Momma," I said and did as she told me. As I leaned forward and my hands gripped the cool tile, Momma tried to explain things to me.

"I don't do this because I hate you, Bree. I don't even do it cause I'm mad at you." Her voice quivered and I knew she was unsuccessfully fighting back the tears. "I do it because I LOVE you. It hurts me more than it hurts you, but I gotta make sure you're a good gurl, so that it neva comes on someone who don't love you to have to do this, or worse. I gotta do something while I still can."

"I kno, Momma," I said, gripping the counter harder and closing my eyes, preparing myself for the blows that were about to come. And then they came, one after another against my back until it burned. When it was over, Momma turned, as she always did, to face the corner so that when I walked away I couldn't see her face.

"I hafta go to work now. I'm late." Her voice was soft, as though it strained her to talk. "We'll talk bout this tomorrow when I get home."

"I love you, Momma," I said as I started toward my room, back aching.

"I love you, too, child. Please kno it."

I thought about Marcus's words again.

What's pain to a warrior is a privilege. To know victory is to know defeat.

When I walked into the bedroom, Nishia was awake, sitting on the edge of my bed. I threw my cap on the dresser and pulled off my shorts without saying anything. I knew it would hurt to pull off my shirt so I moved slowly, pulling it up and over my head and then reaching down for my nightgown and pulling it on.

"Go back ta sleep, Nishia," I said and climbed into bed without pulling the covers down, but she didn't move. "Aye, who made my bed an put my shyt away, you or Momma?"

"I did," Nishia said in a whisper.

"Oh, aiight. Thanks, then. I'll give you a dollar tomorrow," I said. A minute went by and she still hadn't moved, so I added, "Good night."

"Momma beat you bad?" she asked in a whisper.

"Naw, not too bad. I'm koo, jus go ta sleep, man." Nishia climbed between me and the wall and put her arms around me, being careful to rest her arm on my side instead of letting it fall against my back. Reluctantly, I put an arm around her as she started to cry.

"Nishia, stop it, man. You ain no baby. We warriors. An pain ain nothing to a warrior, aiight?"

She pushed her head tight against my chest and nodded, then she continued to cry anyway until we both fell asleep.

When I woke up in the morning, she had already gotten up. I tossed and turned for a few minutes and then walked out to find her and NeeCee watching Saturday-morning cartoons.

"Momma back yet?"

Nishia shook her head no without taking her eyes off the TV.

"You eat breakfast?"

This time she nodded her head yes, again without taking her eyes off the TV.

"NeeCee." The baby turned and looked at me with a big dimpled smile. "You eat breakfast?"

"Yess," she said. Six years old and she still had her baby lisp.

"Good girl." I walked into the kitchen to call Marcus and see what dishes they had left for me. I grabbed the phone off the wall and looked at the clock. Nine o'clock roughly, Marcus would still be at the house. I dialed up his momma's crib and started to rinse the few bowls and glasses in the sink.

"Hello?"

"Hey, Mrs. Johnson, how you? This is Bree. Is Marcus round?"

There was a long pause on the phone, followed by stuttering and then tears. "I'm, I'm so sorry, dear. I, I just thought you'da heard. I'm so sorry . . ."

I couldn't hear the rest. I dropped the phone, letting it hit the floor as all the sounds around me muffled together.

POURIN' LIQUOR

There is a way which seems right unto a man,
but in the end it leads to death.

PROVERBS 14:12

I SLID DOWN in the pew until I could rest my head against the hard
wooden edge of the seat. The pastor was reading from the Bible. I
could feel what he was saying, and logically, at least, it all made sense.
Still, things were never as simple as people wanted you to believe. All
I could think about was revenge, or, alternatively, getting out of that
service so I could blaze some chronic and numb the pain for a
minute. I was in no mood for the lecture, not today. People wanted
to talk about peace in public and nod their head at the good word,
but behind closed doors, even Marcus's mom had grabbed my hand
and said, "Get them, get the mothafukkers who did this to my boy."

Peace was nice in theory, but no one believed in it when shit was
personal, and shit was always personal to someone. I rubbed at my
eyes. My stomach felt queasy, and just trying to hold my head steady
made the pounding unbearable. What are you supposed to believe
when your best friend's mom begs you for justice, or when there are
rumors that Crips are planning to storm the funeral with guns? It
sounds crazy, but it's happened more than enough times to make it
believable. With 800-plus people in the church, covering the hierar-

chy ranging from the OGs all the way down to the YGs, it was a good strategy, and it wasn't just the Crips that employed it. So while the pastor spoke of praying for peace and forgiving our enemies, we knew it couldn't be. How do you forgive someone who doesn't want forgiveness? The rules of survival on the streets had changed. The days of settling things by going "heads up" or fighting it out with fists were pretty much a thing of the past, and now instead of the losers walking away with a black eye or broken tooth, they were riddled with bullets that left them paralyzed or worse. I looked at the casket. It didn't seem real. I looked away, focusing on the ceiling.

I'm sorry to say that I spent the long week between Marcus's death and the funeral doing nothing but drinking, smoking, and sleeping. I just kept pouring the Hennessey into my cup and rolling blunts, trying to drown out how things felt, but even that didn't help much, because the minute I started to sober up, the pain just came right back. Momma would come by intermittently and knock on the locked door, asking me to get up and let her in, but she knew I was hurting and after a few minutes she would let up. Her voice would come through the door, slightly muffled, telling me that God would never put me in a situation that I couldn't handle. Moms knew sometimes I just had to sort through things on my own—she was good like that—although if she knew all that I was trying to sort through she might not have been so willing. Lying there think-ing of Marcus and of Marcus's mom, I knew that God might not put me in a situation I couldn't handle, but I sure as hell might put my-self there.

I lifted my head a little bit, the casket coming back into view. They had gotten him in the head, the chest, and the neck. He didn't die on the street, though; he'd made it to the hospital, where he had been cut into, doctors removing bullets and skull fragments before they finally gave up hope. The damage was so bad that the funeral had to be closed-casket. I looked over at Marcus's momma, dressed in black, sobbing in the front row. I'd been to a few funerals, even some for people I would have claimed to have love or respect for— but no one I was as close to as I was to Marcus. The whole thing was so surreal, and not being able to see him made it worse. When you sit in the church, looking at your loved one stretched out in that box, it hurts, but there is no denying what has happened. Somehow, when you view the body, you are forced to find some level of closure. At the end of an open-casket funeral, friends will place various items in the casket: small bottles of Hennessey, money, whatever they think the deceased might need or want on their journey. I worried about Marcus not having anything with him.

I pulled out my pager and looked at it again to make sure it was on. I had a .38 in my bag, too, just in case the rumors of a Crip attack were true, and the homies posted as security outside the church doors and up the block in both directions knew that I was armed and ready to respond if paged.

Marcus was the one who had given me the gun. It had been a gift from him and my brothers for my thirteenth birthday, back when Terrell and Taye were both still locked up. Mom had made a cake and cooked a nice dinner for me, and she and my sisters gave me Run-DMC's cassette *Raisin' Hell.* Then, later that night, after she had left for work and my sisters had gone to bed, Marcus came over and handed me a small box wrapped in the Sunday comics. It was heavy, and as I unwrapped it, I read the box: Winchester Super X. Marcus looked so proud, but I had no idea what it was. I opened the side flap and tilted it. A Styrofoam holder slid out with five full rows of bullets in it, ten bullets in each row.

"What are these for?" I asked, picking one up and turning it over in my hand. Marcus reached behind him and from the back of his pants produced a Smith & Wesson .38 Special. It was on the small size as guns go, but it was heavy with big wooden grips.

He had bought it in an alley, where guns come in by the crate, trunk, and truckload, usually slightly used and always rubbed clean of any evidence and serial numbers. In the alley (and from a whole variety of "connects"), no ID is required, the waiting period is not enforced, and they don't care if you're a felon or underage. All they care is that you have the Benjamins. Most important of all, they don't register your weapon with your name on it in a government file. If need be, you can just wipe your prints off the gun and it's as if it was never yours. It's easier, faster, and cheaper to buy a gun from a connect than from a legit shop.

"That's from me, Tee, an Taye." I knew that, really, Tee had suggested it and Marcus had gotten it. No one heard from Taye anymore.

I flipped it over in my hand. I'd seen guns a million times. It was pretty much impossible to go a full day without seeing at least one, but I had never held one before. It weighed more than I had imagined. I tried to turn the chamber like they did in western movies, but it wouldn't budge. Marcus laughed at me.

"You have to push this." He leaned over and began to explain how the gun worked in detail.

Flipping through the memorial program now, I tried to remember the feel of his hand on mine, showing me how to hold the gun. Which fingers he wore his rings on. Someone had done a good job on the program. The cover was a color Xerox of a photo of Marcus sitting on the hood of the Monte Carlo. He had on a pair of pressed-up khaki pants and a black shirt. The park was in the background and palm trees framed the top of the image. He had his shades on and he held a cup up to the camera, as though offering a toast. Anyone who knew Marcus knew it was a perfect photo. Marcus loved palm trees. He would often point to them and say, "Look at that. Y'all wanna learn somthin, jus watch that tree. Otha kinds of trees lose their limbs in a storm, or blow over, but the palm tree will touch the ground an bounce right back like nothing. It only gets stronger."

About a month after I first heard him say that, there was a really bad Santa Ana wind. I looked out my window and watched as trash cans blew over and their contents swirled through the air and down the street. And then, just as Marcus said, the fragile lilacs and other pretty ornamentals uprooted or broke limbs, but the palm trees just swayed, bending at forty-five-degree angles back and forth. The next day, when I mentioned it to him, he smiled and nudged me, "Yea, I seen that, too. Told ya." He winked and pointed at an exceptionally large palm on the street. "That's my hero right there, been watchin her since diapers."

I touched the picture, tracing his jaw with my fingertip as though by doing so I could touch Marcus again. I looked from his face to the words just below: "In memory of Marcus Johnson." I turned the page. The inside was a letter from his mom alongside one from the pastor. Both tried to focus on the fact that Marcus lived an overall decent life, that those who knew him would remember him for his kindness and that he was saved and thus would go to heaven. I knew they were right about the middle part; I just hoped they were right about the last part. I wondered if Marcus could see the funeral, and if so what he thought of it. I flipped quickly through the remaining six pages of scrapbook-style photo layouts sprinkled with Bible quotes, a list of all the relatives he left behind, and the order of the service, and sat back against my seat.

They started the music ministry. The woman seemed to sing forever. Every time she paused people would start to clap thinking she was done, only to have her start right back up again. My shirt felt tight around my neck, as though it were choking me. I reached up and pulled at the collar uselessly. When the pastor started to deliver his eulogy I couldn't stand it anymore. I crept down the side aisle and out the door as quietly as I could, hoping that no one noticed.

Outside the doors, I nodded to the homie without even really looking to see who he was. I saw all I needed to: a flash of red that let me know he was an ally. I felt better outside, less overwhelmed, less trapped away from the heat of the crowd. I took a deep breath. My chest felt tight.

"You aiight?" the homie called to me. I nodded and leaned back against the building. I heard his footsteps as he approached me. When I looked up, my eyes taking a minute to focus, it was Slikk, now standing next to me.

"Man," I smiled, relieved somehow by his presence, "I kan't get my breath." The tears almost came, but I refused, fighting them back. Slikk was too well respected in the hood for me to let him see me cry. He leaned back against the building next to me.

"Yea, Blood, it's fukked up," he said. We stood in silence for a moment. I watched his face as he looked down at the ground. His jaw clenched and a few small tears fell from his eyes. He quickly wiped them away with his sleeve. "I miss mah nigga, you kno?"

"Yea, man," I said, not sure what else I could say. I couldn't believe someone like Slikk had tears inside of him. I watched him for another minute, and then I lifted my hand from my side and patted his chest twice. He did his best to force a smile. He pulled a half-burned blunt out from under the rim of his cap and held it up to me.

"Wanna blaze?"

"Naw, man, I think that's why I kan't katch my breath."

"Right, right . . ." he said as he lit it up and took a deep drag. He held the smoke in and then blew it slowly out over his shoulder, away from me. He again held it up toward me, widening his eyes, "You sure?"

I nodded and he snuffed it out on the wall of the church.

"You seen ure bro?" His words shocked me. Marcus was one of Terrell's friends and yet it hadn't even occurred to me to look for him in the swarm of people.

"Man, I guess I'm jus so usta him bein gone . . ." I was embarrassed, didn't know what to say. "You kno where he's at?"

Slikk shrugged. "He ran round the korner wit some the homies. He'll be right back." We sat for a few minutes in silence; Slikk put his arm around me. The eulogy, though muffled, was still audible through the heavy church doors. I listened more to the rise and fall of the pastor's voice than to his words. I was starting to wish I had taken a hit of that blunt when I heard Terrell's voice.

"Oh, shyt . . . Look who it is." He held a bottle of Hen in one hand and a stack of cups in the other. I jumped up and threw my arms around him and he managed to hug me even with his hands full, pressing his forearms tight against my back. "Lil sis . . . How you doin, babygurl?"

I didn't answer; I just held him tight. He smelled of alcohol already and his balance was wobbly. "K'mon," he said, loosening his arms around me, "lemme set this shyt down." Terrell handed me a cup and passed the rest out to Slikk and the other homies who were standing around. Then he opened the Hennessey, poured some on the concrete step, and then filled each cup about halfway, killing off the bottle in his own cup.

"Krazy," Terrell started, everyone's eyes on him. "Seems like we was jus here. I only been out a minute, an already seen two soldiers fall. An next time we're all standin here, it's gonna be one less of us. BIP, homie, I hope you got the peace that you neva had down here."

"Blood in peace," one of the homies said, and then everyone started saying it and lifting their cups up.

"We'll get them niggas back, Marcus. They gonna pay for this," Terrell added, then tipped his cup, letting some more of the cognac fall onto the ground. "This is for you, my homie. I love you, my nigga."

Everyone did the same.

"That's fo all the dead homies, Blood," Slikk said. "Blood in peace." He touched his hand to his heart and then signed the *b* up to the sky.

LOVE AND KONSEQUENCES

A TOUCH OF Santa Ana wind had cooled the August air, clearing the smog a little, but a haze still hung heavy in the sky. A day like any other in this city. Out-of-towners comment on L.A.'s haze constantly, but apart from an exceptionally bad or good day, residents don't really think too much about it. So long as you know the mountains are there, it doesn't really matter all that much if you can see them, they're not going anywhere. Out there in the distance, beyond the freeways and concrete, smog or no, seen or not, they are just as stuck as we are.

My sisters and I had been messing around in the yard most of the morning. I'd recently bought them each a new Barbie and they reveled in their dolls' newness, taking their shoes on and off and brushing their hair. While they entertained themselves I got to play with, and try to train, Cinque. Occasionally I'd sneak from our yard into Rodney's to see Bitch and her newest litter of puppies. It was a happy day, all of us proud of what we had, and not focused on all the things we didn't.

Big Mom really wasn't around much these days, what with her many jobs and church activities. It's not that she wasn't thinking about us. In fact, everything that woman did, she did for us. But, as always, in her absence the job of taking care of Nishia and NeeCee fell to me, all the more now that Denise had left, taking Tiffany and the baby with her. There was no one left but me.

I know it burdened Big Mom's conscience that she had to rely so much on me while I was still so young. In one of the rare letters he did write, Taye said that he prayed to God for forgiveness for the choices he never had. Who's to say who had fewer choices, Mom or us. There are all sorts of ways to be incarcerated, or trapped by the system.

Playing in the yard with my sisters, there was really no way that I could have reached Moms if we needed her. There was no phone at her night job cleaning office buildings, and her day job was forty minutes away, too far if we had an emergency. I had Terrell's pager number as backup, but, realistically, what could he do? He loved us and would drop anything for us once he got the page, but in L.A. things happen fast.

That hazy August day, Big Mom made fried chicken and biscuits for dinner and we ate early, before she left for work at six, so we could all be together. Momma's fried chicken was our favorite, and Nishia and NeeCee clapped when they saw it on the table. We said what we were thankful for and laughed together. Halfway through the meal, as always, Big Mom had to get up and leave. We said goodbye, and when Nishia and NeeCee were done eating, I cleared the table. We watched TV for a while and then I sent them to wash their faces, made sure they brushed their teeth, and tucked them in.

"Night, Nee Nee." Nee Nee, that was my nickname for the two of them when they were together, which was most of the time. As usual, Nishia threw her arms up for a hug, while NeeCee hid under the blankets, laughing. We goofed around a bit, me pinning them down and tickling while they squealed, before I left their room, shutting the door behind me.

"The light, the light. Don't forget."

I turned the hall light on. Nishia's nightmares had started about the same time Taye had left. I don't know if he made her feel safer, for the sake of his being a man, or if it was something else. After my brothers left, vacating a bedroom, I moved out of the girls' shared bedroom. This probably added to Nishia's feeling of being unsettled, but it was the first time I had my own room since I had gone into foster care and I wasn't about to give it up.

After I finished the dishes, I went outside to play with Cinque and Bitch until I got tired enough that I thought I could fall asleep. I patted their big heads good night and then went inside to wash the dirt off with a washrag. I turned the lights off and once back in my room, I looked out the window before lying down. Bitch was by her doghouse, chewing on a plastic milk carton. I tapped on the glass and waved to her, she looked over and wagged her tail, then went right back to chewing. Then I got into bed and pulled the covers up over my head so that the streetlight wasn't in my eyes. I slept.

A few hours later—I sat up with a jolt, startled by the sounds of commotion outside. I was used to all the normal city sounds, but this was different. It was a jumbling of different noises with no beginning or end, a constant loud thundering of strange new sounds. They were so loud that the house shook and all the usual city noise seemed to disappear in the background.

I pulled back my sheet and stumbled to the window. My eyes still blurry, I squinted and looked out through the bar-covered window.

The streetlights cast a slight haze onto the scene outside, enough that I could see the movement but couldn't tell exactly what was going on. All I could tell, to my increasing distress, was that it was all focused on Rodney's house.

"Momma!" I ran through the house in a panic. I whiped my eyes with my hand to try to clear the blur of my tears. My eyes burned from the brightness of the light in the hallway. I didn't know why I was crying. I was too afraid to feel anything yet.

"Momma, help!" I screamed again.

I ran into her room and looked at the bed, but it was neatly made. I looked over at her dresser, where the clock read 5:05 A.M. She'd already left for the Hellermans', to drive the two older kids from Highland Park to their private school in the valley and then watch the toddler and clean their house and do their shopping before the mom came home, somewhere between noon and three. I didn't feel panicked anymore. Instead, I felt a deep weight settle on me. I just wished it all could stop. For a short moment, all the appeal of drug dealing and gangs disappeared. All I wanted was the ability to go back to sleep without knowing that when I woke up in the morning something bad would have happened to someone I loved. I pulled Big Mom's covers back and got into her bed. The blankets smelled of her lotion and hair grease. I closed my eyes as tight as I could and tried to breathe, but then the voices came again. I tried to block them out. I pretended that it was a bad dream and that I had climbed into bed with Big Mom. But it didn't matter, I knew it wasn't true.

"RODNEY SMITH. COME OUT WITH YOUR HANDS UP!" It seemed like the loudest sound I had ever heard. It sounded like it was up above me, like it took up the whole sky.

"WE HAVE THE HOUSE SURROUNDED. COME OUT WITH YOUR HANDS UP."

For a moment, everything was silent. It was as if someone had quieted all the other neighborhood sounds. I pulled the blankets from over my head and got out of Big Mom's bed. If I was scared, surely my sisters were terrified. I remembered again that I had to be the adult. I couldn't pretend that nothing was happening and leave them alone in their room, no matter how badly I wanted to.

I wished Big Mom or Terrell were home, but they weren't. I wished Taye wasn't in juvie, but he was. I took a deep breath and ran down the hall and through the door to check on them.

First I looked at NeeCee. She lay there, motionless but awake, looking up at me, then she lifted a small, fat hand and waved at me.

"Hi, Princess. You scurred?"

She pinched her lips tight together and nodded her head up and down. Yes.

"Yea, all that noise is jus some shyt goin on next door. You wanna kome out? I'll make some cocoa." I smiled at my baby sis, her face was calm. NeeCee was learning to shut down all her emotions and just survive. I knew the routine all too well, and it broke my heart to see it in someone else.

I put my arm around NeeCee and turned to face Nishia's bed. The blankets were crumpled up in the middle forming a big pile. I pulled them back, expecting to find a curled-up Nishia, but instead I found only an empty bed.

I leaned my head forward and looked at NeeCee. "You kno where she's at?" She nodded and pointed to the closet. I walked over and opened the door. Nishia was huddled in the corner under some dirty clothes and cast-off toys, hands over her ears, crying. I remember that her eyes looked huge and dark, like she had just seen something terrible beyond explanation.

"Kome on," I said, reaching a hand out to her. She shook her head no and pushed her hands tighter against her ears. "Kome on, Nishia, it ain here, it's next door," I said louder and then added, again hoping that we had milk, "Ima make cocoa."

She looked up at me, eyes still big and brimming with fear. She reached up her hand and took mine. "Beezy?"

"Yea, baby?" I was still afraid, but I tried to hide it in my voice. I figured I owed my sisters that.

"They gonna take us away?" She couldn't even look at me when she said it. NeeCee's hand gripped the back of my shirt tightly and she looked from Nishia to me, waiting on my answer.

"Naw, where you get an idea like that?"

She shrugged her thin shoulders, her head still looking down at her feet. "Well, las time when the police came across the street they took those kids."

"Yea, but they had kome ta their house and their momma was on drugs. The timas ain at our house, they next door."

"Oh," Nishia said and looked up at me. "What if they see that Momma ain home?"

"Well, I'm here, an I already kalled Terrell, so he prolly on his way." It was a lie, but it seemed to work. Truth was, the kid brought up a good point. "Aiight? Cocoa?" I smiled at her in an effort to be convincing as I pulled her up and started to head for the kitchen.

"Beezy?"

"What, Nishia?"

"They gonna take you away?"

"Maybe, Nishia, but not today." She smiled at me and took my hand again. Somehow we made it to the kitchen without any more questions. In fact, no one talked at all. I took the milk out of the fridge, poured it into a pan, heated it, and mixed in chocolate syrup.

I poured the cocoa into two cups and handed them over to my sisters.

"Can I have marshmallows?" Nishia asked

"Naw, ain got none," I said without even looking. We never had any, but she always asked anyway. She shrugged her shoulders and looked down into her cup.

"You lucky we even got milk." It was sometimes hard to believe her optimism. Nishia was the only person on earth who could sit in a dark kitchen with noise all around, SWAT raiding the neighbor's house, and ask about marshmallows.

"Oh well," she said, "maybe tomorrow we will. Doesn't hurt to ask."

That funny sense of optimism, I realized, was what kept Nishia going, just as NeeCee's and my ability to shut down was what saved us.

"Can you turn the lights on?" Nishia asked.

"Naw, ima leave the hall light on, but I ain tryin to let the po-po see the lights kome on an have excuse to be komin ova here thinkin we awake anyways."

No one said anything after that. I guess they saw the logic. We sat in the dark, listening to the police bullhorns and helicopters, and I watched my sisters drink their cocoa. When they were done, I took them back to their room and tucked them back in.

"But I'm scared," Nishia whined, as she pulled her covers up and buried her face underneath.

I pulled the blanket down just enough to uncover Nishia's face and picked up a ragged stuffed bear, tucking it in next to her.

"Don't be scared, Nish, ima be right outside. Ima stay up an look out so it's nothing to be worried bout. I'd die befo I'd let anything happen ta you two." I looked over at NeeCee, already falling back asleep and then down at Nishia who stared up at me, taking in every move. "You believe me?"

"Yea," she said, sitting up and wrapping her arms around my neck, "I believe you." She kissed my cheek and then lay back down, turning toward the wall and clutching the one-eyed bear. I pulled the sheet back up and tucked it in around her, patted her shoulder, and walked out. She was crying.

I went back into my room and looked out the window. The sun was coming up now, so I could see what was going on outside. Six squad cars and some sort of big gray wagon. The police were every-where, but they were dressed differently than usual. Today the boys in blue wore black instead, complete with masks that covered their faces. Some held shields and some carried large rifles I'd never seen the likes of. One thing I knew for sure, bullets ricochet, and just be-cause you're innocent doesn't mean you can't get hit. I'd been to plenty of funerals for the innocent.

The police looked all amped up like things were about to pop off. They scurried like ants around the perimeter. I could see Bitch run-ning back and forth the distance of her chain, barking loudly, spit flinging out of her giant jaw.

I crept down the hallway and into the girls' room. Nishia was awake, still crying slightly, but NeeCee was asleep. As quietly as I could, I gently lifted NeeCee and laid her down on the floor in the corner of the room where a bullet was least likely to reach. Her eyes opened, studying my face.

"It's okay, baby, jus go back ta sleep."

"They shootin again?" she asked.

"Naw," I said, "sall good. I just wanna play it safe is all."

They were used to it. We all were. The police had come to our street before, this was just the first time they were right next door. Nishia got up and helped me push the dresser in front of the window and threw all the stuffed animals in front of it to create more of a shield. I pulled the sheet off Nishia's bed and handed them each a pillow.

"Go to sleep," I said shutting their door.

I went back to my window and looked out. "THIS IS YOUR LAST CHANCE TO DO THIS THE EASY WAY, RODNEY. ONE WAY OR ANOTHER THIS IS GOING TO BE OVER IN A FEW MINUTES. IT'S ALL HOW YOU WANT IT TO GO NOW." The loud voice seemed to come from the sky. The cops moved again around the house, inching closer and closer while avoiding Bitch's reach on the side next to our house.

In the excitement one police officer got too close and Bitch lunged toward him, coming within six inches of biting him. "Get that fucking crazy dog out of here. How the fuck are we supposed to secure the perimeter like this?" he yelled at someone.

With that my heart dropped. I felt sick to my stomach. I had stopped to think about the rifles and the rounds of bullets that were cased within them. I had thought about the possibility of them piercing the walls and windows and hitting my sisters or myself, but until that moment I hadn't thought about the dogs. I knew that inside the doghouse was a new batch of puppies, and I knew that Bitch would defend their safety by any means necessary, and all of a sudden I realized I didn't see Cinque anywhere.

Dogs aren't like people, they don't think about consequences. If they love you, they'll die trying to defend you, should the situation arise; they don't take a moment to first think about whether you would do the same for them or to ponder what action would benefit them most. They just do it. Rodney taught me that.

"Ima tell you sunnthin," he said one afternoon, sitting on his steps. "Back a few years ago, I koulda named you twenty, thirty niggas I trusted, thought had my back. Now I kan only think ah two, an they the ones I grew up with. That's why I love them dogs."

He lit up the blunt and took a hit off it, then leaned away from me to blow the smoke out. "I'll tell you somethin else, though, a lil bit ah advice. When you got ure back against the wall, it ain a lot you kan do. But in those situations, watch people, kause those are the times when someone really shows you who they are an what they're made of." He looked at me with this sad, wise, stoned look. I didn't understand the weight then of what he was telling me, but I knew he thought it was important.

"Ima remember that, Rodney. Promise." I stood up and held my hand out to him. He grasped it and with a firm grip shook it. I smiled and he smiled back.

"Be up, youngsta," he said.

Looking out the window, I tried to hold on to that moment. I tried to memorize his smile and his eyes. I knew what was happening next door. Adults will close doors, tiptoe around things, whisper, or spell out words, but the truth is, kids, especially in South Central L.A., know as much as any adult. I looked out the window and I knew Rodney was either about to get killed in front of me by the police or else I was going to see him carried off to prison forever. I knew I'd never again sit on the porch with him and learn history or life lessons. I wondered what Rodney was going to do and what that would say about who he was. The hood is full of people who say they won't let the police take them alive, but when it comes down to it most of them do. I rested my forehead against the glass.

Everything seemed slowed down. I know that people always say that about dramatic moments, but it's true. Each minute seemed to last hours and the most painful part of it all was that I couldn't think of anything I could do but stand there and watch.

The cops got closer and closer to the house, motioning to one another in some strange code. Again one got too close to Bitch and again she lunged forward and tried to sink her teeth into him. At the end of her chain, she barked fiercely, her body tensed, each muscle clear and pulling with every ounce of strength against the thick chain.

Then something terrible happened and time seemed almost to stop. A cop turned and aimed at Bitch. I could almost watch the bullet as it flew out of the rifle and hit her in the neck. I don't know if it was the sound of the hit or the shock of what I'd just seen, but I jumped, and then, just the way time had slowed down before, now it sped up again. Bitch let out a high shriek as she flew backward and landed by the doghouse, ten feet away. She didn't get up but I could see her moving as the cop turned and fired another bullet in her direction.

That's when I ran out the door without thinking. I was screaming once I hit the porch.

"No, no, nooooo."

I jumped the fence and almost made it to the doghouse before another cop grabbed me back. He wrapped his giant, padded arms around the front of me and clasped his hands down as tight as he could across my chest to pen me in. I struggled, screamed, and kicked him, the force of which sometimes lifted me off the ground, but I couldn't get free no matter how hard I tried. I felt my tears hot against my face.

I could still see Bitch moving and I struggled against the policeman's grip trying to break free. Then I saw Rodney and I stopped moving. I just stared at him. There were cops all around him, and his hands were locked in cuffs behind his back.

The cop released me and my feet hit the ground with a hard thump. Although I was crying, I was relieved to realize that, if nothing else, with all the chaos outside, my sisters and I were no part of the police's concern. All the commotion stopped. It was over. I watched as they walked Rodney to the black and white. His eyes held mine the whole time. He didn't look surprised or angry, just sad and resolved. I guess Rodney had known that someday, somewhere down the line, this was coming.

One of them put his hand on Rodney's head and shoved him into the car. As they started to shut the door, Rodney leaned out slightly, still looking at me, and said, "Stay up, Bree Bree."

The police slammed the door and I watched it pull away, just like I had watched Rodney pull away so many times. The police on the scene started to disappear. Terrell, who had appeared sometime during the commotion, came over and said he was going inside to check on the babies and that he was going to stay there with me till Momma got home. I nodded. He patted my back and walked up the steps and into the house.

I could still see Bitch moving. I started to walk slowly toward the doghouse. It felt like my feet were made of cement, like each step was a near impossible task. As I got closer I could hear her breathing, but it didn't sound like it usually did. It was strained and slow and it rasped like when Nishia blew bubbles in her milk with a straw.

I could smell the blood. Anyone who has ever been around a vast amount of blood will tell you it's a smell you never forget. I'm not talking about a small cut, or even a pretty bad cut. I'm talking about blood. Blood like when an artery has been severed and there are buckets' worth of blood all around you. It smells hot and sticky-sweet in a way that turns your stomach and burns in your eyes. I dropped to my knees and the blood splashed up on my legs. My chest felt tight and it was hard to breathe. I started to sob.

Bitch's neck hung open, blood and bubbles pouring out of it. She was breathing partly through the wound in her neck and partly through her mouth. In between her strained efforts, her body would tremble and tense and she would let out high-pitched shrill cries.

"Babygurl," I said between my heaving, as I placed my hand on her. She looked up at me with her same begging eyes, and her tail hit the ground softly twice in an attempt to wag. I collapsed into the weight of my tears and lay down next to her, blood sticky and hot on my skin.

It felt like hours that she convulsed and cried and gurgled and struggled to breathe. Every few minutes she would stop breathing for a while and go limp, and I would be grateful that it was over. I would start to pray, to thank God, but then she would gasp again and her legs would go rigid and her body twist and shake. I'd pet her and hold her tight. I couldn't tell if it eased her trembling, and again, each time, my tears would flood my eyes and spill to the ground, mixing with the blood and the dirt in a paste that covered Bitch and me.

I sat up and I started to pray again, this time to beg for her death.

"Please, God, pleeease. Please, God, do something. Take her, God, please, she is my friend. I know she seems bad sometimes, God, but she's good and I love her. Please, God . . ."

But I guess God didn't hear me, or else he had other things he was doing that morning. I cried and I prayed, and then finally I couldn't take it anymore. I grabbed the big heavy chain and un-latched it from her collar. Too sad—to die chained up like that. I took it in both my hands and closed my eyes for a minute.

"God, I don't know if you hear me or not, but if you do, please forgive me for this." I opened my eyes up and slid the chain under Bitch's big, blocky head. She winced and whimpered when I moved her, but then let her head fall sideways onto my lap. Again I closed my eyes, and this time I took a deep breath and pulled as hard as I could on the chain to cut off her air.

I had once saved her from the same thing.

Her breathing became even more labored and her legs stiffened. Her eyes stayed focused on mine the whole time until, after what was probably only minutes but felt like years, her body went limp and her head flopped to the side. I let go of the chain.

"I'm so sorry. I didn't know what else to do." I said it over and over, to her, to God, to myself. Then I just sat there and stared at her until Terrell came outside and told me to come in. I don't remem-ber what he said, just him standing there against the pink dawn sky, his voice. I stood up and he put his arm around me and we walked into the house together. I didn't know if he saw the chain in her neck. I knew it was clear to him that she was dead, but I didn't know if he realized that in the end I had killed her.

I sat down at the table, still in shock. Terrell left and came back with a wet washcloth and wiped my hands clean.

"I put a change of clothes for you in the bathroom." He started to wipe the blood off the chair.

"Terrell." I looked at my brother. I knew he was no angel. His innocence had been robbed from him long before mine. "Where's the babies?" They were getting too big to be called babies and everyone knows that there are no such things as babies in South Central. The word sounded ridiculous suddenly.

"TV," he said and again got up to run water through the washcloth.

"Terrell?" I looked down at my hands. They looked different to me now, red and raw from the tension and strain of pulling, and blood drying under the nails, but different even beyond that. "You ever killed anyone befo?"

He sat down at the table and sighed. "Naw. I mean, I don't know, Bree Bree. I shot at people before. Didn't really go back ta see if they died."

"You think God really forgives?"

With that my brother reached over and took my hand in his. "I sure hope so, lil sis." It was silent for a minute.

"Go wash up. I found Cinque running down the sidewalk. I grabbed him an he's in the bathroom rite now, but Momma ain gonna go for that at all. They got the fence all fukked up on the side. Ima get them two ready an then we gotta go down an get a chain for him."

I nodded. I went off to the bathroom and Terrell went out to the yard. I wondered again if he had seen, if he knew, what I had done. If he hadn't before, he soon would. I narrowed my eyes as I looked at my face in the bathroom mirror. I knew everything had been changed forever. I now knew who and what I was. I was a soldier, loyal and merciful, and capable of taking a life.

TOUGH LOVE

"OH HELL, NAW. Are you fuckin kidding me?" I pushed the bathroom sink's faucet handle back down and up again, but the only thing that came out was a loud clanging noise. It was dry.

It was an early Wednesday morning, the light in the bathroom still dim, my eyes puffy. I had woken to a silent house, Big Mom long gone, having left for work before dawn. NeeCee and Nishia were still asleep. I slammed the handle back down as hard as I could and leaned back against the wall. I took a deep breath and tried not to give in to the anxiety that rose from an ache in my stomach to a fluttering in my chest. Momma always said, if you worry, don't pray, and if you pray, don't worry. I stared at the wall where moisture had begun to make the green- and gold-flowered wallpaper peel.

I tried to sort through the various problems that were about to arise and started to prioritize them. The very first thing would be to get Nishia and NeeCee off to school without their realizing that we had no water. If I woke them up late they would be rushing and if I kept them moving they might not notice. That was important, because NeeCee, at least, didn't get it that if she told her teacher we didn't have running water, the teacher could tell CPS, and then we would really have problems. Nishia and NeeCee were technically in foster care like me since Big Mom was taking care of them, and although it was unlikely that the information would make it to one of our caseworkers, it wasn't worth the risk. If you are receiving any welfare or DCFS money, you are required to meet the basic needs of all children living in the home, and letting the rent, utilities, or phone go unpaid is grounds for removal. I walked to the kitchen and took out bowls, filled them with cereal, and put the milk out on the table. I grabbed the pitcher of fruit punch out of the fridge and poured them each a glass.

Toothbrushing. I grabbed the now empty punch pitcher, got a second one out of the cabinet, and then headed next door. New people had already moved into Rodney's place, and the landlord had assured Momma that he would fix the broken fence in the near future. Cinque was chained outside our kitchen and greeted me with his lolling tongue, as if he were smiling. I patted his head and crossed into the neighbors' yard, where I turned on the hose, rinsing out the dirty pitcher and filling them both. They would never notice. I filled Cinque's water up, too, while I had the chance and he immediately lapped at it, tail wagging thank you, back and forth.

I checked the clock as I walked back in the front door: 7:40. The girls' busses came at 8:00 and 8:10. I took two glasses into the bathroom and filled each with water from the pitcher. I took the pitcher back into the kitchen, poured the milk onto the cereal and then rounded up a pair of shoes for each of them, en route to the bedroom to wake them up.

"Aiight, y'all," I said as I threw the door open loudly. "Seven forty-five, runnin late, get yourselves up. K'mon, only got fifteen minutes. Let's go. I got your shoes rite here. Grab your klothes. K'mon, let's go."

My sisters started to scramble around frantically, looking for pants and shirts and pulling them on as they found them. It was a comical sight and I tried not to laugh as they scurried around. NeeCee stumbled as she tried to pull on a sock.

"You aiight?" I laughed, unable to hold back. She smiled at me and nodded.

"Oops." She stuck her tongue out and made a silly face and started to laugh, too. It wasn't in NeeCee to be self-conscious of her shortcomings. When everyone else laughed, she laughed, too; the laughter was directed at her, but she wasn't about to be left out of the joke, either.

"K'mon, goofies, let's go," I said again, motioning them toward the door, "Cereal's on the table already, go eat real quick."

They ran for the kitchen, and I picked up their nightgowns, folded them, put them on their dressers, and made their beds as they gobbled down Fruity-O's. I looked at the clock again as I walked back to the kitchen.

I grabbed two washcloths out of the hall cabinet and poured the rest of the water from the first pitcher on them.

"K'mon, time ta go."

They came running out and I handed them each a washcloth.

"Get faces, elbows, knees, and hands. Hurry up."

I opened the door as they scrubbed up. They threw the wash-cloths on the counter and headed outside. I followed them and shut the door after them. We made it: I'd pulled it off. They had no idea that the water was shut off, which meant that they wouldn't mention it to anyone.

I was relieved. That greatly decreased the odds of social services coming around the house, which in turn greatly decreased the odds of any of us getting taken away. We walked quickly down to the corner, getting there just minutes before Nishia's bus arrived. Nishia talked with her friends from school, and when the big yellow bus pulled up, she ran back to me and gave me a hug. Another little girl ran following after her.

"Bree, this Sofia."

"It's nice to meet you, Sofia," I said and put my hand out toward her. She smiled a fourth-grade, gap-toothed kind of smile, put her hand in mine, and shook it. With that, they both giggled and ran into the line of kids waiting to get on the bus.

As usual, Nishia's bus left late, and it was a struggle to get NeeCee back in time for her bus, which stopped in front of the house. I grabbed NeeCee by the hand and started walking her back. NeeCee went to a special ed program for kids with behavioral and emotional problems. She had made great progress, but the program's overseers insisted she wasn't ready to return to the regular track yet. NeeCee should have been in first grade, yet they refused even to put her into a regular kindergarten. Big Mom called weekly and argued with them, to no avail. How was she supposed to ever catch up in a program that was designed to stay behind?

"You goin too fast," she complained.

"We late."

"But I don't wanna run, I wanna walk." She struggled as I yanked on her arm, dragging her and forcing her to keep pace with me.

"I kno," I said, feeling bad, but also knowing that we wouldn't make it if I let her just amble along. She struggled a little more and then gave up and started crying.

We got to the house just as the small bus was pulling up. I held up a finger and ran into the house, still holding NeeCee's hand, still pulling her. She was really wailing now. One of the most lasting characteristics of kids who were born addicted to crack is that they are quick to get frustrated, prone to emotional outbursts, and then incredibly tough to console. I grabbed the washcloth off the counter, found a clean spot on it and carefully wiped the tears off her face.

"No kryin, okay? You a big gurl, an big gurls don't kry."

She nodded her head, pushing me away and trying to quickly wipe away her own tears. I held her hand and walked her down the steps to the bus.

"She got regional services today afta skool," I told the driver and he nodded to me that he knew. NeeCee stepped onto the bus and then turned to look at me.

"Bye, sissy."

"Bye bye, baby, I'll see you tonite, aiight? I kant wait ta hear how much fun you have today at skool."

She turned back around and grabbed the rail, then slowly, step by step disappeared onto the bus. I watched and waved as it pulled away just in case she took a seat from which she could see me. Then, as the bus turned the corner, I stopped and walked inside.

I sat down at the table and poured one half-empty glass of punch into the other to get myself a full glass, and then did the same with the cereal turned mush. Still hungry and tired, I got up and shook the kettle, which still had enough water for me to make a cup of instant coffee. At least we still had gas, but if the water was off, it was a safe bet that the gas wouldn't be far behind.

I had a math test in fifth period. It wasn't just any math test, either. I was pulling a solid D in math because I had missed two quizzes and one test. Now that it was the end of the year, I was running out of opportunities to pull my grades up. Basically, I couldn't miss any more Friday quizzes and had to get at least a B-plus on this test. Otherwise I would fail the class, and I wasn't looking forward to repeating ninth grade. The B-plus wasn't so big a problem: I wasn't bad at math. The problem was my not doing the work and not showing up. But as long at I made it to school today and snuck in the back gate by the end of lunch period, I knew I would be fine. The trick was gonna be getting the money to get the water turned back on and paying the bill before 12:20.

Overall, school seemed stupid. The kids in the smart classes, the enriched and magnet programs, had nothing on me. The schools had tested me, and my IQ scores were higher than most of those kids. But I didn't see what putting in all that work could do for me. I'd seen plenty of unemployed people with high school diplomas and I'd seen plenty of people with diplomas working the same jobs as Momma, making the same pitiful wage, and she dropped out in the fifth grade.

The reality was that I could make more in one day with some rock than Momma made in three days. It was easier work, too.

What I'd really learned in the last four years was from my brothers. I'd been watching for years as Terrell and Taye cooked powder cocaine and baking soda down on the stove to make crack while Momma was out working. I learned what precautions they took to avoid getting caught. You could go away for twenty or thirty years if you got caught with enough on you for them to make a case for the feds. I watched as they wrapped the rocks in plastic and carried the smallest of amounts in their mouths just in case the police came and they had to swallow them. I learned to watch where and how much you sold.

I looked around at the house and thought about Big Mom. She'd been up till one or two in the morning after cleaning offices downtown and then gotten up again, before the sun, to drive twenty minutes over the hill to clean white people's houses and take care of their kids till two in the afternoon, when she came home to take care of us. The hours, whose house she was scrubbing, and whose face she was wiping might change a little from day to day, but basically it was all the same. She worked twelve-hour days and still believed in God and begged us to have faith, stay in school, and do the right thing. I respected her for it, but I wasn't about to follow in her path. I wished I believed that God and school could do more for me than the streets and drug money could, but I'd seen a lot more people get out of the hood and move into nicer areas, get nicer cars and clothes, through drug sales than through education.

I took the last sips of coffee, thick and sludgy where the dried crystals had settled, and put the cup in the sink. Yes, Moms could pray for us and hope we'd make it through God's grace, but for me, I was going to go get mine, and I'd pray that when and if the time came, she and the Lord would understand and forgive me.

I grabbed the latest letter I'd started to Taye from the coffee table and tucked it in my back pocket. I could finish it up after I handed in the math test. Then I rifled through Momma's pile of papers and bills until I found the bold, red letters: NOTICE OF INTENT TO DISCONNECT. I put that envelope in my pocket, too. I took a last look at the pictures of Reverend King and Jesus over the sofa, shut the front door, and locked my problems inside. I always felt different the moment I took that first step alone outside of the front yard. Out there, it wasn't about my family, even if what I did, I did for them. Big Mom's rules didn't apply and her love most certainly couldn't reach me out there. Out there any love you had for people had to be tucked deep inside, far away from where anyone else could see it. The less you thought about anything other than what you were doing, the better.

When I first started making deliveries for Slikk, three years before, he had written me a list of rules and laws of the streets.

In red slanted script, it read:

- Always listen before you talk, look before you walk, and observe before you stalk.

- Silence and observation are one a the major weapons in defense. The detail you don't notice will get you killed.

- Trust no one. Even your own momma will sell you out for the right price or if she gets scared enough.

- War has no room for diplomacy, war is outright vicious. Never expect mercy and never show it.

- The best defense is oftentimes a good offense. Stay ready so that you don't need ta get ready.

- There is no greater sin in war than ignorance. Never speak or act on anything you aren't 100% sure of or someone will expose your mistake and take you down for it.

- During war, or peace, never allow your priorities to be misguided. Never drop your defenses and never get kaught slippin.

- In war, strive for rendering the enemy harmless, disrupting the enemy's alliances, and attacking before you are attacked.

- The injuries that you inflict upon the enemy should be considered such a vicious act of terrorism that the damage inflicted causes the enemy to never consider revenge.

In the time I'd been working for Slikk I'd seen enough, learned enough, that even the more excessive of these rules, the ones I had thought curious or cruel in the beginning, were beginning to make sense.

I now understood that the more the darkness of the streets overtakes you, and the more the city makes you feel hopeless, the more inclined you are to hold on because it's all you have. And as my friends became fewer and my enemies more numerous, the idea of putting in work against the enemy somehow began to ease the pain I felt inside. Sometimes the greatest relief came in knowing that you made them hurt worse than they hurt you.

When I got inside the park I spotted Slikk. He was wearing a khaki suit, sitting back at one of the tables surrounded by some other homies. He had a boom box next to him, bumpin' Public Enemy, the volume and bass turned up as loud as it could go. He nodded to me when I walked up.

"Sounds bool, Damu. That's the new one, rite?"

"Fa sho. Ay, I got a blank tape, ima dub you one real quik." Before I could say anything, he was peeling the plastic wrap off the tape and putting it in the dual cassette portion of the boom box so I could have my own copy.

"Aye," one of the homies I didn't know called to Slikk. "Why she get a free one?"

He was younger then the rest, even younger than me, probably twelve or thirteen years old, with long hair braided neatly into cornrows and light-hazel eyes. Despite his age, he was clearly official, not just a wanna-be gang member. He wore a red T-shirt and jeans with red Nike Cortez, and a neatly folded red flag hung out of his right pocket. No one unofficial could get away with that around people like Slikk.

"Kause lil momma is kuter than you," Slikk laughed, and then everyone else started in, too.

"Daymmmn, Blood, he got chu there, dawg," Freddy chuckled and then punched him in the arm.

I smiled, not too sure that I was in fact cuter than him, but grateful for the compliment and the special attention, and the fact that Slikk would give me a gift like that in front of the homies. The homie I didn't know smiled back and extended a hand.

"What that B like? They kall me YG Dog."

"Bree." I put my hand out and we shook.

Slikk smiled, first at the homies, then at me. "That's a down ass lil bitch, too, don't let that innocent face fool ya. Lil momma an I real kool. That's Taye's lil sis, matta a fact."

The constant fights I was always getting into at school with other girls from different neighborhood sets had earned me a level of respect, despite the fact that I hadn't been officially jumped in like Terrell and Taye had. I felt proud that someone like Slikk would talk me up to the homies, and proud that my name was associated with my brothers'.

"What got chu skippin skool today? Nigga like me might even go ta school if I had ure momma. She scurrey." He pretended to shiver. "I'm already known'n she gonna beat yo ass if she think you fukkin up."

I didn't say anything; the answer didn't matter.

"You in a hurry, then?"

"Kinda," I said.

Slikk smiled and switched the dubbing to high-speed. For a minute, Chuck D, Terminator X, and Flava Flav sounded like Alvin and the Chipmunks. Everyone laughed, and then Slikk hit the radio switch and K-Day blasted Boogie Down Productions.

"Well, let's talk business." Slikk motioned for me to follow him and we walked over to the next set of benches.

"You got any deliveries?" I came right out with it. "I need it, man, like . . . right now. Today."

I pulled the disconnect notice out of my pocket and handed it to Slikk. He took it, pressed it flat against his leg, and read it.

"Letter of intent to disconnect," he said out loud and sighed. He shook his head and handed it back to me.

"I ain really got nothing. I mean, I feel you." He looked me right in my eye, shook his head again. "I jus made all my moves, ain gonna have nothing for at least a few days."

"Aiight." I felt defeated. I couldn't wait.

"You gonna be aiight? What you finna do?"

It was nice of him to ask. I knew it wasn't his problem to solve. In fact, it wasn't supposed to be mine, either. But here we were.

"Dunno. If my social worker find out our shyt turned off, we all finna get bounced."

"Walk wit me." Slikk put his hand on the small of my back. I knew by the gesture and effort that he would help me. The relief rushed through me and I wanted to cry. But I didn't. I couldn't.

We went across the street, through the alley, up three flights of stairs, and down another hallway to the apartment Slikk stayed in. Slikk was young, probably seventeen or eighteen, but he had been from the hood for a long time. His dad came and went, and his mom was one of the first to get strung out on crack and take off. The big homies had taken him in and looked out for him and as a result of that history he was one of the most well-connected people from the set.

"Look," he said as he shut the door behind us, "all I got is some raw."

I nodded my head. Slikk watched me, trying to read my expression to gauge if I knew what he was talking about. I stared right in his eyes to fake confidence and after a minute he smiled at me.

"Aiight, thas a gurl." He shook his head and walked to the corner of the apartment, past an unmade bed, and opened the top dresser drawer. My eyes followed him and then wandered as I looked around the studio apartment. It was dark, with just a few cracks of light coming through the vertical blinds. A red Pendleton shirt lay on the bed and a stack of folded starched red flags rested on top of the dresser. On the wall beside me, five flags were tacked up in the shape of a cross. To the sides of it were pictures and funeral programs, so many of them that they overlapped. I stared at them, fascinated, unable to look away. Some of the people I had seen before, some I hadn't. Some were people I remembered coming over to the house with Terrell, but they were now in pictures that clearly came from different correctional facilities.

"You eat anything today?" Slikk had finished digging through the drawer and was standing next to me. He held a small plastic baggie of white powder in his hand.

"I ain got no money," I said, holding my hand out toward him.

"I'm knowin. Ima front you this time, but don't neva tell no one that, aiight?" He placed the powder in my hand like a salvation, like a pastor handing out Communion, knowing just as certainly that he was saving me.

"K'mon, ima make some food. Aye, you kno, my pops left me in foster kare for a minute, too. That's some shyt." He grabbed a pan out of the sink and put it down on the stove. I noticed the baking soda on the counter and a pot with a mason jar in it still sat on the back burner. I knew that meant he had been cooking cocaine into crack. He reached into the fridge and took out some bologna and began to fry it in the pan.

Twenty minutes later I was walking out the door with a full stomach, an extra sandwich in hand, and the assurance that Slikk would get me my Public Enemy tape later on. The food made me tired and my feet seemed to drag, but it felt good to be full.

Still, I couldn't afford to be slow. I was on a tight schedule and now I had to add processing coke into crack to the schedule. I'd never done it by myself. Plus, he'd fronted it to me. I owed him money back. I couldn't afford to mess up. Pride may be one of the deadly sins, but I still couldn't admit I didn't know what I was doing. Plus, I should know, I'd watched a million times. I psyched myself up as I walked home. By the time I reached the corner, I was almost excited to try it solo.

I pulled out my keys, and then reached into my pocket, touching the baggie of powder, double- and triple-checking that it hadn't fallen out. I looked at the kitchen clock: 10:30.

I knew I was running out of time and that I wasn't going to be able to make the money and take the test. It was a choice at this point, one or the other.

I walked into the kitchen and got out a pot and a mason jar. I knew that Momma would notice if I used the almost empty baking soda that she used to bake with so I took the one out of the back of the fridge and carefully cut it open with a knife. I mixed the powder, baking soda, and water to make a base and began to boil it, to separate out the solids. Then I took down a bowl and filled it with the rest of the neighbor's water from the pitcher, along with some ice from the freezer.

As I watched over my product, pleased with my abilities, my mind drifted from the unpaid bills and my math test to Slikk. I turned back and grabbed the pot holder off the stove and began swirling the jar around.

I turned the front burner off and placed the jar into the bowl of ice water; then, while I waited for my product to cool, I grabbed the plastic wrap, a lighter, and a pair of pliers so I could wrap the rocks up securely and carry them in my mouth.

When I sat down at the table and looked at the clock it was 12:15. In five minutes my teacher would be handing out the test. I didn't care. I should, but I didn't. I looked at the crack waiting to be broken up into pieces. My stomach felt queasy.

I got up and tossed the last of the extra sandwich out the door to Cinque. At least in a few hours I'd be coming home, bill paid, a little extra money in my pocket and able to jump in the shower.

URBAN SURVIVAL

BECAUSE OF ALL my extracurricular activities, and because I had missed that last math test, the summer that I was to turn fifteen found me sitting in summer school. In fact, my school counselor had offered to let me skip summer school and proceed to regular tenth-grade math track the following year since I could easily pass the ninth-grade proficiency, but Momma and the woman in the gray jacket had refused. They said that summer school would do me good and took every opportunity to let me know how disappointed they were, that I was too smart to be failing, and that I needed to focus on what was really important. The woman in the gray jacket also let me know that I was one false move from being sent to a "continuation school" on account of my behavior and lack of concern, and with that would come a change in placement.

I knew at this point that a change in placement meant a group home, and from what I heard, that wasn't good. At all the foster-kid events and picnics, when kids talked about the group homes they stayed at, they made them sound like something between a prison and an orphanage—livable, but institutional. They were places where you got the bare minimum and nothing else. I would do whatever I needed to do to avoid that. I had all the usual conflicts with my family, but I loved them and was grateful for them. I knew that I needed them, and I knew that they, especially Nishia and NeeCee, needed me.

Summer school was more relaxed than the regular school session, although rumor had it they had still confiscated a bunch of guns on the first day of classes. Things in South Central were changing fast. Legendary hustler Freeway Rick Ross had greatly increased the quantities of crack being brought into the hood and put it in the hands of gang members; the guns arrived in mass quantities soon after. The crack fiends were growing in number and desperation, but so was the desperation of the dealers and all the people who had spent a lot of hungry years in the hood, waiting on a chance to finally get some money. Turf became ever more important, because whoever had the most territory to sell in made the most money and wielded the most power. It was a deadly game, the stakes rising continuously in the late eighties and early nineties. South Central became a different, even more deadly, place than it had been just five years ago. The number of homicides and violent crimes was out of control. The police responded by turning the hood into almost military zones. There was an urgency that hung in the air in Los Angeles as evening news programs showed footage of the police using their new battering rams to get through the front doors of dope houses that were popping up everywhere.

Marcus's death and the raid on Rodney's house were just the first in an escalating string of shootings and raids that showed no sign of letting up. It was becoming clear to me that we all had to change our way of thinking, just to survive in this urban Third World. Hard as Momma and the woman in the gray jacket tried to get me to look to the future, all I could see was what was right in front of me, and as the summer passed, the future became harder and harder to envision.

The numbness that I had felt as a young child, when I first came into the system, had returned. I was making money, and I found comfort in that. It felt good to have something in my pockets besides holes and lint, not to have to worry about disconnect notices or an empty fridge. I lined the bottom of my closet with new kicks: Nike Cortez; low and high-top red, white, and black Chuck Taylor All Stars; and Adidas. I kept shoe cleaner on hand and extra pairs of thick red laces so that I could keep them fresh. I bought clothes— Kross Kolors and Dickies—and still stacked some money off to the side hoping that I could get a car—and the Daytons and beat to go with it—when I turned sixteen. At summer school I had almost perfect attendance, and even though I did nothing but sit in the back and draw, I gave the impression that I was turning my life around. In reality, however, I lived my life one rock at a time, dreaming of the joys I could buy.

At the beginning of July, I went to the woman in the gray jacket's office and told her that I decided to opt out. "Opting out" is a term that describes a foster child who has decided to pursue an independent living path, forgoing the social worker's efforts to find an adoptive family for them. It means taking a series of classes that teach foster kids how to cook, fill out job applications, and balance a checkbook, with the understanding that no parental figure is going to be there to advise them of these things later on. To me it meant acknowledging that the best person to rely on was myself.

My fifteenth birthday came on a Friday that year. Denise had disappeared again about two weeks before, so Tiffany and little Tray were back staying with us. Denise would often show up asking if Big Mom could watch them while she ran down to the store or to pay a bill and then fail to return, but she usually popped back up after a week. As the days went by this time, Momma started to really worry, and somewhere in all of that, with no mention of my birthday, and no plans made, I knew that my day was going to pass unnoticed as a result. So on the morning of July 29, Momma still asleep from her night job, I got up, ate some cereal, and slid my backpack over my shoulder for authenticity, just in case my sisters were watching.

"Bye, y'all," I said as I walked out the door. Nishia halfheartedly waved and NeeCee said "Bye" back without taking her eyes off the TV.

As much as I told myself that it didn't matter, I felt bad as the screen door slammed shut behind me. Shake it off, I told myself, just shake it off. I hopped on the bus as it pulled up and made my way toward Rosedale Cemetery to visit Marcus.

I hadn't been to his grave since they laid him in the ground. I missed him and I wanted to visit, but there was this acknowledgment of finality to it that I just hadn't been ready for. The nervousness grew on the bus ride over, and by the time I was walking in I was shaking. The ground felt unstable under my feet as I wandered around, looking for the spot where he was buried. Rosedale is one of the oldest and largest cemeteries in Los Angeles and was the first in the area to be open to all races. Because of that, a number of famous African-Americans were buried there, including Henry Armstrong and Hattie McDaniel. Marcus's mom had chosen it because it was close, but even more because it was filled with the palm trees he loved.

"Hey," I said to the air as I located Marcus's headstone, my voice no more than a quiver. I hadn't been wrong. There was something deeply sad in seeing his grave and knowing, in seeing it, that he really was never coming back. Almost instantly the numbness lifted and tears came. I stood for a while, not knowing what I was supposed to do, thinking about his life and about my own life. These days it was hard not to think about what it would be like to be dead. A big part of me had resigned myself to the idea that I wouldn't live to be any older than Marcus had.

It wasn't long before someone walked past me on their way to visit someone they had lost. How weird it seemed, that whole huge field of people who weren't with us anymore, and everyone in there was somebody's loved one. Bloods, Crips, and civilians. I couldn't help but think of what I looked like, standing there crying. And then, just as quickly as it had lifted, the numbness returned.

I set my backpack on the ground and unzipped it, taking out my PeeChee folder and producing a drawing I'd made of the hills.

"I got somethin for you, Blood."

I looked the drawing over in my hand. I never got to tell Marcus about where the lights end. "Tell me about it tomorrow," he had said, but tomorrow never came for Marcus. I bent down and set the drawing carefully against the headstone, and then I grabbed my backpack and ran out of the cemetery as fast as I could.

There was still some time before school was out and I didn't feel social enough to go to the park or the burger place, so instead of taking the bus, I walked home. When I got back, hot and exhausted, the door was locked. I took out my keys and went inside to wash up. When I came out of the bathroom, Terrell was standing in the living room.

Last I'd seen Terrell was when Rodney's had been raided, and we hadn't really had time or heart to do anything other than talk about how fucked up things were.

"Where's everyone at?"

I shrugged my shoulders. He smiled and put his arms out. I fell into them.

"Well, west up wit it, sis?" He picked me up and spun me in a circle before he put me down.

"I miss you, Tee."

"I miss you too, babygurl, please believe." He kissed my forehead. "Ain't it your birthday today?"

I released myself from his embrace, rolled my eyes, and nodded. "Yea."

"Momma at the store gettin dinner stuff?"

"Naw, she been stressin over Auntie. I guess she forgot."

"Man," Terrell said. He put his hands on my shoulders but avoided my eyes. "I seen Denise the other day walking down Arlington. She's on the rock again, but she's around."

I looked up at my brother's face hovering above mine, again shrugging my shoulders. Terrell was twenty now. He had gotten so tall that my main view was of his chest. I searched his features. He had become a man, skinny with sharp angular features, no traces of boyhood or baby fat left.

"Bree, I gotta tell you something, but you kan't tell Momma. I mean, ima tell Momma, but jus not yet."

Terrell leaned back against the wall, his slouched posture bringing him closer to my height. His eyes were red and puffy, a combination of weed smoking and lack of sleep.

"Shawna's pregnant." He looked up from the floor again. He and

Shawna had been dating since before he had gone to juvie. "A baby, you kno? My baby. Man," his voice trailed off and he shook his head. "I ain told no one yet. You the first. I mean, it's fukked up ta think about. You know Shawna's momma hate my ass. I'm broke. Every bit of money I get Shawna thinks she needs for maternity klothes and baby stuff, and I'm trying to put some up to get us outta here. But all I kan think about is that baby. That lil me: Lil Tera or Terrell Junior. That piece of me that lives on no matter what else happens— flesh of my flesh."

Terrell stood up straight again, and the sentimentality of what he'd said quickly vanished, replaced by the arrogant self-assurance of a general.

"Anyway, I kan get money. My seed ain gonna want for nothing. My kid ain gonna have no raggedy ass shyt like this." Terrell's face showed anger and resentment, the hurt and desperation of a life of going without. He gestured around the house with his hand. "An Shawna wants go ta skool an shyt—she bout sunnthin, and she smart as *fukk*. I figure I'll jus do what I do, slang them rocks until we get her through all that, then I'll quit. Work some lil chump job. Straight life. I told you, ima get us the fukk up out the hood. My kid doesn't need to know nothin bout this place."

He began pacing up and down the hall anxiously. It was hard to think of what to say. I had never heard him talk about leaving the hood. Terrell continued pacing and planning out his soon-to-be family's future. I watched and thought about him raising kids, having his own family instead of being part of ours. Then Terrell stopped pacing, stood directly in front of me, looking deep into my eyes.

"I ain gonna be like our parents, or Denise, pawnin my baby off on someone else to raise." His clenched jaw and firm tone showed his emotions. "An my kid won't *eva* be no banger either, end up dead before his time like Marcus or in juvie like Taye, or drop outta skool like me. My kid, my kid's gonna have options, choices we neva had."

I took a step forward and wrapped my arms around my brother.

"I'm happy for you, Terrell. I know you gonna be a good daddy." I wasn't sure that I really believed it, but I knew he needed to hear it. I let my arms go from around his waist and took a step back. "An, hey, I'll watch my niece or nephew anytime you need."

He smiled, looking relieved.

"Really, you think it's good? You think I kan be a good dad?"

"I dunno. Seem like if you kare enough to worry bout it, you prolly will be. I mean, I don't guess that our parents sit around out there wonderin if they're good parents, right?"

My brother nodded his head, thinking it over. "Yea, I mean ima try. It's funny kause ain like I do shyt fo y'all. And I know you're hurtin. But it don't even really bother me when I think about it. I done gave up on the whole family thing long ago. I mean I tried an tried again when I first got out. Y'all prolly hate me, but I jus hit this point where I got sikk of all Momma's hypocritical shyt, all the demands. I jus figured that karin bout people was a bitch and I get all I need from the block and the homeboys."

My brother's face looked tired. He suddenly looked like an old war vet, eyes deep and full of sorrow. I didn't know what to say. His words hurt, but I understood them, too.

He hung his head low and dropped his voice. "When you write Taye, tell that nigga I'll bee him on the outs. Tell him what I toldt chu. That he finna be an uncle."

His mention of seeing Taye made me think maybe somehow he knew something I didn't. "He getting out? He got a release date?"

"Naw," Terrell said, "but it's juvie, they kan't hold him forever. Worse that happens is at twenty-three they have to let him go."

Taye was seventeen, and six years seemed like a long time. Terrell stood there for a minute, staring down at his hands, then reached in his pocket and pulled out a small brown box.

"What's that?" I asked as he handed it to me.

"Oh," he said, pulling his hand back, smiling now, "you don't want it?"

I slapped his arm and jumped up to grab the box from him. I was excited and relieved. I smiled more at the fact that Terrell had gotten me something—that he remembered—than at the thick gold bamboo hoops he had bought me.

I smiled as I put them on, happy too that when Big Mom asked where they came from I could tell her that Terrell had bought them for me as a birthday gift.

"Terrell?"

I looked up at him. He was smiling at his gift, proud, and I couldn't be mad at what he'd said about it not bothering him that we were doing badly and that he got all he needed from the hood. I bit the inside of my lip and squinted my eyes, gave him my best mad dog stare and then shook my head, the gold earrings swinging and hitting my cheeks. If he really had given up on us, he wouldn't have remembered my birthday.

"What ya think?"

"You're a foo," he said, all teeth, and I hugged him.

"Hey, Bree, when you write Taye, tell him I love him. I love you, too, Blood."

It was silent for a minute. Then he kissed the top of my head and turned to leave. "Don't tell Momma I was here."

"I love you, too, Tee," I said as the screen door shut, and I listened to the sound of his footsteps on the creaky stairs as he left.

I must have been more tired from the heat and the long walk home than I realized, because it wasn't long after Terrell left that I leaned back into the overstuffed couch and fell asleep. When I woke up, Big Mom was shaking my shoulder to let me know dinner was ready and that I needed to go wash up and come to the table. She was clearly in a bad mood, still worried about Denise and further annoyed by the fact that I was sleeping. Naps, according to Big Mom, were for lazy people and babies.

I sat down, still sleepy-eyed at the table. Red beans, rice, and cornbread. Momma said grace and NeeCee recapped an entire episode of *The Smurfs* between bites while the rest of us ate, only half listening. When the food was gone, my sisters ran off to put on pajamas and Tiffany gave Tray a bath. I started clearing the table. The third time I passed by Momma she noticed the earrings.

"Where you get those?" She asked leaning in and squinting to see if they looked real.

"Terrell dropped them off for my birthday." I watched her, knowing the words would sting, and somehow, as she gasped and clasped her hand over her mouth, I didn't feel glad like I thought I would. I felt the same. Her pain did nothing to lessen my disappointment.

"Don't worry about it," I said as she tried to hug me.

"I'm so sorry, baby." She was quickly at the counter fumbling through her purse and pulling out her wallet. "You, you don't have to clear the table. And here"— she pulled the full contents of her wallet out and extended six dollars toward me—"go see a movie or something."

I hesitated.

"Take it." She pushed it into my hand.

A part of me wanted to tell her I didn't need her money and that six dollars wasn't enough for me to do anything but see a movie by myself, which I wasn't going to do. I looked at Big Mom. I knew she felt bad and I loved her, so even though my feelings were hurt, I kissed her and said thanks.

"He seen Auntie, too," I offered, looking down, not wanting to see the look on her face. "She smoked out, but she alive." Momma didn't ask where he had seen her, or how he knew she was smoking, but I watched as her slippered feet shuffled on the floor, approaching me.

"Okay." She kissed my forehead and then turned toward the sink of dishes that would usually be mine to wash.

I went to my room and started a new letter to Taye, glad that the day was almost over. When I got to page five the house started to smell really good. Sometimes, since Momma didn't work on Saturday, she would stay up late Friday night and make muffins to freeze so that we could have them for breakfast or as snacks during the week. I finished what I was writing and walked into the hallway to say good night and maybe get one still hot out of the oven.

"She comin, she comin!" NeeCee, who had apparently been sitting in the hallway on lookout, unusually quiet, ran toward the kitchen, and almost tripped on her nightgown. Nishia looked up from the table, where she was helping Momma finish icing a cake with thick white frosting.

"I made you a card, too!" NeeCee ran over and grabbed my hand, pulling me toward the table.

"Thanks." I looked at Big Mom as Nishia pulled out my chair for me and NeeCee handed me her card.

"You like it?" NeeCee asked as Momma cut the cake and Tiffany served us.

"I love it."

NEVA BE

IN MAY 1989, Shawna gave birth to a baby boy. Little Marcus Terrell, Jr., came into the world with his fists balled up, trembling with the strength of his first scream: a straight soldier. We called the baby Lil Tee because from that first moment, he was the spitting image of his father's looks, expression, and temperament.

Lil Tee's arrival was a blessing on many levels. Most of all because he forced us all to dig deep down inside and find those last traces of hope and joy that we had abandoned. Lil Tee made us want to see the world differently because he was so perfect and innocent and because we all loved him so much more than we could ever love ourselves. We couldn't stand to think that he was doomed to the same lousy choices and opportunities that we had, so we each took it upon ourselves to dig down and give him the best parts of ourselves and to do what we could to change the world, or at least the part of it he saw.

We would sit and watch him sleep, talking about how he was going to have a life full of luxury: air-conditioning in the summer and heat in the winter. He would never be hungry, have the lights cut off on him, or wear hand-me-downs, at least not any so old that other

kids made fun of him. Lil Tee gave us a reason to feel pride, something real and more lasting than the clothes and shoes and jewelry,
or even our neighborhood, which we were realizing more and more
was anything but ours. Lil Tee was something that would last beyond
us and live to tell about what we did. He was the first thing that we
loved that couldn't judge us.

His birth made Shawna eligible for welfare, Section 8, and food
stamps. Since that covered the expenses and Tee was still hustling on
the side, they were living well. They got their own two-bedroom
apartment, a second car, a forty-two-inch television, cable, a stereo,
and pretty much whatever else they wanted. I stayed over there a lot,
too, to help out with the baby. Lil Tee seemed to prefer to be at his
most fussy and awake at night, and then sleep for the first part of the
day. Shawna was a good mom, but she was also grateful for the help.
We'd take turns during the night, sleeping and staying up, holding,
rocking, comforting, and feeding my brother's son, while Terrell was
standing out on the block. He'd return in the morning, eyes puffy,
and place take-out containers full of breakfast on the table.

"Give me my son," he'd say as he pulled his gun and a roll of bills
out of his pants and put them away in a drawer. Terrell would cra-
dle the baby in his big arms and kiss his face, speaking to him in an
unusually high-pitched voice while we ate. "West up, lil man? You
miss ure daddy? What you do all night, huh?"

When we were done eating, Shawna would go lie down for a
nap and Terrell would strap the baby into the car seat and drop me
off at school. Lil Tee was a sucker for the feel and sound of the big
350 block engine. It always managed to rock the baby to sleep within
a few blocks, which Terrell loved because then he could bring the
sleeping baby back home and lie down himself with Shawna. There

is not much that is more physically or mentally exhausting then spending the night out on the block, and even though Terrell was the happiest he had ever been in his life, his fatigue showed in his face. He had developed deep furrows on his forehead and his jaw was perpetually clenched.

"Stop it," I said, pushing my pointer finger into his cheek.

"Stop what?" Terrell turned and looked at me. We had just pulled up in front of my school.

"Biting down like that. That's what you got all them headaches from." Tee clicked his tongue in his mouth and pushed out the air in front of him with his hand.

"Get outta here. You don't know nothin, shorty. Think you all smart an shyt." He shook his head. "Ima bee you later?"

"Yea, I guess Shawna is set on pickin me up at Momma's. She wanna go shopping and get a dress for homekoming. I'll be at ure krib later on after that."

Homecoming was a few days away. Part of me thought the whole thing was stupid and not worth the bother, and part of me wanted to go anyway. Shawna had dropped out of school at the end of her pregnancy and was now studying for her GED. She was the popular, pretty type and had been heavily into school events, much more so than I was. My homecoming dance gave her the chance to live vicariously through me, and she repeatedly insisted that I go. Somewhere around two or three A.M., as she handed the baby off to me, Shawna had decided she wanted to pick me up after school that day and go to the alley to buy a dress. The alley is where anyone in the know, from hoodrats to suburban housewives, to over-made-up, blond, wanna-be models and actresses went to buy designer knock-offs. From the sound of things, Shawna had been plotting this over

the last several hours of feeding, pacing, and bouncing Lil Tee. I figured she would forget about the plan by morning, but when the sun
came up and Terrell was coming in with food, she was still on it. By
then she even knew exactly what style of dress I should get, and how
I should do my hair.

I listened for a minute, and then, as she began to debate dress
colors and types of jewelry, I just tuned her out and let her have her
vision. Shawna was really the first female friend I had, and it felt
good to have someone to gossip with and confide in. I had a hard
time refusing her things she wanted. It didn't mean all that much to
me if I wore a dress or shoes I didn't really like.

Tee had never gone back to school once he got out of juvie. He'd
certainly never gone to prom. He shook his head as I told him about
Shawna's plans. He was laughing, but I knew he was proud. I felt it,
too; we were doing well enough to go shopping. Sometimes we even
bought things we weren't sure we'd ever use, just because we could.

"The big dance, huh? That's what she was karryin on about this
morning." Terrell laughed, leaning back in the driver's seat. "Aiight,
Bree Bree."

"Be up." I patted the door and walked toward the high school as
he pulled off.

I was late, but had forged an admit slip. One of the kids I sold
weed to worked in the attendance office, and I'd given him extra
and knocked money off in return for the stack of admit slips that I
now kept in my backpack. I slipped into the building, down the hall,
through the metal detectors, and took my seat in the back row of
health class. This class was beyond ridiculous. It was all the same shit
they tried to tell us in the independent living classes I had to go to
for foster care. Mostly it focused on how not to get pregnant, or con-

tract chlamydia or HIV, and how fucked up our lives would be if we did. I'd trip sometimes on how much energy they would put into telling us about sexually transmitted diseases. At least those things took a long time to kill you, and having a baby actually made some people try a little harder to stay alive. The teacher would throw out a few quotes that might have struck terror into the hearts of kids in the suburbs, about how much tougher a baby made things at our age, about how much more likely someone with a kid was to drop out and never even get a GED, but in South Central, where half our community dropped out anyway, and where we saw people get shot down and killed every day in the street, it all seemed like bullshit. No one wanted to talk about the real and immediate problems and dangers we were facing just living day to day.

I shut it all out and spent the allotted class time drawing pictures or daydreaming about the shoes and the clothes I was going to buy for myself, my sisters, and Lil Tee. I'd just dropped a flat Benjamin on a Kolor jacket for Nishia. My sisters were now showing a bold confidence, proud to step off the bus with all the nice things they had. They loved looking fresh and showing up the other kids, and I loved watching their pride in what I had got them just as much.

I took out a drawing I was working on. It was a picture of Jesus. A homie looking to get it tattooed on his back had asked me to draw it for him. The picture showed Jesus looking up at the sky, hands held up in prayer, his wrists handcuffed. His robes dripped blood on top of the words "Father Forgive Me," the cloth falling around the edges of the letters. I felt the message. I hadn't had a lot of time to work on it, though, since I'd ditched class the last few days. I took out a pencil and began to shade and shape the image, and by the end of the class it was starting to come alive.

When the bell rang I tucked the drawing into my notebook, put the health textbook back on the shelf on my way out of the room, and made my way to English class. By the time I got there all the books were already gone. Even more of an excuse not to care and do my thing. I took the drawing back out and started in on it again. By the time math class came around, at the end of the day, I was almost done coloring in the blood on the robes with a red ballpoint pen. I was finished, and happy with it, when the bell rang.

I took the bus over to Momma's house to grab some things and wait for Shawna to pick me up. I could hear Nishia and NeeCee fighting before I could even make it up the walkway, and as soon as I had the door open NeeCee was on me.

"It's not faaairrrrrr." She had on some Kross Kolor overalls and a yellow and green shirt I had bought her, one strap done, the other thrown back over her shoulder.

"Give me a minute, daymn. At least let me walk in the door."

The more I was away, the more chores ten-year-old Nishia was having to do in the house. She cooked a little, cleaned a lot, and nagged at poor NeeCee even more. NeeCee, of course, wasn't cool with the fact that now everyone in the house was telling her what to do.

"Tell her to stop bossin me." NeeCee was losing it. Her chin jutted out and her arms flew up and down at her sides.

"Well, tell her to pick up her stuff. I ain tryin to do *everything* round here," Nishia said, stomping a yellow Converse All Star on the floor, interrupting her. I stood in the middle, watching them bicker and yell until they both stopped and looked up at me, waiting for me to intervene.

"Jus knock it off, y'all." I wasn't about to get in the middle.

"Nobody lissens to me," NeeCee started up. "Everyone bosses me." The sadness of the whole situation brought tears to her eyes and she flopped down on the sofa dramatically. "Even Cinque don't lissen to me."

"Cinque doesn't listen to you? Are you serious?" I looked at her, and shook my head. "Give me a break." She sniffled a little and wiped at her face. Nishia ducked into the kitchen and started in on some dishes in the sink.

"Look, shorty, I ain't tryin to kall you out, but you ain a baby. NeeCee, you're eight. You need to help Nishia out round here. She's not that much bigger than you. Aiight? You kan't just expect everyone else to do for you all the time. You kan chill out a minute, an then go in an help her."

NeeCee threw a pillow off the chair and onto the ground. "Well, great," I said, starting my way out of the room, "that kan be the first thing you pick up, then."

I walked into the kitchen and patted Nishia's head on my way into the yard, where Cinque bounced around at the end of his chain. I kept thinking that as he grew older, he would inherit his mother's demeanor, but Cinque seemed pretty set on staying a puppy forever. Tee said I had made him into a pussy, holding and petting him all the time when he was a pup, and while it might have been partially true, most of it was just his nature.

When Shawna pulled up to the house, I held up a finger to let her know I would be another minute. Shawna sighed in clear irritation as I ran inside to grab new clothes and say goodbye.

"The baby's here," I said as I threw the door open. Before it could swing back shut, both girls were running out at top speed toward Shawna's car. I grabbed a shirt, socks, underwear, and pants and

stuffed them all into my backpack and zipped it closed. Confident
that my sisters were outside and not watching, I knelt down on the
floor, pulled out the bottom drawer of my dresser, and reached
through to the wall. My hand groped until I found my roll of bills.
I counted it and divided it in half, putting just over 200 dollars into
my pocket and returning the rest to its hiding place.

I walked out into the hall just as Nishia was walking in. "Why's
ure bag so full?" she asked, looking down at her feet.

"Grabbed some klothes kause I'm goin shopping with Shawna
and then ima stay over there tonight."

"You're always gone." She sank down and sat against the wall. I
wasn't sure if it was legit or good acting, but I felt bad.

"I'll be back tomorrow after skool. I'll even take y'all down to the
movies, aiight?"

"Okay," she said, still not looking up. I had hoped for more of
a reaction, something to make me feel less guilty, but she didn't
even get up. I stood for a minute, watching her, then walked out
the door.

"Go inside, NeeCee. I told Nishia ima take y'all to the movies tomorrow when I get home." Momma had changed the rules on them.
In her abject fear that they would follow the rest of us into the streets,
she had forbidden them to even go outside without her supervision.

"Can I get candy?" NeeCee smiled ear to ear, showing her two
missing teeth.

I shook my head at Shawna. NeeCee was something else. She
knew how to work it. She was going after hers in life. "Yea, you kan
get kandy."

"Thanks, Bree!" NeeCee smiled and took off up the stairs, and
into the house.

"West up?" Shawna said as I got into the car. She was laughing. "That kid is off the chain. You excited ta go shoppin, tho?"

"*You* are." I turned to look in the back at Lil Tee, who was awake, batting at the air, his whole body moving with his jerky efforts. "I gotta find some Kross Kolor shirt for Nishia, too. She buggin out," I said, turning back around, and settled into the seat as the engine started up.

Thirty minutes later we were walking around the alley, Tee fussing, grabbing at everything, going from one set of arms to another while we looked at countless dresses. I couldn't blame him. It was getting boring, even for me. Finally I tried on a dark burgundy one. It wasn't my favorite, but Shawna smiled, content. "That's the one," she said, and so it was.

I tried to hide that I had a crush on Slikk, but Shawna knew, and by teasing me about it she had let Terrell and most of the rest of the neighborhood know as well. It made me feel even more embarrassed and nervous when I was around Slikk, but he always acted so confident and kind toward me that my anxiety quickly faded. I couldn't remember having ever felt that way about anyone before.

On the way home, I asked Shawna to take the dress back to the apartment and drop me off at the park. She smiled and nodded.

"What?" I looked at her. She was smirking. "I gotta drop off a drawing I did."

"Mmmmmm-hmmmm." She looked at me out of the corner of her eye.

"I do. You want me ta show you the drawing?"

"Nope," she said, pulling up to the curb. I took my binder out of the backpack and the drawing out of the binder and held it up to her face.

"I see it. I see it," she said, but then added, "But I ain't stupid, either. You gone ask him, right?"

"Yea, yea. Ima ask him," I said, getting out of the car and gesturing down at my backpack. "Ima leave all that here. I'll be over later."

"Ask him," she said and laughed as she pulled away.

Once inside the fence at the park, I delivered the drawing. The homie looked at it, shook his head, surprised, and passed it around the table. I listened as it went around. A few of the homies reached across the table and shook my hand. "Daymn, that looks good—you did that?" they asked; or, "Shoot, draw *me* sunthing." I smiled and thanked them. I won't lie: it felt good to be good at something and to have people recognize it.

When I spotted Slikk over by the park building I excused myself. The homie held a fifty out toward me for the drawing.

"Good lookin out," he said.

"Fa sho, good lookin on the bread." I shook his hand with one hand while I took the bill with the other.

On the walk across the park I went over what I was going to say in my mind. I couldn't believe that I was that much of a girl that I was getting nervous and stressing over this sort of thing.

"What up, Miss Lady?" He smiled at me and I forgot everything for a split second, smiled back, and then got nervous all over again.

"Aye." I sat down on the table a good foot and a half away from him. "I was thinking bout going to this homekoming dance, you know?" I looked at him and then dropped my eyes back down quickly, focusing on a Fritos wrapper that lay crumpled on the grass. "Well, I kouldn't think of anyone else to go with."

I looked over at Slikk again. He sat on the bench, looking at me, confused. I got nervous and I could feel my stomach churning under the pressure. I started to sidestep quickly.

"I mean it's no big deal, if you don't wanna go. I'm not even sure I wanna go. Jus, Shawna, she really wants me to go."

Slikk stood up. I hadn't even thought about how I would feel if he said no, and now here we were. I was so sure he was about to walk away without saying anything, but instead, he stepped up on the bench and sat down next to me on the table. I could hear him breathing in and out.

"Hey, mama, you really askin me kause you kan't think of anyone else? Or you askin me kause you wanna ask me?" I turned my head and looked at him. His eyes looked different, softer than usual. He looked far from gangsta. He looked like I could hurt him as easily as he could hurt me.

"I guess the second one."

He smiled at me, then leaned in and kissed me on the forehead. "What day, then?"

"Friday."

"Aiight," he said getting up, "meet me here Friday at noon."

"It ain't till night."

"I know," he said tilting his head and smiling. People were calling him from the tables impatiently. I loved his face. There was something about it that just made me feel tender and want to hug him, to seek him out in hard times when I needed someone to hold me. I wouldn't say that he was handsome; that wasn't it. He had a big, kind of square head that seemed large on top of his tall, too-thin body, but there was something to him that made him seem more appealing than the other, more proportionately handsome guys. He leaned over and gently kissed me again, this time on my lips. "Just meet me here at noon."

His lips tasted like Olde English and chronic smoke. I nodded my head and watched him walk across the park, pants sagging hard, hanging over his shoes and dragging slightly on the yellowed grass. When he got to the table, the homies were laughing and obviously teasing him. He looked back over at me and smiled. In a city where they are quick to say "Fuck a bitch," it was a nice acknowledgment. I smiled back, then started over to Tee and Shawna's crib.

Friday, after second period, I walked down the hallway amazed at how empty the school seemed. Usually, between periods, the narrow halls and staircases were packed with students struggling to make it to their next class, bumping into walls and each other, but a lot of people had used the dance as an excuse to miss school. I held my hands out at my sides, reaching out to the walls of lockers on either side, and smiled. I couldn't wait till noon.

When I got to the park, I started looking for Slikk before I even passed the gate. He saw me first, though, and was already approaching me when I spotted him.

"You soft, my nigg," Freddy called after him as he made his way to me.

"What's ure boy sayin?" I joked with him. He reached over and took my backpack from me, slinging it over his shoulder.

"Ah, I ain't trippin," he smiled at me, batting the air with his hand. "They know I ain't soft. K'mon, ma, let's get outta here."

"You wanna know where we goin?" he asked as he shut the door of his silver Caprice and we began to roll toward Crenshaw.

I nodded.

"Well, I ain't tellin ya."

I leaned back and watched the streets roll by. "You bee that?" I said, pointing out a piece of graffiti that had been X'd out and tagged over. "They trippin."

"Shhh," Slikk placed his finger over his lips. "Today, don't worry bout all that. Today, we gonna jus do you kause this Lady Slikk stuff's no easy gig, feel me? We gotta make sure you look just right."

I thought for a minute.

"I'm Lady Slikk?"

He looked at me for a second, furrowed his brow, and then looked back at the road. "What, you ain't my baby?"

As the car slowed to stop at the light, I leaned over and kissed him, all that he was saying and trying to do suddenly clear to me. "So," I said, slowly pulling back, "where ARE we going?"

"Get ure hair an nails done." He bit on his lower lip. His eyes were soft, almost as though he could cry all the hurt out if he let himself. I reached up and touched his cheek, but as the light turned green he turned his head away and sped off down the Shaw.

At the beauty shop I sat down while he talked to the lady at the counter. I flipped through a magazine, pretending not to watch as he pulled a roll of bills out of his pocket and peeled three twenties off the top. The lady flirted with him and laughed as he gestured with his hands around his head trying to show her what to do with my hair.

He sighed as he sank into the small sofa next to me, like what he had just done had been exhausting. He held his hands, palms pressed together, in his lap and looked down at them. "They gonna do something nice with ure hair an nails, aiight?"

I smiled. A lot of females expect boys to do things like this for them, but it just wasn't in me to think someone would not only pay for me, but also arrange the whole thing. I was speechless.

"Hungry?" he asked, turning his head to look at me. I was, but for some reason I didn't want to admit it, so I shook my head no.

"Well, I'm starving." He showed an exaggerated flash of teeth, trying to be cute. "Church's, Johnny Pastrami, or Dollar Soul Food?"

"Pastrami's bad for you." I looked at him and stuck my tongue out, teasing.

"Ooh shyt, Snow White's gone Muslim now, huh?" He jumped up and tried to avoid a playful slap I threw in his direction.

"I ain't Muslim"—I was laughing—"and I don't *think* pastrami is pork, either, is it?"

"Hell if I know. It's good, though, and just for all that, that's what ima go get, too. Want one Ms. Shabazz, or you jus want a bean pie or sumthing?"

"Wooow. Naw, I'm bool. I'll have a sandwich or whatever you wanna get. Want some money?"

"Naw, I got ya," he said and walked out the door. After a few minutes, the lady from the front desk walked me back to a seat where someone else started cutting and filing my nails roughly.

By the time Slikk came back in carrying the grease-soaked paper bag, my nails were dry and they had started on my hair. He held the bag out to me.

"Where's yours?"

"Ate it on the way. Had to stop off and handle some business."

I held up my nails.

"They look nice." He smiled at me proudly as he reached in his pocket and pulled out his pager. "Hold up, I gotta go make a kall real quick. I'll be right back." He placed the bag of food by the side of the chair and walked out the front door. In twenty minutes, when he walked back around the corner, I was sitting outside, hair done, halfway through my sandwich.

"Koo"—he reached a hand out to help me up—"you done. Ima take you home to finish getting ready then."

"I mean, I'm moreless ready. I just need ta get my dress on an do some makeup. You done doin business? Kan we drive around a lil while?"

I missed driving around with Marcus. I missed talking and watching the neighborhoods change, and the freedom of letting my mind wander.

"Okay, mama, where you wanna go to?"

"Turn on West Adams." I gave directions as we drove. "Straight, straight. Aiight, Arlington. Now park."

"You tryin to go to Second Avenue Park?" He looked confused.

"Naw, look at that house." The house I pointed at was referred to as Elegant Manor. It was a brick-and-wood mansion of a place with small balconies and bay windows that sat on over an acre. It had been a lot of things over the years. When the original owner died, her son inherited it and turned it into a nightclub. After too many noise and nuisance complaints, the city revoked its permits and shut it down, but it continued to operate anyway. Parts of it were trashed, and rows and rows of junked-out cars sat in its side yard, including a fleet of delivery trucks from the forties, but to me it seemed a fairy-tale place. "Ima buy that house one day."

Slikk looked at me for a minute without talking. "Fa sho"—he nodded and pointed up to the top-right-hand window, "Cinque be up there barkin at all the people as they walk by."

In that moment it was done; I let go and I fell in love. In Slikk I found the only person, outside of Marcus, who saw my dreams and played along instead of telling me I was stupid or unrealistic. I thought about it and scooted closer, resting the back of my head against his chest. He wrapped his arms around me and we sat for a while on the hood of the car, looking at the house and dreaming of a life where we had a future.

PROSPECTS

"BREE BREE," Freddy waved to me, motioning me to come over and talk to him. He and a few of the homies were sitting out in front of the chicken place, leaning up against the wall of the parking lot. Patches of bricks were painted all different shades of off-white where gang members and business owners had battled it out. Even from twenty feet away you could see the layers of graffiti and paint overlapping. I quickened my step a little and smiled as I walked up to them.

"West up, west up, west up?" I gave Freddy a small sucker punch to the arm and then hopped up to sit on the ledge of the waist-high wall next to where he stood. At five-foot-nothing I was actually taller sitting. "Kloser to eye level," I said and winked at him.

Freddy smiled at me. "You're a fool. You know that, right?"

"Why I gotta be a fool?" I raised my eyebrows and tilted my head. Freddy just shrugged. "Aye, I learned it from you, big homie. I learned it from watchin you," I said, mocking the newest in the series of commercials from the "Just Say No to Drugs" campaign in which a father finds weed in his son's room and irately questions the boy about where he learned to do drugs.

Freddy looked around at the homies. "You all know Bree, b.k.a. Lady Slikk." It had been over a year since the homecoming dance, and Slikk and I were still going strong. I smiled, proud of the title, and extended my hand to the one homie I hadn't met before.

"West up, Blood?" he said, chewing, one hand over his mouth, the other extended out to me. "I got madd respect for ure man. He good people, so you must be aiight, too." He gestured at a box that sat near me on the ledge. "Pie?"

One of the local bakeries made sweet potato pies for a bunch of L.A. restaurants and sold off the burnt slices early in the morning for a quarter apiece. They weren't really burnt, either, just slightly browner than the higher-end restaurants would accept. The new homie had about two pies' worth piled up in the box. I reached in and took out a piece.

"Good lookin out," I said, breaking off the burnt edge of crust and throwing it out to the curb for the pigeons. I bit into it and smiled as I thought of Big Mom.

"Lemon extract," she would always say whenever she tasted other people's pies. "That's my secret ingredient. That and just a touch of cardamom in with the allspice. That's what makes mine so much better." She said it like she was the only one to ever think of it, and like it was the kind of information that could save your life someday.

Freddy held a cup out to me. I took it, looked inside and, unsure, sniffed it. "Apple juice and Henny?" I scrunched up my nose.

"Hell, yea," he said.

"Naw, man"—I handed it back to him—"that's nasty. Plus I'm bout ta go to school." I wasn't about to have a teacher smell alcohol on me and suspend me—or, even worse, call Momma. I could probably get away with it, but I didn't want to risk anything. I had a year left of school, and even though I was sometimes apathetic about it, I knew how long Momma had been waiting on seeing one of us finally get that diploma.

Freddy looked at his watch and then reached out for the cup. "You know you late, right?"

"Yea. I got an admit slip."

Freddy laughed. "Oh, like that? You got a slip without goin in to the office, huh? Now, *that's* the shyt you learned from watchin me pimpin."

"Yea, I don't know bout all that," I said, meaning that I wasn't really sure I was pimpin', not that Freddy wasn't ahead of the game, but instantly I realized how it sounded when everyone else started laughing. "Naw, I just meant"—I could barely talk through the laughter—"I meant I ain't pimpin like that. Sorry, homie."

Freddy nodded his head, trying to look serious. "Kome on, smart ass, I'll give you a ride.

"You a trip," he said as he grabbed a button-down shirt off the passenger seat and threw it into the back so I could sit down. We talked as he drove me the few blocks and he shook his head as he slowed to a stop in front of the school. "You got a smart mouf, for real. You a down ass lil bitch, Glo-worm. When you get sick of Slikk, holla at me. See, nigga like me kan see the potential in a female like you."

Yeah, the homies got at me sometimes, but never in a way that sounded serious. If I told Slikk, he would probably react in the worst kind of way, as though it were a personal affront to him. I was never sure the right way to respond, so I pretended just to blow it off, treating it as though they were joking, and throwing whatever game they threw at me right back at them.

"Oh yea?" I said, grabbing my admit slip out of my pocket and trying to straighten out the folds against the dashboard so that it looked crisp and new, or at least crisp and new enough. "*What's my potential?*"

"Girl like you kould do a lot."

"Mmmm-hmmm, sounds good," I said, getting out and shutting the door. "Thanks for the ride, homie."

He nodded, "Right, right. Be up, Miss Lady Slikk."

I thought about the difference between what my real potential was and what someone like Freddy thought my potential was as I walked up the steps, through the metal detectors, and down the hall.

"You got your homework?" my English teacher asked as I tried, unsuccessfully, to slip into the back of the class and take my seat unnoticed. I shook my head no. "Admit slip?"

I nodded and held it out. She walked up the aisle and took it, looking it over as she sat back down at her desk. "See me after class. I need to talk to you for a few minutes."

The class let out an echoing "Ohhhh" as I leaned back in my chair, trying to at least look like I didn't give a fuck. I sat through the last half of class dreading the impending conversation and thinking of what to say to end it as quickly as possible.

"Yo, teach," I said walking to the front as the bell rang, "what's up?"

"Why were you late?" she asked, looking through a pile of old assignments, pulling out one and then another. I had been absent when she had handed them back in class. They were A's. I always got A's on the work I turned in.

"I had ta get my lil sisters to skool, you know?" It was a lie, but a good, solid excuse, not really anything you could argue with too much.

She sighed. "Well, you have to get yourself to school, too. You're missing . . ." She paused as she looked through her grade book and counted up the blank squares. "It's five assignments now."

"Yea, I jus need ta sit down one weekend and katch up. Ima do it, though. Just been busy the last few weeks."

She took her glasses off and set them down on the desk. "Do you ever think about the future, Bree?"

I couldn't quite figure out what she was talking about, or why. "Sure. I mean, I said ima do the homeworks."

"No," she said, raising her voice slightly. "About *the* future, *your* future, about what you're going to do with the rest of your life?"

"I mean . . ." I paused and looked at her, trying to think of how to explain it. "I'm basically doing it right now."

"Doing what?"

"Living my life."

She looked down at her grade book, at the five blank squares amid the row of A's. "You're a really smart girl. You could go to college."

I started laughing.

"The idea of college is funny?"

Suddenly I was the one who was frustrated with the conversation. It didn't make any sense to me that she could sit there and not grasp the reality of what went on in the community around her. I tried not to yell at her, tried to keep my voice calm and steady as I spoke: "Kollege takes bread. I mean, if you think me or my people got that kinda money, you krazy. Plus, I'm the only one in my fam-

ily to make it past tenth grade so far. My people gonna be happy as
fukk if I even graduate from here."

She looked at me as though she hadn't heard a word I had said.
"There are all sorts of grants and scholarships available. I'd be more
than happy to help you look into it as an option. You would probably be eligible for a lot of help and only have to take out a few student loans."

"Look, man, I only know one person went to kollege, and he
workin the same weak security job as someone else I know who
doesn't even read. I ain't tryin to take out no loans when there ain't
no jobs round here anyway to pay em back."

"You don't have to stay around here; that's the beauty of it.
College could help you get out. You could apply to schools in other
cities—other states, even."

I looked at her like she was crazy. Clearly she didn't know or understand me at all. I thought quickly about Marcus and about where
the lights ended, and then I thought about Momma and Slikk and
my little sisters. They needed me here. They had never given up on
me, so how could I ever consider leaving them? I thought about all
the people I knew, and the streets that I knew and the way I knew
my way around L.A., and then I remembered what Marcus said to
me just before he died.

"I am L.A. Ima die in this bitch," I said proudly.

"But you don't have to. You have other choices."

I ran my hand over my face. I knew she was trying to help, and
since I had to sit in the classroom with her for the rest of the year, I
needed to keep things civil.

"Just think about it. Roll it over in your head."

"Yea, aiight," I said just to end the conversation. "I'll think about it."

She smiled. "Good. Go ahead and get to your next class, then. No need to be late for that, too."

I turned and was almost out the door when she called after me to remind me to get my missing homework assignments in. My head and my heart and my stomach hurt, and I wasn't even completely sure why. Instead of going to my next class I left the school and caught the bus over to Slikk's apartment.

I had to knock on the door a few times before I heard him come to the door.

"Who dat?"

"It's me, baby. Open the door." There was the sound of one, two, then three locks and the chain being undone and then the door flung open to reveal Slikk, standing in his boxers, still half asleep.

"You aiight?" he grabbed my arm and quickly looked both directions down the hallway before pulling me into the apartment and redoing all the locks. "Why ain't you in school? Something happen?"

"I'm fine, baby." He walked up to me, looking deep into my face to make sure I was telling the truth, and then put his arms around me. I reached my arms around his waist and held tight, pulling him tightly against me, instantly feeling a little better.

"You sure?" he asked, leaning over and kissing the top of my head.

I nodded, my head rubbing against his bare chest. "Yea, I'm sorry I woke you up. Long night last night?"

"Yea, long night, but that's how it be sometimes."

I looked up at him, half naked and sleepy-eyed. "Kan I lie down with you for a while?"

"Yea, we kan do that." He rubbed his hands up and down my arms as I leaned back against him and then he walked me over to the bed. He knew I was upset, but he knew better than to push it too much. I hated questions. I never much asked them, and answered them even more rarely. "Kome here, baby." He lifted up a side of the blanket and we crawled under. I pushed my head up against his chest and he traced his finger along my neck above my shirt collar.

"You wanna tell me what's wrong?" His voice sounded muffled as though it was a strain to stay awake and try to speak. I shook my head no. "No?" He started to fall asleep, and then, with a slight jerk, started to talk again. "You're smart, baby. You kan't just be ditchin skool like that all the time. You almost there, you should go ahead and graduate, get that diploma."

"I know. I'm gonna." I closed my eyes. "You really think I'm smart?"

"Hell yea you're smart." He pulled away from me and propped himself up on his elbow so that I had to look up at him and see his face, see how serious he was when he said it. "I ain't never met a female like you before. You always make me think, and you always telling me something I didn't know."

"You think I kould go ta kollege? I mean, you think I'm that smart?"

"I don't think—I *know* you are. You should go ta skool, kollege or whatever. My one auntie got some nursing degree an moved to Atlanta. Makes good money, too, I guess." Family was an even harder subject for Slikk than it was for me. "I don't wanna do this shyt forever anyway, Bree Bree. I'll help you get thru skool, and then once you done I kan get out the game, get some lil security gig. Fukk it, man, I don't kare. I'll work at Foot Locker."

He laid back down and I snuggled closer to him. He let out a deep sigh and patted me on the back. I closed my eyes and listened as his breathing became slow and steady and then turned into a slight snore.

My thoughts ran wild. It was easy for someone who didn't go to school to think I could make it in college, but I wasn't so sure. I remembered Big Rodney sitting down and reading half of a big thick book in an afternoon. It took me that long to read one chapter, if I even got that much read, and then after I set the book down, I would only remember about half of it. Going to college would mean going to classes every day, and turning in all the work on time. It would mean giving up on what I was doing now and trying to keep up with kids who had been preparing for college all their lives. I squeezed my eyes shut and listened to Slikk's heartbeat until I fell asleep.

The next few months moved quickly, and although I didn't tell anyone, I thought a lot about college and all my different options. I knew I had to be a hundred percent sure of what I wanted to do before I could tell anyone. If I chose to do it, I would have to follow through, just to keep my word and my pride intact. I also needed to build up my confidence so that if anyone told me I couldn't do it I would be able to look them in the eye and tell them they were wrong. The thing is, college was this big, almost unimaginable idea. It felt so far beyond my reach that I couldn't really picture myself doing it, yet it seemed to be enough within my reach that I knew I should at least try.

I tried not to let my thoughts distract me too much, because, as always, the game continued all around me, and more so than ever.

The minute you stop noticing the details, someone, be it the Crips or the police, was there to catch you slippin'. The LAPD had started a program called CRASH, which stood for Community Resources Against Street Hoodlums. It was the CRASH team's job to get to know the gang members and their dealings, and, as the world found out (though not till a decade later), they used any means necessary to achieve their goals. It was commonplace in South Central to hear about people getting beaten up or robbed of whatever drugs or cash they had—by police. Sometimes, the police would try to finish the job off by dropping their victims in a rival neighborhood. As a result of their presence, and also thanks to increased poverty and racial tensions, the block was hotter than it had ever been before.

Suddenly the thought of maybe leaving L.A. made me see things from a new perspective. Most of the people who were making enough money were finding places to live outside the constant dangers of South Central—"in the cut," they would say, where at least once they handled their business in the city, they could go home and sleep without watching their backs. I began to look around and wonder if I really wanted to spend the rest of my life running around in the streets, selling dope, making deliveries, and playing different roles in robberies, in cons. I was tired of watching and hearing about murders, and I was tired of seeing people go to jail. I began to wonder if I really did have other prospects or if it was my fate to die in L.A.

Then, in March, as the weather heated up and I started to prepare to graduate, a series of events happened that forced all of us to rethink our world, to question whether there was any real justice out there for poor folk.

The month started out with the Rodney King beating—though, really, outside of the fact that the police got caught in the act on videotape, there was nothing out of the ordinary about the incident to us. Police brutality happened every day throughout South Central, Compton, and Watts, just as it had for a long time. There was nothing shocking about it. The real turning point came just thirteen days later when fifteen-year-old Latasha Harlins walked into the Empire Liquor Market on South Figueroa and put a bottle of orange juice into her backpack, then walked toward the counter, with the money in her hand to pay for it. The store owner, Soon Ja Du, began to yell and accuse Latasha of stealing, grabbing her shirt as she tried to run away. A scuffle ensued and Latasha ended up hitting Du in the face, and then, as she tried to leave, Du shot her in the back of the head, killing her.

The orange juice had cost $1.79.

The store's security footage was leaked to the press and played often, alternating with the King video. I would sit up at night after Shawna took Lil Tee to bed, or while Momma was at work, and watch first the ten o'clock and then the eleven o'clock news, the footage of Latasha getting shot in the head running over and over again, while the tension and outrage built within me, as it did with every other sane human being in Los Angeles.

It was at about that time that Terrell and Shawna started fighting all the time, and I usually found myself caught in the middle of it. Shawna felt that Terrell was always gone, leaving her to take care of the baby and do everything for the house. Terrell was mad because, as he saw it, the only reason he was gone so much was because Shawna was always blowing money on things. It got so bad that the only times they spoke were when they were fighting. By the beginning of my senior year, Shawna packed up, took Lil Tee, and moved back in with her mom.

Terrell took it hard. At that point he couldn't stand to be near Shawna, but he still loved his son. What made matters worse was that Shawna would barely even pick up the phone when we called, let alone help us set up times to see Lil Tee. She was trying to get at Terrell, and it was working. Lil Tee had brought out the kind, loving side of my brother, and without his son, Terrell withdrew from everyone. He threw himself full force into the hood and street, hustling just to stay busy. When he wasn't doing that, he was at the apartment, drinking and smoking weed until he passed out. I wished so much that I could hug him or talk with him about things, but that wasn't really Terrell's style anymore, so instead I went by every few days and tried to clean up and at least make sure he ate something other than Hot Pockets and Ramen. That was about the most Terrell would let anyone do for him, and although it broke my heart, Big Mom said that we had to face the fact that he was a grown man and was entitled to handle his own pain the way that he saw fit.

"Just pray for him," Big Mom told me. "The only way Terrell is gonna let you hold him is in prayer."

I felt so torn about everything in my life. My family needed me, and Slikk and I were talking about maybe getting married and having some kids of our own. I liked the idea of something that was half-me and half-him running around, but I couldn't help but to be worried about the future, too. Anyone in the game knows the odds are always good that you'll end up in the funeral home or doing life. One of my biggest fears was having to raise a son to be a man on my own. One day on my way home from school, as the deadlines were getting close, I decided to secretly purchase money orders for the application fees and begin the process of writing out my applications for college. I told myself it was just to give myself more options. Within a few days I sealed the envelopes and applied to four schools: two in California, one in Arizona, and one in Oregon. From there, I settled in for the long process of waiting. I still didn't tell anyone that I was close to what I was doing: not Big Mom, not my homies, not even Slikk. The only people I told were the two teachers I had to ask for recommendations, and that was just out of necessity. I wanted to see what the colleges had to say before I got anyone's hopes up.

I began to check the mail every day, rushing to Big Mom's house to make sure that if the envelopes came, I'd be the one to find them. When the first letter came from UCLA, I took the thin envelope back into the bedroom and opened it. All I had to read was the first line, which said that although they thanked me for my interest, they regretted to inform me that I did not meet their criteria. I crumpled it up and shoved it in the back of my top drawer, where I knew no one would ever look. It wasn't beneath Nishia to borrow some socks or a shirt on the sly, but I knew she would never take my underwear. I tried my best not to think about college after that. Slowly, the rest of the letters showed up, and as I saw their thin envelopes, I crumpled them up without even opening them and put them with the other one.

Soon after I got the last one, I really did stop thinking about college. I figured Slikk was my future, and I was pretty much okay with that. I thought a little about looking into one of the nursing programs he kept mentioning, but there was still plenty of time for all that. They weren't like college, where you had to apply months in advance.

Then on April 29 of my senior year, an all-white jury found the police innocent in the Rodney King beating and the city rioted for five days. Even after the flames began to die down, living in the city just went from hard to harder. In many spots, everything burned to the ground. You couldn't find a market or a laundromat. Over 13,000 soldiers were deployed to the city to maintain order, and a curfew was put into effect. The news reporters and commentators took every opportunity to call us savages, and point out as proof the fact that we had burnt down our own community, and with that, Los Angeles suddenly hit a standstill.

Although some of the news programs featured the feel-good efforts of a chosen few to rebuild the First AME Church, that little photo op was hardly the norm. Anyway, one church didn't begin to make a dent in our needs. Most of the city stood barren; businesses were scared to build within the urban center and some neighborhoods found themselves without even the basic necessities. The things that did get rebuilt looked different and clearly expressed a reaction to recent events, with their addition of thick security gates and bulletproof glass. We did what we'd always done and made the best of a bad situation, trying to adjust to living in what felt like a police state. Terrell and Slikk kept slanging, Taye was still locked up, the little ones kept growing, I kept going to school, and Momma kept on working and praying. We maintained like that for about a month, and then, as we began to adjust to the new obstacles and changes, we got hit with a few more.

Nineteen ninety-two was a record year for homicides in the City of Angels, and my family was one of those that helped make up the statistics. A month before I graduated, Terrell became one of nearly 1,100 killed in Los Angeles that year.

Shawna had started dating someone else, and although you couldn't really fault her for that, when Terrell got a glimpse of his son holding some other guy's hand, he just flew off the handle. After that, the only way Shawna would let him see Lil Tee was when she dropped him off with Big Mom. She said that she was scared of Terrell's anger and that she never again wanted to be in a room alone with him. Despite the friendship I once shared with Shawna, it was hard to feel anything positive toward her as I'd watch Terrell sit out on Big Mom's front steps, looking at his gold watch every two minutes, waiting for the chance to see his son for a few hours.

But just as sure as Shawna knew the routine, and knew that Terrell would be waiting on the steps, so did the Crips. As Slikk and Freddy had taught me, back when I started in the game, the love that Terrell had in his heart became his weakness: he was killed while sitting out in front of Big Mom's house, waiting to see his son for a weekend visit, shot by some little BG Crips looking to get their stripes and move up in the ranks.

Growing up in South Central, you learn to accept the violence. You attend the funerals and know that life, truly, is fleeting. But no matter how often you say, "Next funeral, one of us won't be standing here," nothing prepares you for what it feels like to lose a member of your family. For the next few weeks I walked around in a haze of emotion and chronic smoke. All the dreams I'd had before of shoes, cars, and clothes turned to dreams of revenge.

Yet for all the murderous thoughts I was having, it was Slikk who got arrested for attempted murder. He hadn't done it, and they had no proof, except for the testimony of an elderly woman who, tired of seeing him out on the corner across from her house selling dope, was willing to say she had seen his car fleeing moments after a shooting that had left two people dead.

When I found out, I went to his apartment and buried my head in his pillows. They still smelled like him. I couldn't believe I'd lost both Terrell and Slikk. An OG told me once, every time someone uses a gun at least two people lose their lives: one goes to the funeral home and one goes off to do life in the pen. I looked around the apartment. I couldn't even imagine a life without Slikk in it.

My pager went off. Momma. I put it on silent and placed it on the floor next to the bed. I knew she was worried and upset and I felt ashamed of myself for putting her through that, but I needed a last time alone with Slikk's things. I needed to think.

I got up and walked around the apartment, picking up different things and then putting them back down, when suddenly something on the kitchen counter caught my eye. It was the copy of *Manchild in the Promised Land* that Big Rodney had given me. Slikk had asked me to lend it to him. He must have been reading it that morning, while eating breakfast.

I thought about Rodney, how long he'd been locked up and how he was never coming back. That's when the reality of it hit me and the tears came. After a few days, I dragged myself back to school. I wasn't about to let poor attendance keep me from graduating. I knew if there was a heaven for us ghetto kids, my brother and Marcus were watching me, and I knew how much it would hurt them if I didn't go get that piece of paper. Plus, suddenly, I wanted that piece of paper more than ever. I wanted something, anything that could put me on a path to something else. I thought about how Terrell dreamed, in good times, of getting his family out, and how Marcus never made it past the lights. I decided I really would look into one of those nursing schools.

When I got to Big Mom's house, I was surprised to find the door unlocked and her sitting on the sofa, looking at a stack of papers. She had the strangest expression on her face, not happy or sad. She looked confused.

She picked up the top paper and held it out to me. The stationary had an official-looking letterhead. I took it in my hand, which shook, making it hard to read.

"Why didn't you tell me you applied to college?" Now I was the one looking confused.

"What?"

I quickly read the first paragraph. After all the no's, I had been taken off the wait list and accepted. It was a yes.

"Momma," I said, clutching the paper, both of us in tears and yelling at the same time. "Momma, I got in!"

AFTERLIFE

I SAT ON the hood of my car in the visitor's parking lot. The shiny black paint absorbed the Central California sunshine all around me, upping the temperature even more. The area in and around Bakersfield is hot like nowhere else I have ever been. It is a vast expanse of dusty farms, rednecks, and migrant workers, among which, at some point, the powers that be decided to build prisons. Concentrating the facilities within the corridor between Highway 99 and I-5 actually made sense. It eases the transport of inmates from place to place, and with the almost constant gang and race riots inside, it is necessary to be able to separate incarcerated enemies quickly. The San Joaquin Valley has more prisons concentrated within it than anywhere else in the United States. Between family members and friends, I have sent mail into all of them and been inside the visiting rooms of most.

I was at Wasco State Prison. The small town consisted of a hotel, a Rite Aid, and a small family-style restaurant. There wasn't even a gas station. If you needed gas you had to haul yourself the eight miles back to the highway. As the water crisis in California grew, the farms became more and more depressed-looking. It was easy to see that the area welcomed the business and jobs the prisons brought. I looked around, thinking of the vast political problems of the state, from the inner cities to the farms. California broke a lot of people's hearts and dreams, and the town of Wasco was just one small place where people were forced to look each other in the face and realize it: rednecks, immigrants, and inmates.

The sun caused me to squint and burned my skin, but after several winters of being up north in college, the heat felt good: instantly familiar, reminiscent of everything I once knew and accepted as truth.

The prison looked like most of them do. This one was built in 1991 and sat in the center of over 600 barb-wired acres. A small 1970s-style rectangular building interrupted the path from the parking lot to the main facility. A big sign in front said: VISITING. It wasn't just the place for visiting, though; it was also where they released inmates. Taye had gotten out of prison in 1992, just in time to see me graduate from high school, but six months later, as we were about to celebrate the New Year, he got popped for distribution of a controlled substance and was right back in prison. Now he was being released again.

Upon arrival, I had practically run up the ugly cement walkway, which was futilely lined with rosebushes. Inside, I had given Taye's name and ID number and asked impatiently what I should do and where I should go. I was told with a half smile that I should simply "wait."

I sat down for a minute. We'd all waited and prayed for this day for so long it was hard to believe it was actually here. Taye was coming home. Not that there was much of a home to come home to, with Terrell gone and everyone else having moved on with their own lives, but at least he was about to be free. I looked at the clock and then at the desk where the guards stood sorting paperwork. I was painfully aware of the outside temperature and the precious cargo I'd brought as a gift for my brother and left in the car: an eight-week-old red-nosed pit bull. She was brindle with deep orange and brown stripes, the pick of my last-bred litter. I watched as more people filed in through the doors, filled out visiting forms, and waited for their names to be called to go through the metal detectors. I thought of all the times I had put my name and signature on those papers, stating that I understood that if there were to be an outburst the prison would not negotiate for hostages and that I entered at my own risk. California has the second-highest prison population in the United States, housing more people than the entire federal prison system. They play for keeps and let you know from jump that despite all the different battles that go on inside between Bloods, Crips, Sureños, 415s, Noturos, and the rest of them, there are really only two sides: officers and felons. You have love for your people, and they have love for theirs. You are either with the system or against it.

I watched as a woman took her toddler son's shoes off and placed them on the counter for the CO to examine. Smuggling something into the prison in a baby's shoes would be a low move, but I'm sure the CO had seen all that and worse. The man behind her, whose name had also been called, took off his chain, earrings, and belt, putting them in a small plastic container already waiting on the counter. Then he removed his shoes and waited his turn to go through the metal detector.

It was a relief to sit there in my jeans and red Chuck Taylor All Stars and not have to go through the process or worry about what you can and can't wear. The metal detectors are super-sensitive.

Anything at all sets them off: barrette, underwire bra, metal buttons on the pants or shirts. Then there are all the other things that are forbidden: red, blue, denim, khaki, Calvin Klein ("Crip Killa" logos), British Knights tennis shoes, and the list goes on from there. I actually had a special pair of preppy-looking, drawstring black pants and a pink shirt from the Gap that I called my "prison outfit."

Just as I decided to go back outside and take the puppy out and wait with her, a little old lady who reminded me of Big Mom sat down next to me and gently laid a hand on my knee.

"Baby, they ain gonna let you in with those jeans on. I have an extra skirt in the car if you need it. It might be a little big, but it has an elastic waist, so it'll stay on."

Her eyes looked straight into mine; her face was so kind. I could tell she'd been doing this a long time. She was a pro at it, a self-appointed caretaker of those facing the same insurmountable, heartbreaking force: the Prison Industrial Complex. I looked into the old woman's eyes. I wanted to hug her but something about her, about her eyes and her life and what she might see in me, scared me, so I quickly looked down.

"Yea, I kno. I ain goin in, though. I'm pickin my brother up today."

It was silent. It's not every day that someone gets out. Come to think about it, in all the time I have spent sitting in the visiting room I've never seen anyone leave. The CO called out three names and the old woman patted my leg.

"That's real good. I'm happy for you and for your brother."

She stood up and walked over to the counter. I went outside, unnoticed, and walked slowly past the rosebushes. At least they tried, I thought, as I plucked a peach-colored petal and rubbed it between my fingers the way I used to when I was a kid.

I let the puppy out of the car and poured some water into a cup. She instantly knocked it over and lapped the water up off the ground. She still had her big floppy ears, and they bounced as she pawed and dug at the water soaking into the ground.

I kept thinking about the old lady's eyes, about her face, the way she walked to the desk. It was like she was accepting a sentence of her own. In a way, I guess she was. Taye was about the only person I hadn't visited in prison. Not since the time during his stint in juvie when the woman in the gray jacket had taken me to visit him and he told me he needed to do his time alone. Looking at that old lady, I finally understood what he had been saying and the love it took to say it. How much time had she done, side by side, with her son, husband, or brother? How much longer did she have left?

I knew the statistics.

I saw some movement out of the corner of my eye and turned my head to see the door push open. I stood up and my breathing stopped for a minute when I saw my brother step out. It had been over four years this time since I'd last seen Taye. He was being released off a five-and-a-half-year bid for possession of crack cocaine, 5 grams' worth, with a little time off the top for not getting too many write-ups. The street value of 5 grams of rock was about a hundred bucks. You'd have to be caught with *500* grams of powder cocaine to serve roughly the same amount of time my brother had. I stood frozen for a minute as I took him in. He looked self-conscious and confused, clutching a cardboard box that held all his worldly possessions. California prisons are arranged according to four classifications, level I being the lowest-security and level IV being the high-est. Points are assessed based on gang affiliation, type of crime, crim-inal history, and what type of life and family support system you had on the outside. Someone with no enemies and who didn't want to lose his weekly visits with his loved ones was a lot less likely to get into a fight than someone from a set who had to prove himself—and wouldn't get any visits anyway. Taye had spent the first two years on an IV yard, but after that, his classification had been reduced to level III. He had clearly spent most of the last two years on the yard lift-ing weights. Big brother was swole up—looked like he could bench press 300 pounds easy.

"Taye!" I screamed his name and ran through the parking lot to-ward him. He turned and looked at me but I couldn't make out his expression. My vision blurred as the tears welled in my eyes. I heard the box drop and he grabbed me, lifting me up off the ground.

"I see you, lil momma. I see you . . ." He said it over and over as he held me, and then I began to really cry. I couldn't help it. I hated myself for it, but I couldn't stop it from happening.

"I see you, momma, it's really you. Hey, stop that kryin, Blood. What you doin all that for?"

My brother set my feet back on the ground and looked down at me. He gently wiped my tears from my cheeks and then cupped his big hands around my face. "K'mon, stop that now. It's aiight, Bree Bree."

I tried to look away but his hands held my face steady, his eyes staring right into mine. He had tattooed two tears under his eye. I knew one he must've gotten for Big Mom. She had passed earlier that year. No one knew she was sick, she just went to sleep one night and never woke up. I didn't know if the second tear was for Terrell or for someone else, and I didn't want to ask. I couldn't imagine what it was like for him, knowing that Momma was gone and not having had the chance to say goodbye, to walk past the casket and touch her hand or kiss her cheek; to live knowing that he hadn't been there to throw a shovel full of dirt into the grave after they lowered the casket. That was Taye's luck. He joked about how upset he was that he had missed the riots, but it was left unsaid how he had missed his brother's funeral, and then his grandmother's.

"Bree"—Taye smiled, and then shook his head—"I see you."

He started laughing, and I smiled, too. Convinced that I was done crying, he let go of my face.

"Oh shyt!" I looked around quickly and found the puppy scratching at the grass a few yards from my feet. In all the emotion and excitement, I'd forgotten about her. Taye's eyes followed mine and he caught sight of the puppy.

"She's beautiful." Taye was instantly on his knees petting her as she climbed up onto his lap and started trying to lick him, tongue flapping after his face.

"She yours?" Taye asked, looking her over. "That's one of the nicest lil pups eva."

"Naw," I said, leaning down and patting her, then resting my hand on my brother's shaved head. "She's yours."

I smiled at him, truly happy for a moment. My brother was free again. He picked the puppy up in his arms and cradled her like a baby. She looked so small, lying against him. I reached over and gathered up the letters and books that had fallen out of the box and motioned with my head to the parking lot.

"Let's get outta here."

"Hell, yea," he said, clutching his puppy tightly. "Hell, yea."

We walked the short distance and I pointed out the car. I was driving a 1976 Chevy Caprice Classic. It was a nice whip and I knew it. As it turned out, my fears about college had been right. It wasn't that the material was so hard, but I just couldn't keep up with the other students. I didn't get how anyone could keep up with the hundreds of pages of reading per week per class. Even pulling all-nighters, falling asleep book in hand, it didn't take long before I was too far behind to ever catch up.

When I had left for college an OG had handed me a wad of bills and said, "Go represent to the fullest in that skool. If it don't work out, the hood will always have you back. Nothin changes in L.A. cept the time and the date." A year and a half later, when I came back, my tail between my legs, he fronted me what I needed to get back in the game. I spent the next year reading as much as I could and stacking my money. I read everything I could find until I knew I could keep up, then I shook the OG's hand, bought the Caprice and went back to school, this time set on finishing.

Taye nodded his head in agreement and approval as he eyed the car, with its candy-red paint job, tinted windows, and, most of all, the gold Dayton hundred-spokes.

"Gold D's?"

"You know how we do," I said, shrugging my shoulders like it was nothing and unlocking the door. I set the box in the back, got in, and unlocked the passenger door.

"Shyt, I ain trippin," Taye said, getting in and kissing the puppy on the top of her head before setting her down on his lap.

"Ima kall her Justice," he said and looked at me, as if for approval. I nodded my head and started the car up, engine shaking the frame as it turned over.

"Sounds right." I put the car in drive and we started on our way out of the prison.

"Yea." Taye stroked her head, his eyes switching suddenly from joy to sadness. "When I was leaving, this bitch female CO said, 'See you next time.' I mean, what the fuck? She don't know me. I ain neva even seen that bitch before in my life. Neva." He shook his head. "That's the world, though, right? They don't give a fuck. All they see is this black skin and a rap sheet a mile long. They figure that's all I'll ever be. Thug nigga."

Taye tilted his head and looked at me. His eyes seemed different than I'd ever seen them look, and for a moment I was taken aback. I thought about how strange it must be to walk back into the world at age twenty-two, after years of being gone. All the little things that change so fast we take them for granted—living out in the world— must seem so big and new, so different and overwhelming to him now. It was hard enough just readjusting without everyone doubting and judging, but he was right, that was the world. The statistics said that he would go back, and his file suggested as much. I hoped they were wrong, but even I had my doubts.

"Prove em wrong?" I said, suddenly turning my gaze back to the road ahead.

"I guess," he said. He shifted his weight away from me and leaned his forehead against the window. "You got beat in this? I know you got beat."

"Yea, two tens." I reached behind the seat and handed Taye a case of CDs.

He nodded and started flipping through pages of bootleg CDs, titles written on them in pen. I tried to think of something to say that would make my brother understand that I got what he was going through, but really, the more I thought about it, the more I realized I had no clue. Taye had lost his entire adolescence to the system. He had grown from a boy to a man behind the walls.

"Hey, sis, what the fuck is *this*?" He laughed and held up a CD with no writing on it. I looked over and laughed, too.

"Anyone's guess, right?"

"Yea, and you got a grip of em like that too. Lazzzy."

I smiled, but I was still fixed on what that CO had said to him and how that must have felt. "There's this lady, rite?" I started, unsure exactly of where I was going with this. "Audre Lorde. Actually, she dead now, died of cancer, but she wrote this shyt once, said something bout how we made it, 'those of us who were never meant to survive.' That's us, bro, world don't expect much of us really. Don't kare what happens to us as long as we stay out of their way."

"Real talk." Taye straightened up a little, looked back at me, still unsure, but then finally decided to smile. "Baby sis"—he shook his head in an exaggerated disbelief—"baby sister got an edumacation, beats, and gold Daytons."

Beats and Dayton wire wheels were two of the surest status symbols in the hood. Daytons range from 72 to 180 spokes, in various patterns and finishes, from chrome to custom-matched powder coat to the 24-karat goldplate. Even if you had a good connection, a set of gold D's was going to set you back at least a grand, and once you went through the trouble of buying them, you still had the problem of how to keep them. Daytons are a prime target to steal because they aren't locked up, are worth good money, and are easy to resell.

"Aye, I got some lil odds and ends fo ya in the glove." The Daytons and beat were from old money, back from before I went back to school. Truth was, I was hurting now that I was in college and trying to get my square business on. I thought about pawning the Daytons daily, and the money I had scraped together to get some things for Taye was most of what I had left from my financial-aid check.

"Good lookin!" my brother said as he reached over the puppy and started pulling out the contents: a case of burned CDs, a gold Cuban link chain that had been Terrell's, and a starched and ironed red bandana.

"Oh, daymn. I got CDs, an a chain." My brother fumbled excitedly with the clasp, big fingers on small metal parts. "How I look?"

He puffed his chest out under the chain and held his hands up.

I shrugged my shoulders. "You aiight, I guess."

Taye laughed and punched me hard in the arm. Then he unfolded the flag and held it up, flapping it out in front of him and looking at it.

"Ain had one these in a while." He folded it carefully, kissed it, and then tucked it into his right back pocket. Red bandanas were another thing you couldn't give to prisoners. "Not a real one at least. We be makin bootleg ones inside with T-shirts and Kool-Aid as dye."

"Got this fo you too, big bro." I reached around in my purse till I found the box with the wallet in it and handed it to him. I had placed a hundred-dollar bill, and photos of Terrell's son, Tee, and Nishia's new baby daughter, Mya.

"Pretty lil gurl," Taye said. "Who that?"

"Nishia daughter." I said it and Taye's eyes grew wide. He flipped the plastic photo holder and smiled. "Daymn, look at Lil Tee! He huuuge!" He glanced from the photo to me and said, "We finna go by there when we hit L.A., aiight?"

I nodded my head. I had planned on it anyway.

"Pizza place, pull over."

We stopped and got a large pizza with peppers, sausage, pep-
peroni, and onions and a ten-piece bucket of chicken with four biscuits. Taye was so excited not to have prison food that he made me
stop at every place we passed that sold food. It was amazing to watch
him pack it away: burgers, doughnuts, tacos, Doritos.

We ate and chatted and the three hours back to L.A. became
more like five. We got there just as the sun was going down and the
city lights were coming on. L.A. was on its night vibe: kids inside, and
the smokers, prostitutes, pimps, and dealers walking the streets and
standing posted on corners.

My brother sat on the edge of his seat, close to the window.

"That's it, that's it," he said, tapping his fingers against the glass,
his words sounding almost like a mantra.

"Remember when that lil store usta be there? When we was kids
we usta be robbin them for chips an Laffy Taffys?" He pointed at the
empty space.

"Man, I'm still sorry I missed all dat," Taye said, referring again
to the riots. "Musta been sumthin. If I regret anything, it's missin
that." Taye had only been home for a short time right after the riots,
not long enough to really adjust to the new L.A. before he went back.
"I thought they woulda rebuilt a lil more by now," he said, looking
sad and excited out the window.

"Stop! Stop the kar." As he said it he threw the door open. I hit
the brakes and slowed as fast as the heavy old car would let me. Taye
took off running into the park, red flag waving out his back pocket.
No other choice, I parked the car and walked into the park. He was
talking to some homies, a bottle of Hennessey already in his hand.

"Babygurl," he called to me, gesturing with his hand as I approached. When I caught up, he pointed the flask at me, offering me a sip. I took it and handed it back, the alcohol burning in my mouth and throat. Taye put his arm around my shoulder.

"Trip, huh? The two ah us bickin back at the park again?"

It was a trip.

The thing is this: unlike most of my homies, I made it out of L.A. with my life and without a prison record. Wait, let me reword that, as it is not entirely true as it stands. I made it out of L.A. with what life I had left. I wake up in the morning, and where I live, in a little house on a dead-end street in a small Oregon town, I hear birds singing in a big-leaf maple outside my bedroom window and I thank God because I know it shouldn't have been so. So many people I knew and loved are dead or stretched out in prison, doing long sentences with words attached that are hard to swallow. Words like "armed robbery," "murder," "gang-related homicide," "triple life," "twenty-five to life," and "death row." I, on the other hand, beat the odds. I was getting by in college, pursuing a career; and yet, despite the obvious success that I've made of my life, there are some parts of me that did die in L.A. and that I'll never get back, and other parts of me that die daily because I exist away from the city, in a world where people can't begin to imagine what it was like where I grew up.

I looked around the park; so many memories sprang to mind. The homies gave my bro the rundown of who was beefing with who and why, who had been killed in his absence and what their funerals had been like. Your greatness in life, by L.A. standards, is determined by your funeral and how many people show up to view your body. They talked about females and gave him hook-ups to the ones he used to mess with. Then they each reached into their pockets and broke my brother off fifty- and hundred-dollar bills.

"Good lookin," Taye said pulling out his wallet and putting the money in.

I watched my brother and felt a sudden deep sadness and fear rise in my chest. Taye was back on the block. "Kant stop wont stop," we used to say, but in that moment all I could see was my brother's life in and out of prison, or worse. I looked around at the homies. Things change fast in L.A. Soldiers keep falling—dying, and going to prison—and there's always a little homie stepping in to take up the curb space. I'd been gone a while and only recognized two of these homies, but I knew the odds. Out of the six people standing in front of me, two would be going to prison like Taye had. Some, like Slikk, who was convicted of murder, would go off to do life bids and never stand on the grass in the park or walk freely down the street again. I squinted my eyes and tried to see outside the park. I blocked out the conversation and visualized the streets as they led out from the park. I probably had a memory on every street in the area.

"Everything looks different, but ain shyt really changed," one of the homies said, and then started a blow-by-blow rundown of enemy activity in the area.

"Fukk all dirties, filthies, sissies, and fukk Mesikans."

I closed my eyes and let my head rest against Taye's side. My heart felt cold. It was hard to care about the catalogue of who had shot who in this slow-motion genocide. This was home, and while this was what made me who I was, as I listened I couldn't help but think and hope I had become something more, too.

Taye and the homies started to plan their night out. I almost told him that Nishia was probably waiting up, but he had years of living to catch up on. I knew she would still be there when he made it in.

I said my goodbyes and drove around for a little while, finally pulling up in front of Elegant Manor. I let the car idle while I looked up at the old house and thought about all the hopes and dreams I'd had as a kid, all the times I'd lost hope and fought to find it again. I thought about how we had to come up, and how countless kids are still coming up.

A few years later, I found love again. Ironically, it was with a Crip. A Crip healed my heart in places where I didn't even know it was broken and gave me back the self-confidence that had been systematically stolen from me since diapers. A Crip showed me that my past didn't define me or make me a bad person, that it made me a warrior and that I was as good as anyone else.

When I reacted irrationally and panicked that he was going to disappear, he reassured me. When I lashed out at him, he still loved me, and although it took years on my part and endless patience on his for me to believe in that love, it changed every detail of my life. Suddenly, the Calvin Klein logo (ck), which for me had always meant "Crip Killa," lost its brutal edge now that it was attached to his life. I was forced to see that we are not each other's enemies. We all face the same social, economic, political, and spiritual problems. We were just born into different streets and neighborhoods.

I guess it's true what they say, that understanding can only come with the evolution of self. I still have hopes and dreams. You're holding one of my dreams in your hand right now and if any of this book has touched you or opened your mind, then that, for me, is a hope fulfilled. Most of the rest of my dreams have to do with getting back to L.A. and figuring out a way to give back. To begin to make

up for all I've participated in. I've perpetuated a lot of hate and darkness in the world, and because of that I must bear some of the weight
of the many dead soldiers.

I got a letter yesterday from a friend in prison. He has done
about fifteen years in the penitentiary now. It's amazing how much
someone can change in fifteen years, or how long fifteen years really
is when you think about it. The sad part is, he's got at least another
ten to go to make it to the gate. He's my rock, though. He learned all
his lessons at the greatest of costs and I respect his wisdom and feedback dearly. I don't doubt that if it weren't for his love, guidance, and
support, I would be sitting in the same kind of place that he is now.
I'd written him to tell him of some problems I was having, and in
his return letter my homie told me to do what he always does: to
maintain. He told me that he was proud of me, that my OG and I
were among the few who made it out. I read his words and tears
flooded my eyes. I wondered if it was right or wrong to tell him that
OG was back in the hood selling rocks. So few of us will ever get the
chance to see what it's like outside L.A., he wrote me, be our eyes.

I'll tell you a secret I wasn't going to share. I woke up in the middle of the night last night, still thinking about that letter. My head
was so full of thoughts that I couldn't focus on any particular one,
then I tried to shut them out, but that didn't work, either. I tossed
and turned for a few minutes until I gave up, turned on the nightstand lamp, and sat up in bed. I tried to call Taye, but his phone
went straight to voice mail. I wanted to call Big Mom, but she was
dead. I wanted to call Terrell, but he's dead, too; and Nishia's phone
is disconnected. So I looked over and picked up Big Mom's Bible.
Someone gave it to me after her funeral, but I hadn't had the heart
to look through it or read it. I ran my hands over the worn leather

cover and gently opened it. How much of Big Mom was in that Bible. I pictured her, hand raised toward the altar in church, saying "Amen" whenever the pastor said something she particularly agreed with, or jotting notes into the margins based upon the sermon. The Bible fell open to 1 John 3:18, and I looked at what was underlined.

"My children, our love should not be just words and talk; it must be true love, which shows itself in action."

In the margin, Momma had written: "Without love we are bankrupt." She wrote it later in her life. I could tell because the letters were hard to make out. In the end, her arthritis became so bad that to the untrained eye her writing was illegible. I had to look at it for several minutes to make it out. After that, I closed the Bible and fell back to sleep.

AFTERWORD

TODAY, when people find out where I'm from, they always ask, "What is Los Angeles like?" It's a difficult question for me to answer. The Los Angeles of my youth has evolved. Crenshaw Boulevard, one of the main streets through South Central, has been cleaned up considerably, and chain stores like Wal-Mart and Starbucks have begun to pop up where once were only vacant lots of rubble and ash. In this way, I suppose it resembles more of the rest of the U.S. than it used to, but in other, more important ways, it's still like nowhere else I've seen. We used to say that South Central was separate from the luxury of America—it was an urban Third World—and that's still true. And as tough as it was in the eighties and nineties, in many ways, today's kids have it worse.

Over the last decade, the government has imposed new legislation—from the three-strikes law to gang injunctions—in its attempt to combat gangs, but the actual effect has mostly been an increase in the hostility hanging over the city. Membership among street gangs continues to soar, as do the violence and racial tensions that come with it. In today's Los Angeles, police come through and raid projects with tear gas in the early mornings, arresting forty-plus people at a time—leaving children and old ladies waiting for the smoke to clear. Generations of men and women are being incarcerated, and with new law enhancements they are now receiving decades- or life-long sentences. Even with over thirty adult facilities, California prisons have run out of room for all those sentenced and have begun to pay other states to house inmates. Guns continue to flood the community, only they are getting cheaper and easier to obtain, which means they're not just landing in the hands of more people, but younger ones, too. A conflict that once would have been resolved with a fistfight now goes straight to gunfire.

And no longer is this activity limited to L.A., or places like New York or Chicago. Los Angeles gangs are being franchised across the country—even around the world. In Portland, Oregon; Charlotte, North Carolina; or Indian Reservations all over the country; and even in Grenada and Belize, there are growing gang sets emulating what they know of the South Central Bloods and Crips. They name their local sets after streets in Los Angeles that their members have never seen, and many of these kids know L.A. gang history better than most L.A. gang members do. Instead of lessening, the dangers of L.A. gangs are spreading.

The idea of a gang truce did not end with the much publicized and quickly shattered peace treaty that rose out of the aftermath of the 1992 riots. Many people still want to see the violence end, and as gangs continue to grow, as the racial divide widens and tensions increase, these efforts have in fact become even more critical. There are a number of organizations, big and small, working toward gang truce, each with its own vision of how to create change. There are organizations run by the City of Los Angles, by mothers who have lost children to gang violence, by gang members, by church members, and by the community at large. One thing that seems clear, though, is that real and lasting change is most likely to come from within the neighborhood, from those who truly understand what we face.

I work with the organization International Brother/SisterHood, founded a few years ago by gang members with the intention of reducing violence through mentoring and outreach. We work not only with youth who are in gangs, but also with those at risk of joining, and concerned parents looking for advice. Part of what we offer is the perspective of having been inside the gang ourselves. It is from this perspective that we try to help these kids stay focused on education, a trade, the future.

For more information on different gang truce organizations and how to get involved, please visit www.brothersisterhood.com.

ACKNOWLEDGMENTS

I am a firm believer that I am able to write this today only because of all those who have stood behind me over the years and shaped me into the person I have become.

I'd like to thank God, who makes all things possible and who gave me strength and put me on this path; my family, without whom, on so many levels, I would be nothing; and Christi Jones, who is my anchor. This book would never have been possible without the other side of my winning literary team: my agent, Faye Bender, who just gets me when no one else does; my editor, Sarah McGrath, who had the courage to believe in a no-name author like me and put so much of herself into this book; Sarah Stein and the entire staff at Riverhead; and Inga Muscio, who believed in this book before even I knew it was a book.

My deepest appreciation goes out to Madd Ronald, who taught me at least half of what is in my head, for supporting me always and through everything; and to Ase Kapone, aka Keith Ty Fudge, the wrongfully kkkonvicted one, for keeping me on my path and telling me he'd always roll with me right or wrong. On many a bad day it was that thought alone that kept me on track. Enormous thanks, too, go to Big Brother, aka Komrade Sadiki, for inspiration and wisdom deeper than any sorrow; and to the homeboy JaBerri Bratton, for always checking in on me and having faith in my endeavors even when I don't. Thanks to YG Agony, who is always willing to read things and give me feedback, or just be a friend; Michael "the don" Harvey; Brotherhood Entertainment; and Michael Lapointe. Thanks to Gully, for just being Gully; Ol Skool Ray, now Professor A, for being the person I can always count on to keep me humble; Tray; Rod; Clarence; Stew; my mentor, professor Jayna Brown, for more than she realizes; the homeboy Solo, for teaching me that true friends stick around; Kristin, for always lending a hand; Andre Brown; Rick; the homie Swift; T-Bone; D. Will; Fernie; my girl Kameko; Zacch; Legacy; Cecil Murray; Pastor Thomas; Pastor Green; Pastor Johnson; Khalid Shah; JoJo; Tyrone Homes, who always makes me laugh even in the darkest times; Brooke and Brian; Vinyl Richie; Eizabeth; my fellow writer homies Angela Newman and Antoine McAdoo; Unity One; Gangsters for Christ; Julius; and Markell, for everything and with all my heart.

The deepest gratitude goes to Michael Butler and to Steven Moore, the two best friends anyone could ever be blessed with, and without whose love and support I would be completely lost in this life.